Austin Financial Group

AF778849

The Best Trendline Methods of Alan Andrews and Five New Trendline Techniques

By Patrick Mikula

Copyright © 2002 by Patrick Mikula All Rights Reserved
First Edition: Second Printing

ISBN 0-9650518-3-8

Published by
Austin Financial Group
www.marketwarrior.com
P.O. Box 152672
Austin TX 78715-2672
USA

Important Notice:
No claim is made that the trading methods or ideas in this book will result in profits and will not result in losses. The contents of this book are not guaranteed to produce profits. Commodity futures or stock trading is a risky business and may not be suitable for all recipients of this book. Although the financial correlations contained in this book have been reliable in the past there is no guarantee by the book's author or distributors that they will work in the future. Each trader is responsible for his/her own actions in the markets, if any. The contents of this book are not, and should not be considered as an offer to buy or sell any commodity or futures contract or stock. Purchase of this book constitutes your agreement to this disclaimer and exempts its author and distributors from any liability or litigation.

Copyright Notice:
No part of this book may be reproduced without written permission from the publisher. No part of this book may be reproduced, stored in a retrieval system, or transmitted in any form or by any means, photocopying, electronic, mechanical, or otherwise, without the prior written permission of the publisher.

Contents

Introduction

I am fortunate to have been involved with trading before computers completely took over technical analysis and I have read many trading books written between 1950 to 1980. There is a much greater discussion of trendline methods in those older books than there is in trading books of today. My first encounter with a reference to Alan Andrews was in the 1986 book, "Technical Analysis of the Futures Markets," by John Murphy. I have been researching Alan Andrews trendline methods ever since and present my findings here. In my book, Alan Andrews will be referred to simply as Andrews.

In my consulting work as a Commodity Trading Advisor (CTA) I encountered several people who attended the Andrews Action Reaction seminar. This provided me the opportunity to examine Andrews original material but more importantly, it allowed me to converse with traders who have used Andrews trendline methods for many years.

In his seminars, Andrews said his trendline methods were based on the work of Roger Babson. In the 1930's, Roger Babson was publicly credited with forecasting the crash of 1929 more accurately than any other person. The exact nature of what Roger Babson showed Andrews no one can know. My research leads me to believe Roger Babson gave Andrews the concept of financial action and reaction. Then Andrews developed his trendline methods based on this idea.

The methods used by Roger Babson and Andrews may have been based on the same theory of action reaction but the actual methods are very different. Roger Babson used a method which measured how far the price moved above or below a line drawn through the center of previous price swings. This allowed Babson to calculate the average distance above or below the center line that a price swing should move before it turns the other direction. It is believed that Babson used this method to make a fortune in the markets by identifying when markets were over extended either upward or downward. This is also believed to be the method he used in 1929 to give many public warnings that the stock market was greatly over extended and a large decline was coming. When the 1929 crash finally came, Babson was heralded as a genius.

The methods used by Andrews appear to be based on this same idea of the price moving around a center line but are different from the methods used by Babson. The Babson methods are for long term stock market and economic analysis, while the Andrews' methods are for short term trading. The end result for Babson and Andrews was similar, because it is reported that Andrews also made a very large amount of money trading. The traders with whom I have talked, who attended the Andrews seminars, indicated that Andrews made well over a million dollars trading.

The biographical information on Andrews of interest from a traders perspective is rather meager. Andrews did not become involved with sharing his trendline methods and his ideas on trading until after he retired. I have not encountered any investors who dealt with Andrews for trading purposes before the mid 1960's. The documentation from his Action Reaction Course and his seminars is dated in the 1960's and 1970's. This 20 year period seems to be when Andrews became active as a financial educator and trader.

This book is written in two sections. The first section presents the material which can be directly attributed to Andrews. I refrained from inserting my opinions and ideas into the first section and included only Andrews' methods. In the greater body of Andrews' work, there are ideas and methods which were suggested by his students. Andrews encouraged his students to share their ideas. This material has been left out of the book because the methods suggested by Andrews' students are not the methods Andrews used to make a fortune in the markets.

The second section of this book deals with new trendline developments made at Austin Financial Group. In this way, the reader can separate clearly the original Andrews' ideas from the new ideas. After becoming a CTA, I was asked to develop a trading method for the Eurodollar futures, which I did. Since that time developing trading or prediction models has become the largest part of my business as a CTA. In the second section of this book are five new ways to apply trendline methods.

There was a time when I thought computers would replace all the old trading methods. After years of watching advanced computer models come and go I no longer believe that. After you read this book I hope you will agree that trendline methods, both old and new, still have great financial value to traders. The computer is a powerful tool for doing repetitive work and time consuming tasks but nothing replaces simple methods which work and trading experience.

Section 1:
The Best Trendline Methods of Alan Andrews

Bar Charts and Pivots

In this book we will use the standard financial bar chart to present the trendline methods. The chart seen below is a bar chart. The price scale is on the left side. The time scale is across the bottom. Each vertical line is an individual price bar. In this book we will often make reference to a price pivot. A pivot is a point where the price bars change direction. On the chart below there is a label “Top Pivot” and a label “Bottom Pivot”. These identify simple examples of pivots.

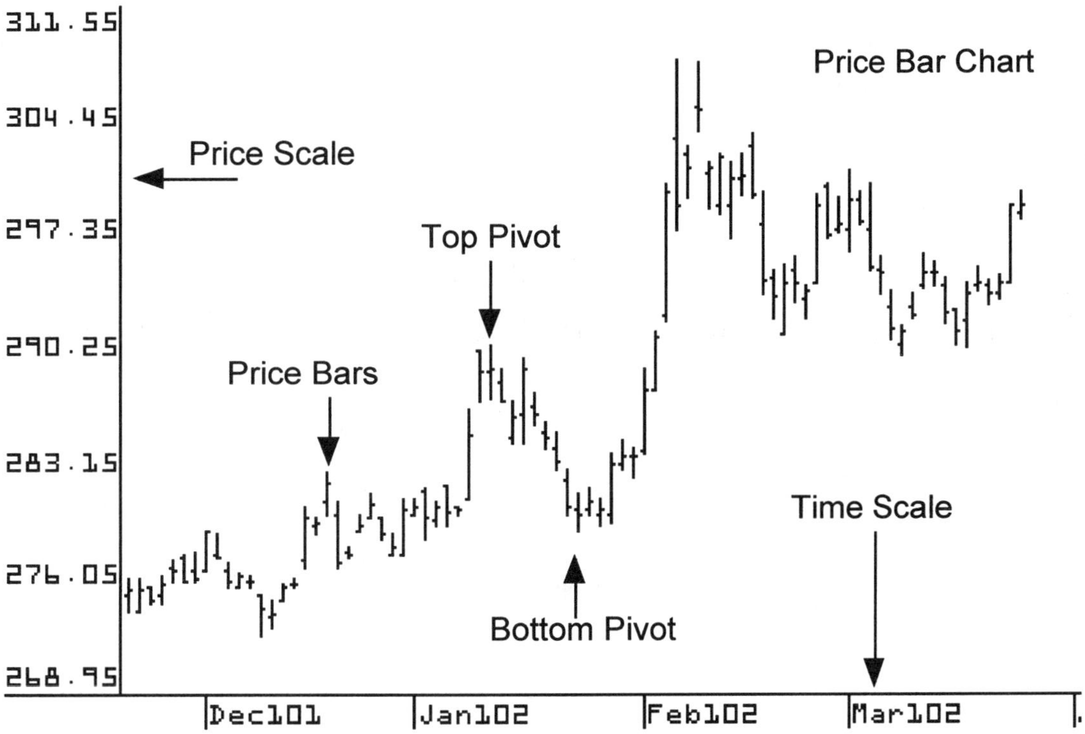

The picture below shows an individual price bar. The bar has an opening tick mark on the left and the closing tick mark on the right side. The high and low price are used to create the vertical bar.

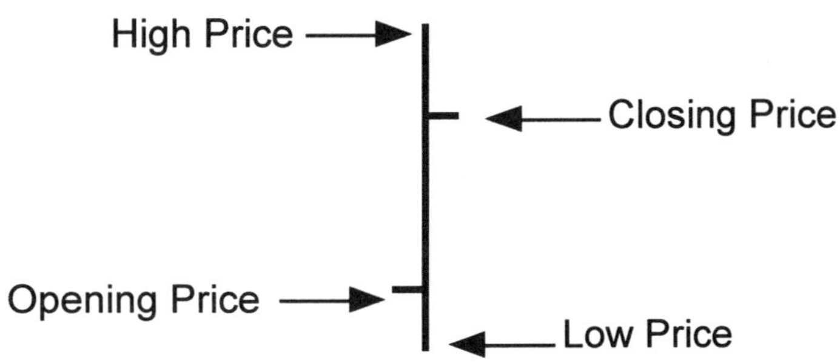

High to High and Low to Low Trendlines

The chart on this page shows four trendlines. One of the trendlines is connecting pivots B and C. This trendline has two characteristics. It is upward sloping and is connecting two high pivots. This line is identified as an upward High to High trendline.

Also on this chart is a trendline connecting pivots A and D. The two characteristics of this trendline are that it is upward sloping and is connecting two low pivots. This line is identified as an upward Low to Low trendline.

When a trendline connects two of the same pivot types, such as two high pivots or two low pivots, there are six basic trendlines. These are: 1) downward high to high, 2) downward low to low, 3) upward high to high, 4) upward low to low, 5) horizontal high to high and finally 6) horizontal low to low.

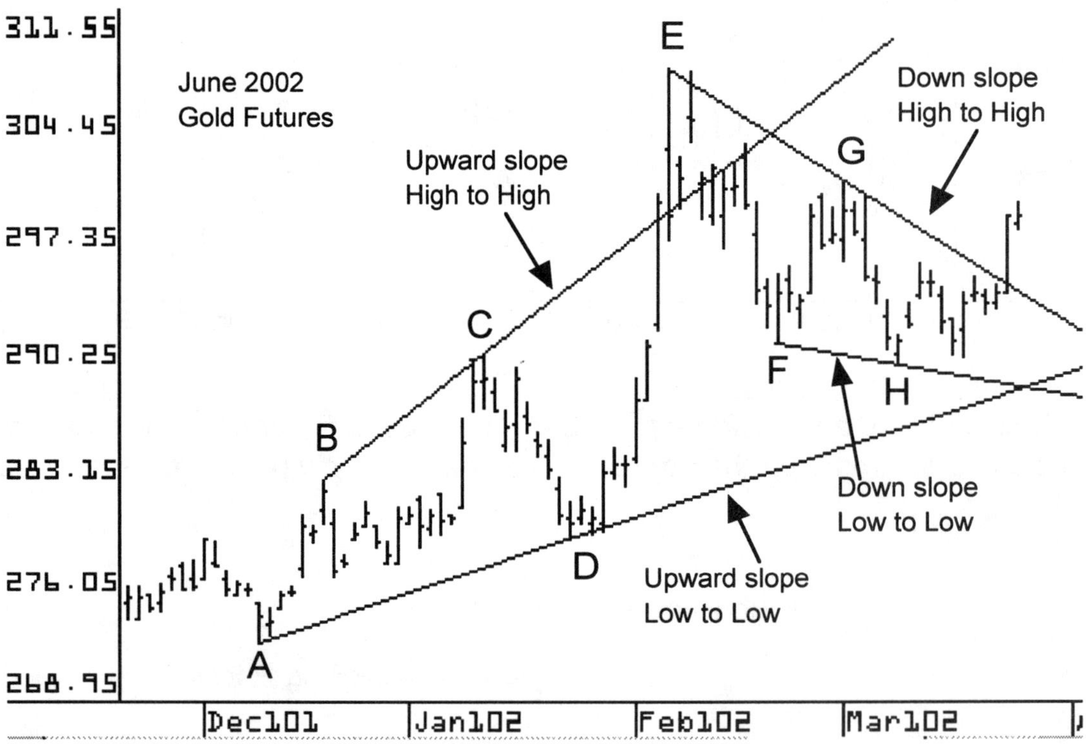

High to Low and Low to High Trendlines

The chart below shows a trendline drawn from pivots A to B. This line has two attributes. It is upward sloping and is connecting a low and a high pivot. Also on this chart is a trendline connecting pivots C and D. The two attributes of this line are downward sloping and connecting a high and a low pivot.

When a trendline connects two pivots of the opposite type such as high to low there are six possible trendlines. These are: 1) upward high to low, 2) upward low to high, 3) downward high to low, 4) downward low to high, 5) horizontal high to low and 6) horizontal low to high.

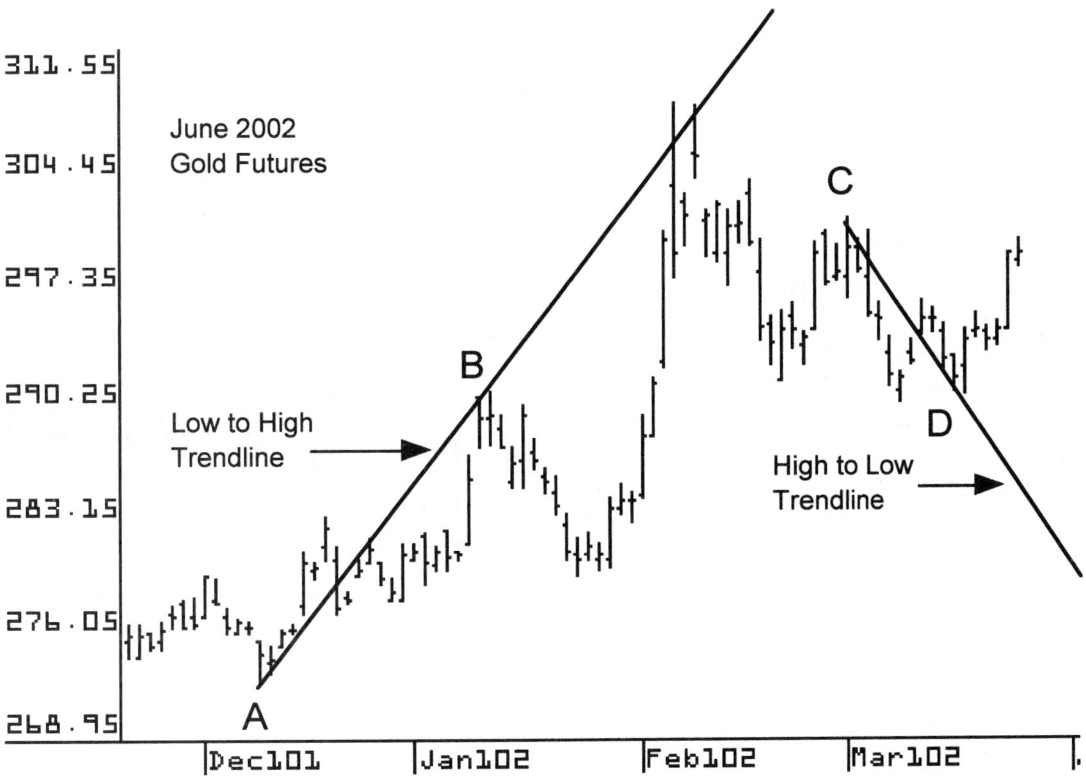

Multi-Pivot Line

Andrews used a trendline that he named the Multi-Pivot line. This is a trendline which runs through more than two pivots. This trendline does not have to run through the exact high or low of each pivot; it only needs to be close to each pivot. Andrews believed that the greater number of pivots through which a trendline runs, the more important the trendline is for finding future support and resistance levels and pivots.

The chart below is for General Motors, symbol GM. On this chart there is a trendline which runs through five pivots. This is a Multi-Pivot Line and should be considered more important than a standard trendline which uses only two pivots.

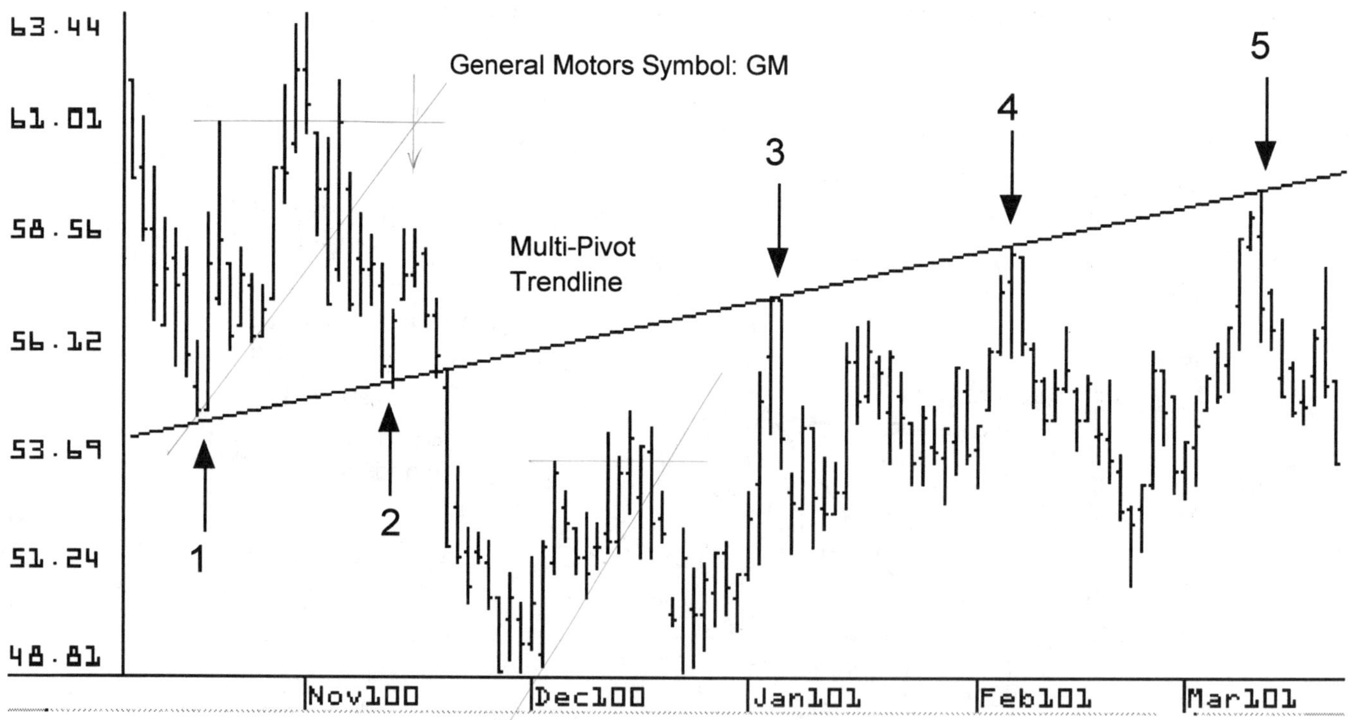

Median Line

The trendline for which Andrews is best known is the Median Line. The chart on this page shows an upward sloping Median Line. Three pivots are needed to draw a Median Line. Two of the pivots must be the high and low of a price swing. The mid-point between these first two points must be calculated. This is calculated through simple division and addition. The range between the high and low is divided by two and added to the low value. The same is done for the amount of time between the high and low. On the chart below, the middle point between pivots B and C is used to draw the Median Line.

Next, a third pivot which occurs before the price swing described in the paragraph above is selected. Usually this is the pivot immediately before the price swing described in the paragraph above but can be any pivot. This third pivot is the Median Line starting point. On the chart below, pivot A is the starting point for the Median Line. The Median Line is drawn by connecting the starting pivot A and the middle of the B - C price swing.

Note that the line between pivot B and C is not required to draw this Median Line. This line has been added to help the reader easily see the pivots used to draw the Median Line.

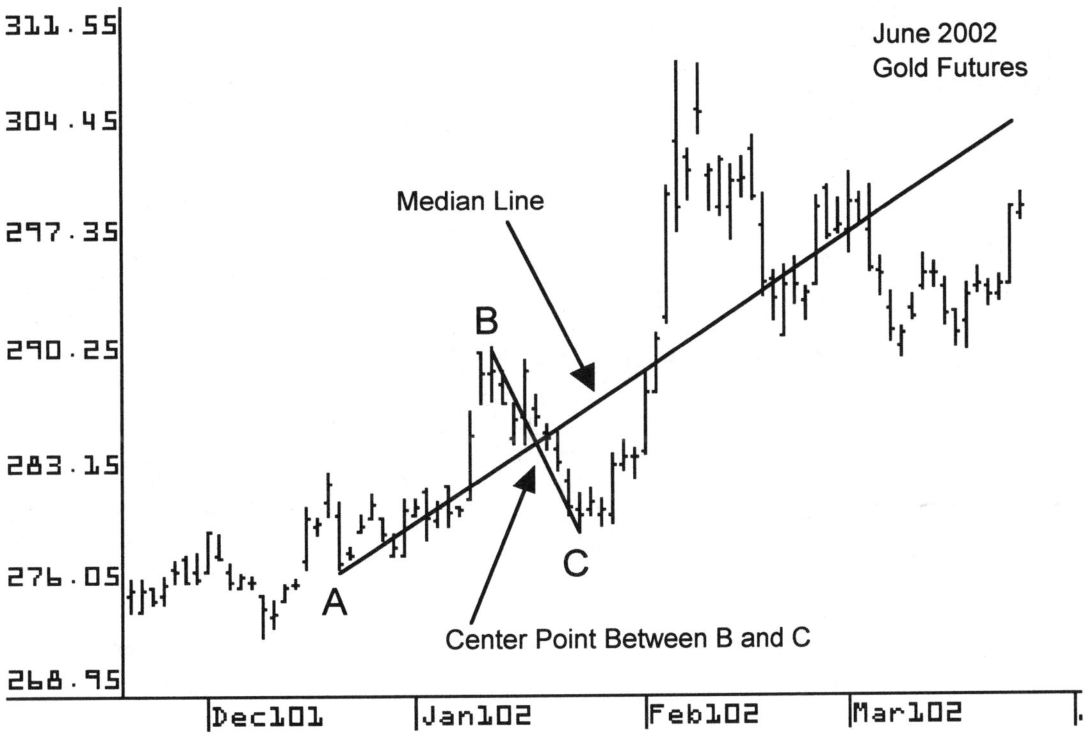

Median Line Theory

Andrews always held that the Median Line is based on the laws of physics. He believed that principles from physics could be applied to financial markets. The diagrams below show the principle on which the Median Line is based. These principles are that natural cycles return to their centers, and for every action there is a reaction.

The top and bottom diagrams on the left show a sine wave cycle which is only partially complete. In these diagrams, A is the starting pivot and the Median Line is drawn through the center of B and C. In the second two diagrams on the right, the sine wave moves back to the Median Line at point X. At point X, the sine wave completes one cycle. When a swing in the financial market returns to the Median Line, it also complete one cycle. Andrews believed that the price returns to the Median Line about 80% of the time.

Upward Sloping Sine Wave with Median Line:

Downward Sloping Sine Wave with Median Line:

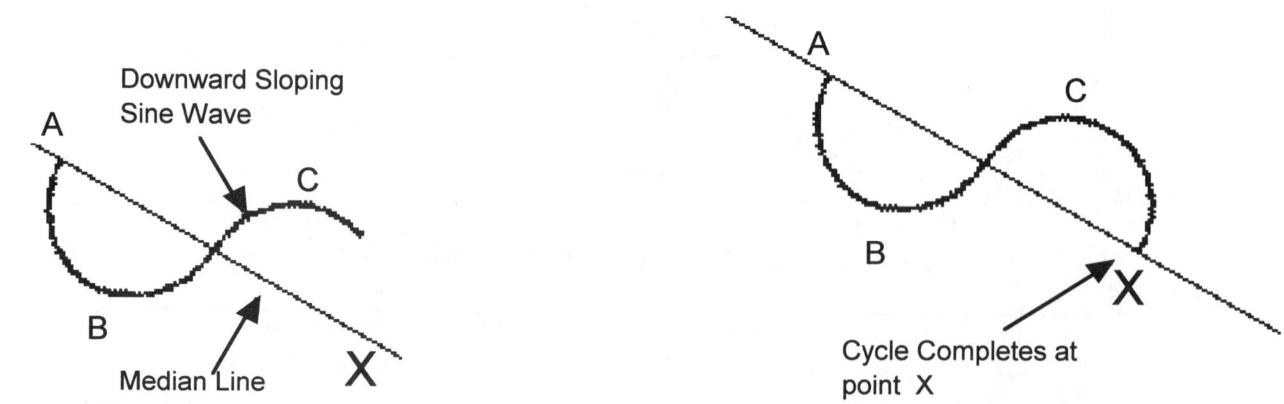

Median Line Trading Principles 1-3

Andrews made several observations about the Median Line which are important for traders. These are not absolute rules; they are general observations made by Andrews which will help a trader know what to expect when using the Median Line.

Median Line Trading Principle 1: When a Median Line is drawn from the most recent swings the price should return to the Median Line approximately 80 percent of the time.

Median Line Trading Principle 2: When the price returns to the Median Line there often will be a pivot made on the Median Line.

Median Line Trading Principle 3: When the price returns to the Median Line the price often will form several small swings around the Median Line and touch the Median Line more than once before moving on.

Here are a few examples of these Median Line trading principles. Below is a daily chart for May 2002 wheat futures. The Median Line is drawn using pivots A, B, and C. After pivot C, the market moves back up to the Median Line at point D. When the price reaches the Median Line, a top pivot is made and there is a fast reaction downward.

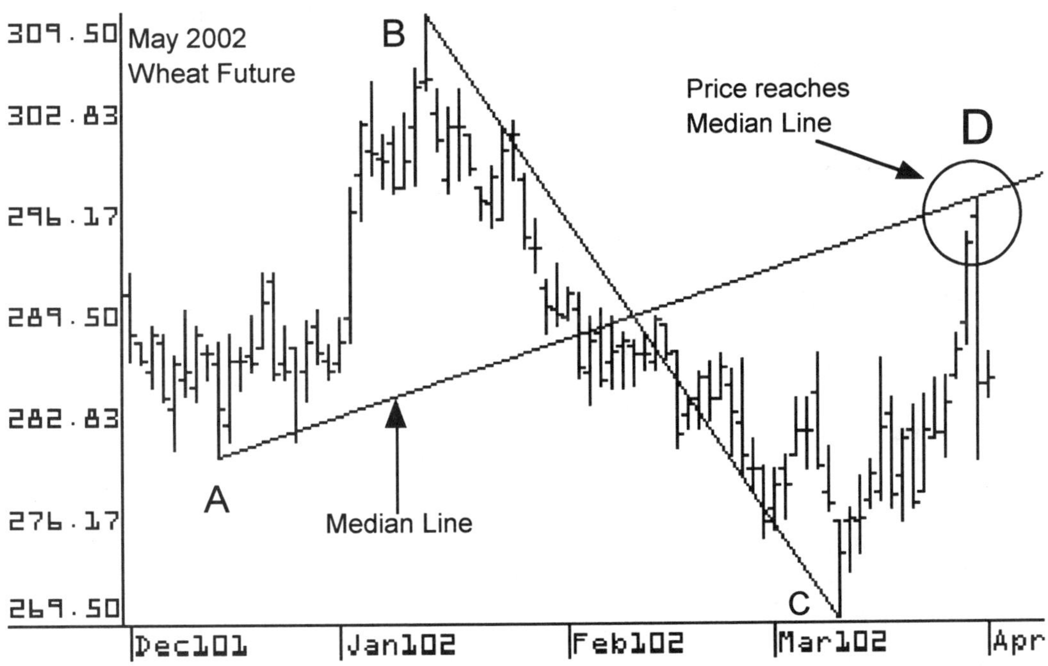

The first chart below shows a weekly stock chart for General Motors, symbol GM. A Median Line is drawn using pivots A, B, and C. After pivot C, the price moves up and returns to the Median Line at point D.

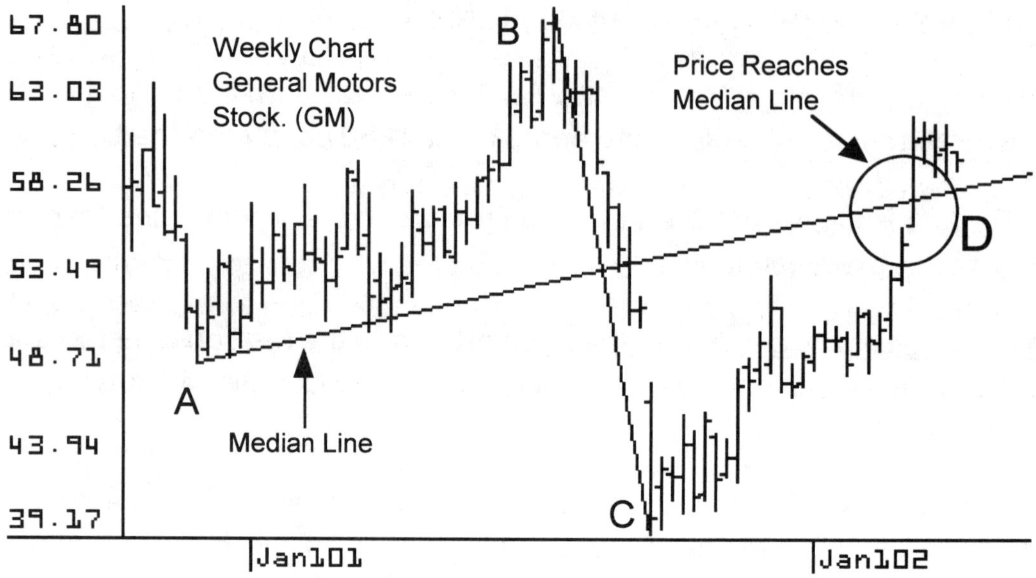

Below is a chart for May 2002 Copper futures with a Median Line drawn using pivots A, B, and C. After pivot C, the price returns to the Median Line at point D. When the Median Line is drawn from the most recent price swing, the price returns to the Median Line in the majority of cases.

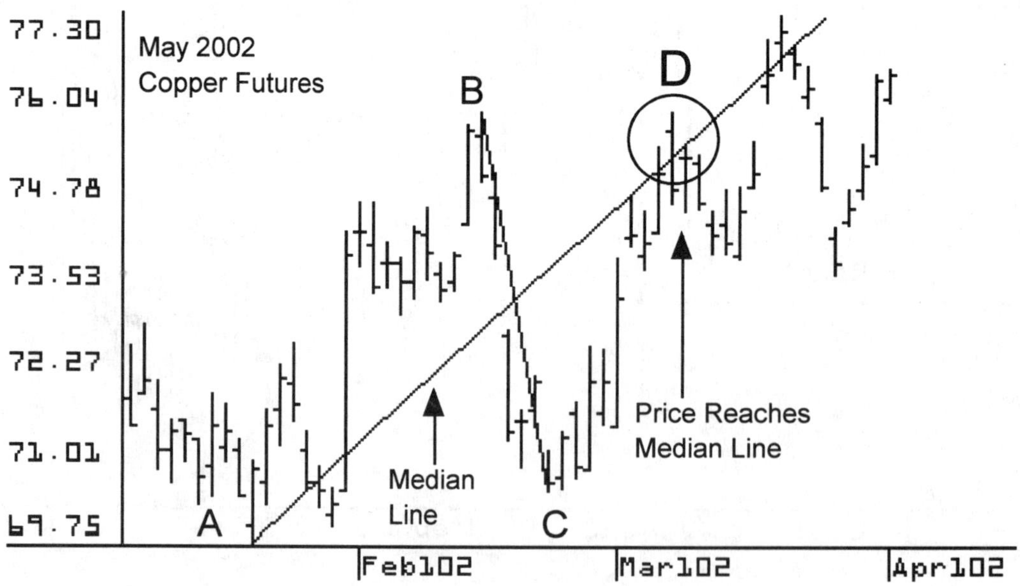

Median Line Trading Principle 4

Another observation Andrews made about the Median Line deals with situations in which the price fails to reach the Median Line. In these situations, Andrews observed the price reverses direction and moves a greater distance than the size of the previous swing. This observation can be used to set a price target after the price fails to reach the Median Line.

Median Line Trading Principle 4: If the price does not reach the Median Line, the price moves in the opposite direction more than the previous swing size.

The chart on this page shows June 2002 Eurodollar futures. This chart shows a Median Line drawn using pivots A, B, and C. After pivot C, the price falls but fails to reach the Median Line. After the price fails to reach the Median Line, the first price target is the high price at pivot C. This chart shows that the price moved back up above the price target at pivot C.

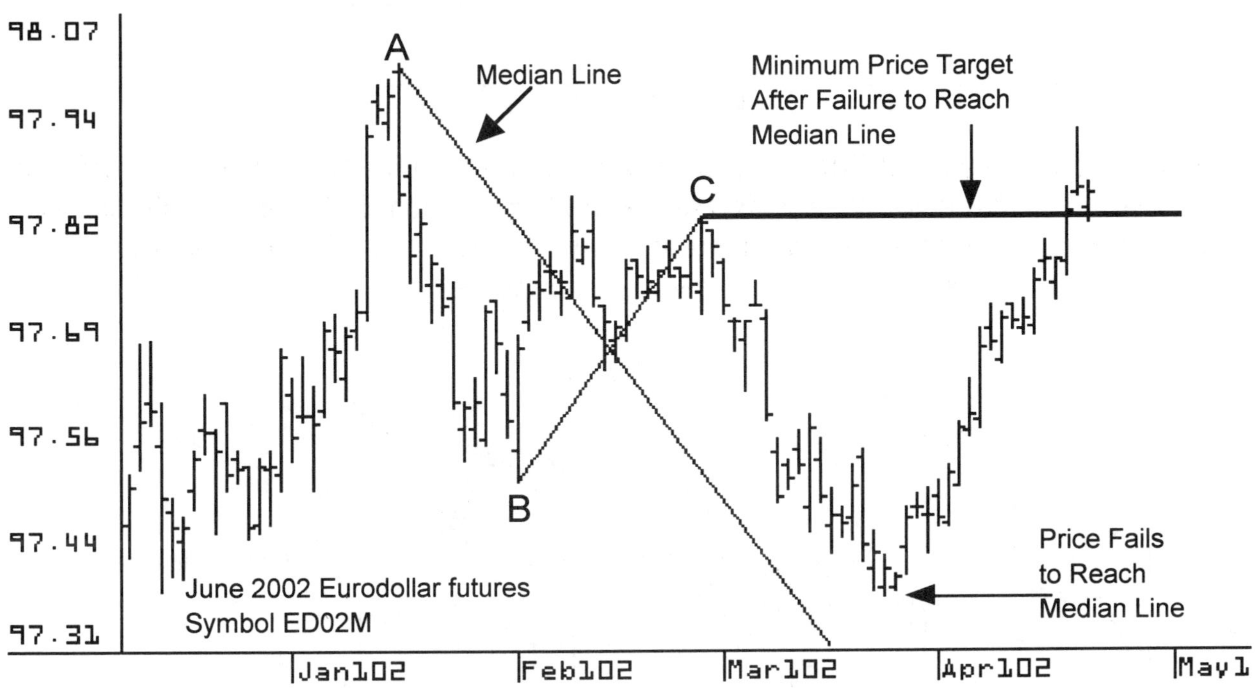

The top chart on this page shows the stock for McDonalds, symbol MCD, with a Median Line drawn using pivots A, B, and C. After pivot C, the price declines but fails to reach the Median Line. After the price fails to reach the Median Line, the first price target is the high price at pivot C. The price moves up and touches this price level twice before the price breaks through to higher price levels.

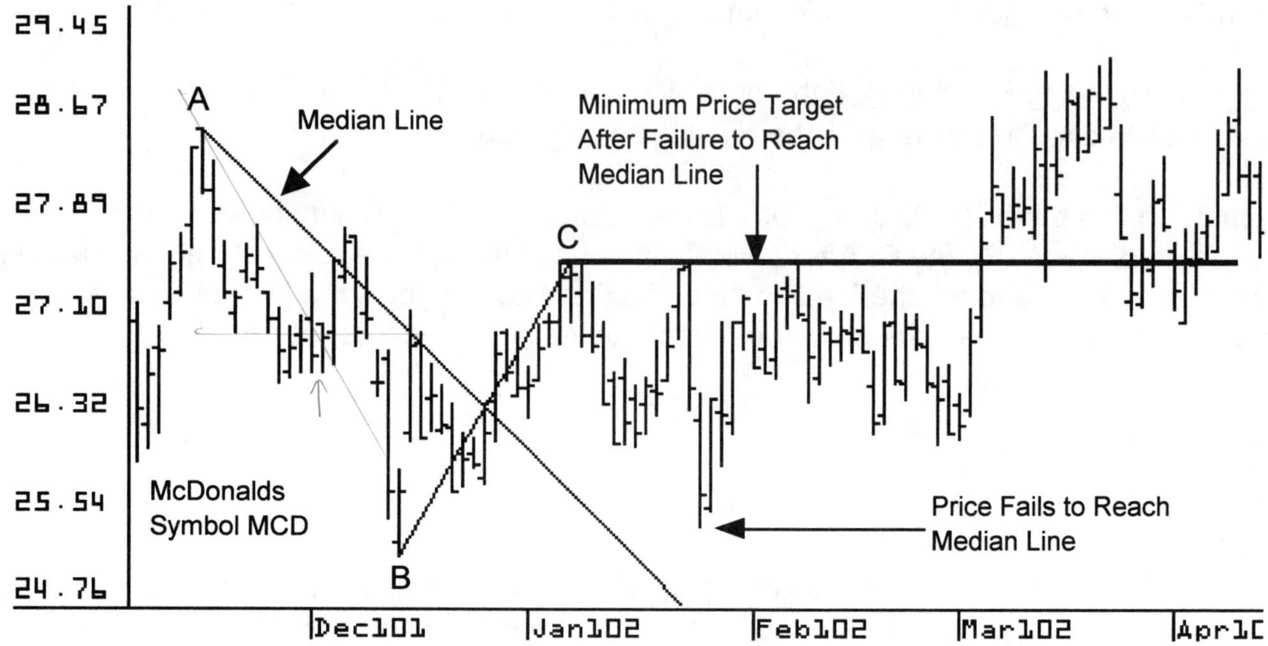

The chart below shows the stock for Compaq, symbol CPQ, with a Median Line drawn using pivots A, B, and C. After pivot C, the price moves up but fails to reach the Median Line. After the price fails to reach the Median Line, the first price target is the low price at pivot C. This chart shows that the price falls below this pivot C price target.

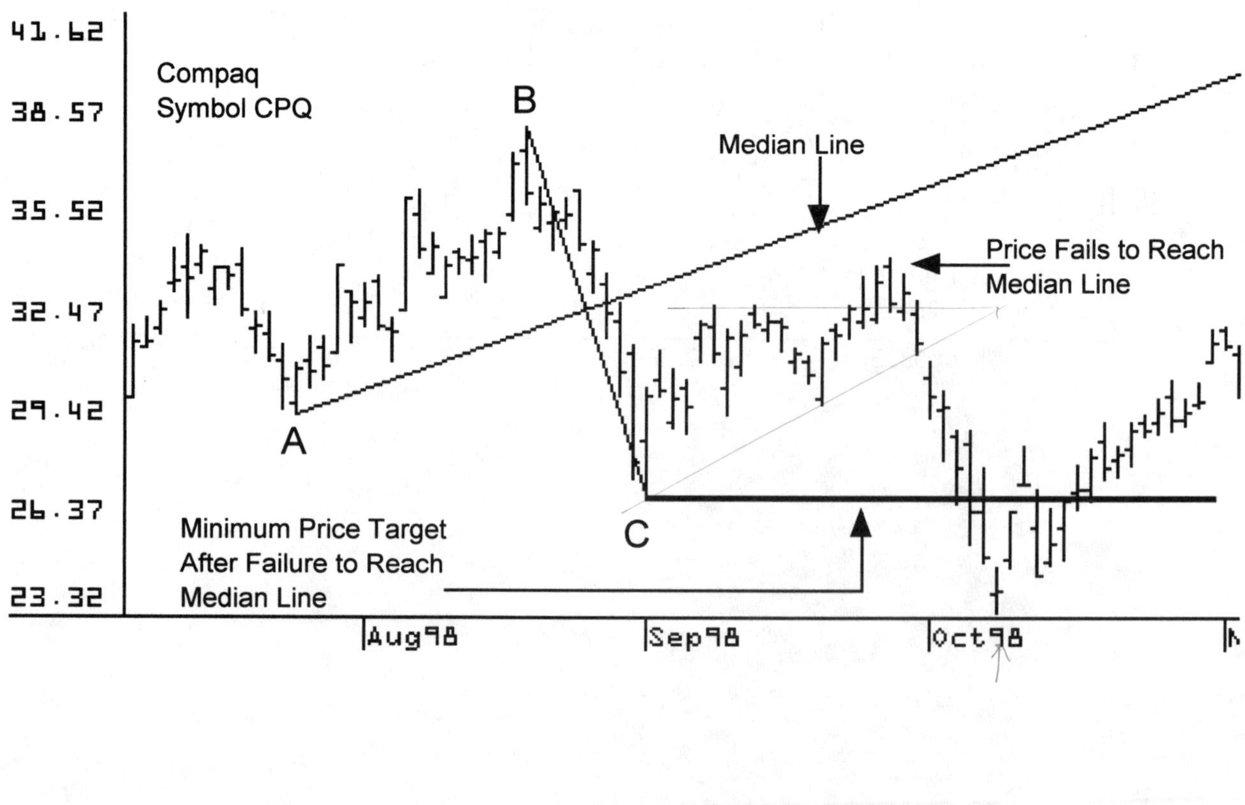

The top chart on this page shows the stock for Xilinx Inc., symbol XLNX. There is a Median Line drawn using pivots A, B, and C. After pivot C, the price falls but fails to reach the Median Line. After the price fails to reach the Median Line, the first price target is the high price at pivot C. The chart shows that the price moves up above the pivot C price target.

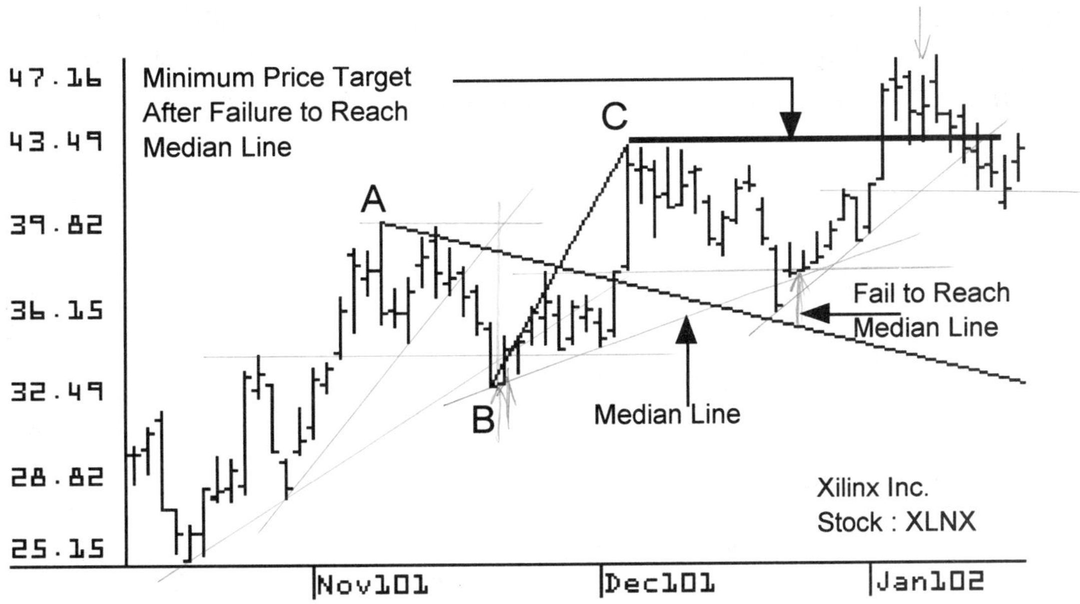

The chart below is for Ameritrade, symbol AMTD, with a Median Line drawn using pivots A, B, and C. After pivot C, the price moves up but fails to reach the Median Line. After the price fails to reach the Median Line, the first price objective is the low price at C. On this chart, the price falls below this pivot C price target.

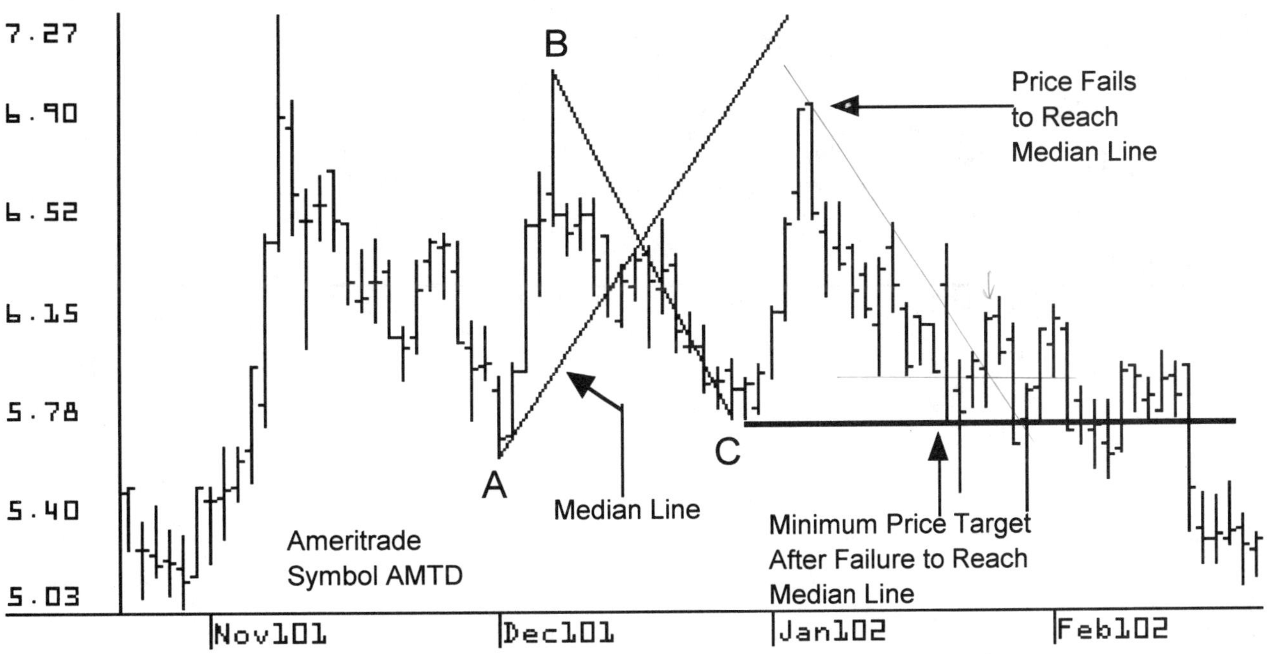

The Pitchfork (Upper and Lower Parallel Lines)

The chart on this page shows a Median Line drawn using pivots A, B, and C. After drawing the Median Line, Andrews added 2 parallel lines starting from B and C. This creates an upper parallel line and a lower parallel line. The three lines on the chart below make what is now known as the Alan Andrews Pitchfork. As far as I can determine, Andrews never used the name Pitchfork. It is included in this book because the term is widely applied to the lines and is well known.

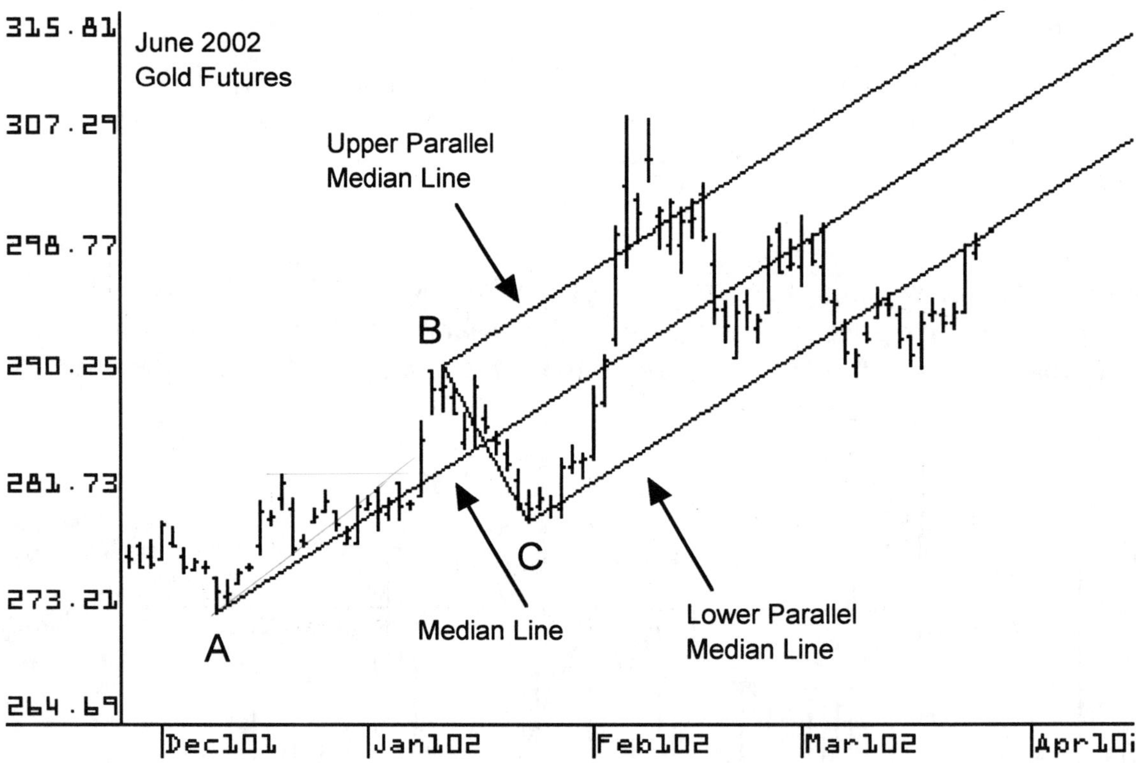

Trigger Lines

Andrews used the lines on the next chart but did not have a name for them. An appropriate title for them is Trigger Lines. On the chart below, there is a standard Pitchfork using pivots A, B, and C. There are two additional lines on this chart. One is a dotted line connecting pivots A and B. This is the upper Trigger Line. The second is a dotted line connecting pivots A and C. This is the lower Trigger Line.

Used with several trading rules, these two lines trigger signals to buy long or trigger signals to sell short. Thus they are aptly named Trigger Lines.

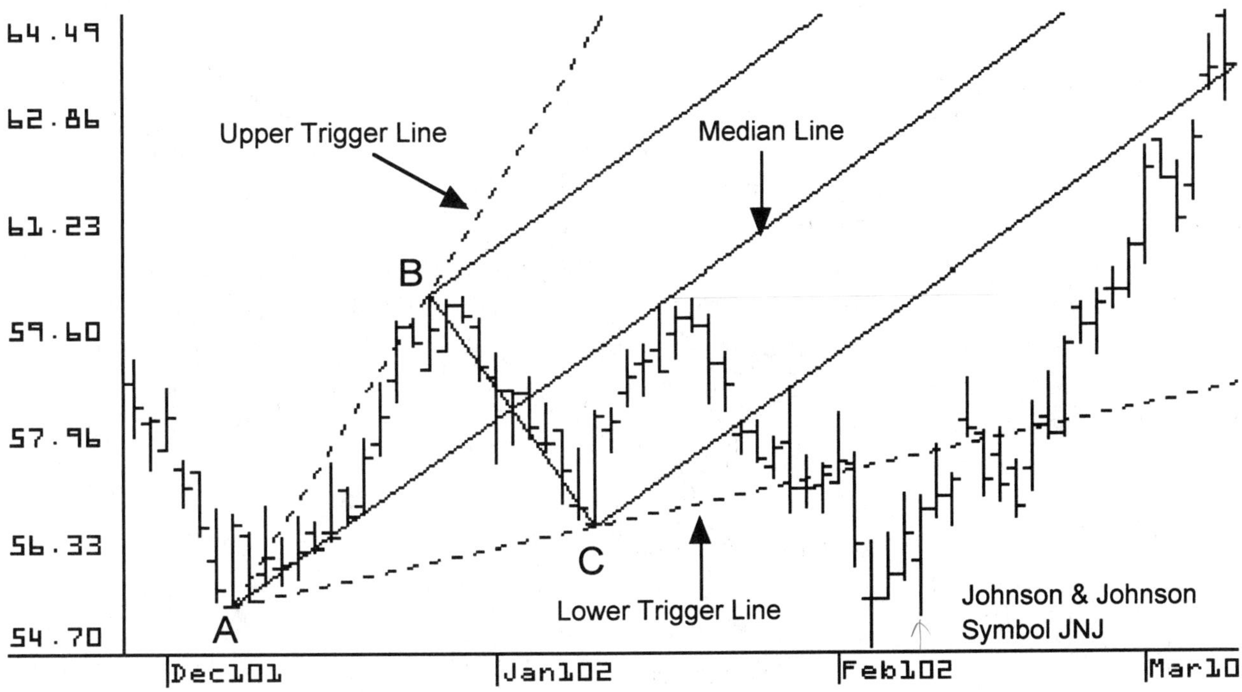

Pitchfork and Trigger Line Trading Rules

Below are some of the rules Andrews provided for using the Pitchfork and the Trigger Lines.

Buy Rule 1: When the price breaks above a downward sloping upper parallel line it is an indication of market strength and can be considered a buy signal.

Sell Rule 1: When the price breaks below an upward sloping lower parallel line it is an indication of market weakness and can be considered a sell signal.

Buy Rule 2: On a downward sloping Pitchfork and an upper Trigger Line, if the price does not fall to the Median Line and then rallies and breaks above the upper Trigger Line, this is a signal to buy.

Sell Rule 2: On an upward sloping Pitchfork and a lower Trigger Line, if the price fails to rise to the Median Line and then falls and breaks below the lower Trigger Line, it is a signal to sell.

Below is the first example of these rules. This chart shows May 2001 Corn futures. On this chart there is an upward Pitchfork using pivots A, B, and C, plus a lower Trigger Line. The price moves up from pivot C but does not reach the Median Line. When the price falls below the Pitchfork lower parallel line, it can be considered an early sell signal or simply an indication that the lower Trigger Line may give a sell signal soon. When the price falls below the lower Trigger Line, the sell signal is given.

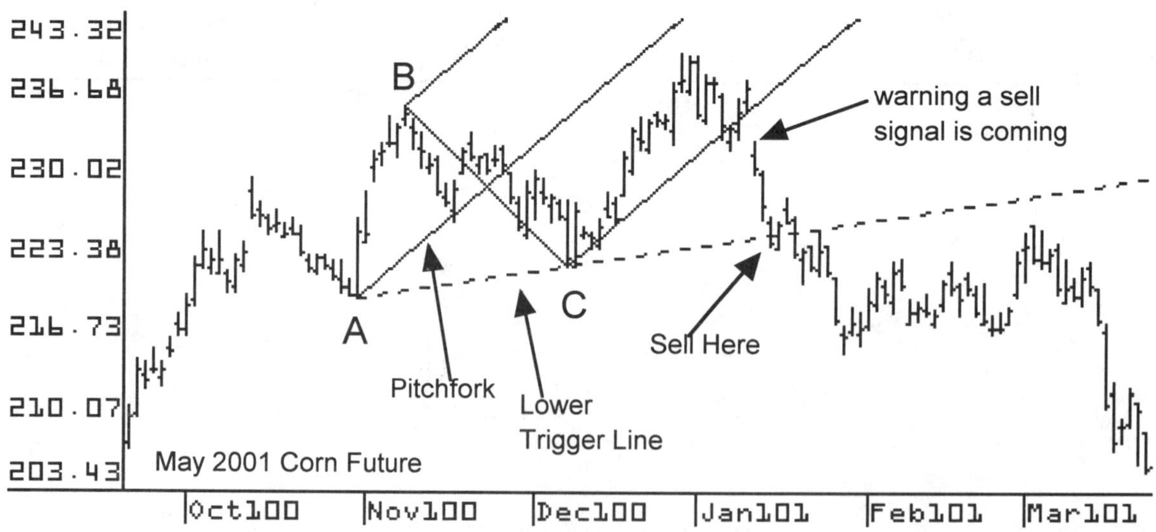

The top chart on this page shows June 2002 Eurodollar futures with an upward Pitchfork drawn using pivots A, B, and C. Also on this chart is a lower Trigger Line. The price moves upward from pivot C but does not reach the Median Line. When the price falls below the Pitchfork lower parallel line, it is an indication that a sell signal is coming. When the price falls below the lower Trigger Line, the sell signal is present.

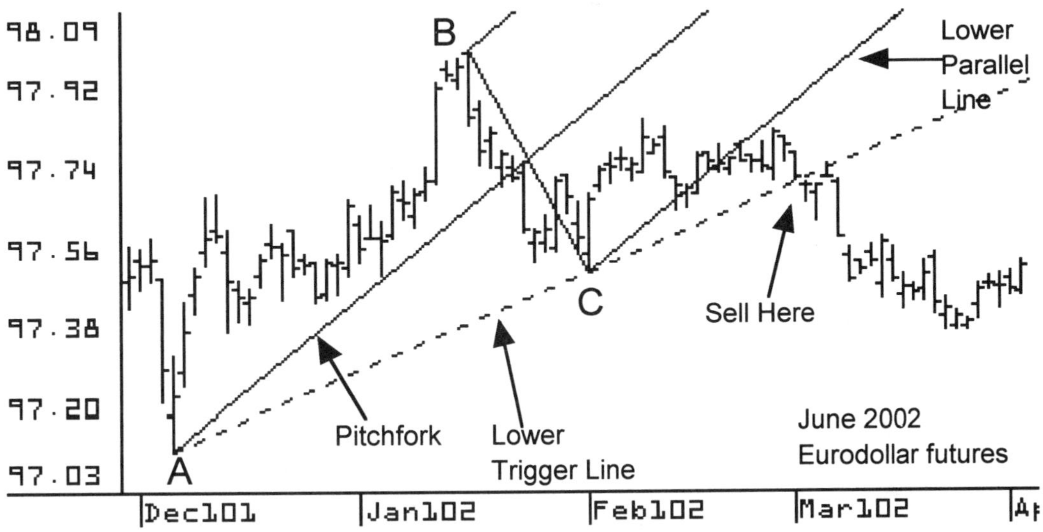

The chart below shows March 2002 Soybean Oil futures with a Pitchfork drawn using pivots A, B, and C. There is also an upper Trigger Line. After pivot C, the price falls but is unable to reach the Median Line. When the price moves above the Pitchfork upper parallel line, it indicates a buy signal is coming. When the price breaks above the upper Trigger Line, the signal to buy is triggered.

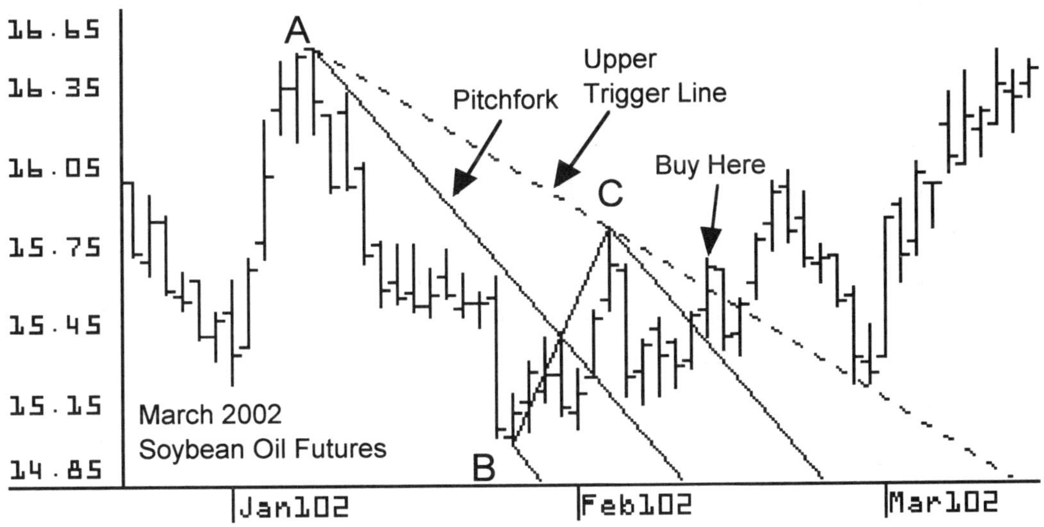

The top chart on this page shows June 2002 Crude Oil futures with a downward Pitchfork drawn using pivots A, B, and C along with an upper Trigger Line. After pivot C, the price falls but is unable to reach the Median Line. When the price moves above the Pitchfork upper parallel line, it indicates a buy signal is coming. When the price breaks above the upper Trigger Line the buy signal is given.

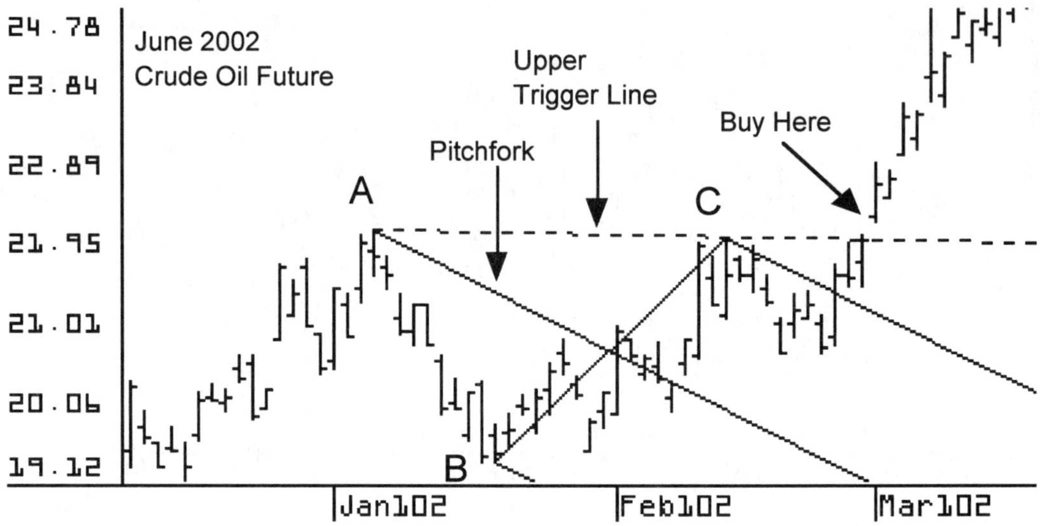

The chart below shows June 2002 Euro-Currency futures with a downward Pitchfork drawn using pivots A, B, and C and an upper Trigger Line. After pivot C, the price does not fall to the Median Line. When the price moves above the Pitchfork upper parallel line, it is an indication of a coming buy signal. When the price breaks above the upper Trigger Line, the buy signal is activated.

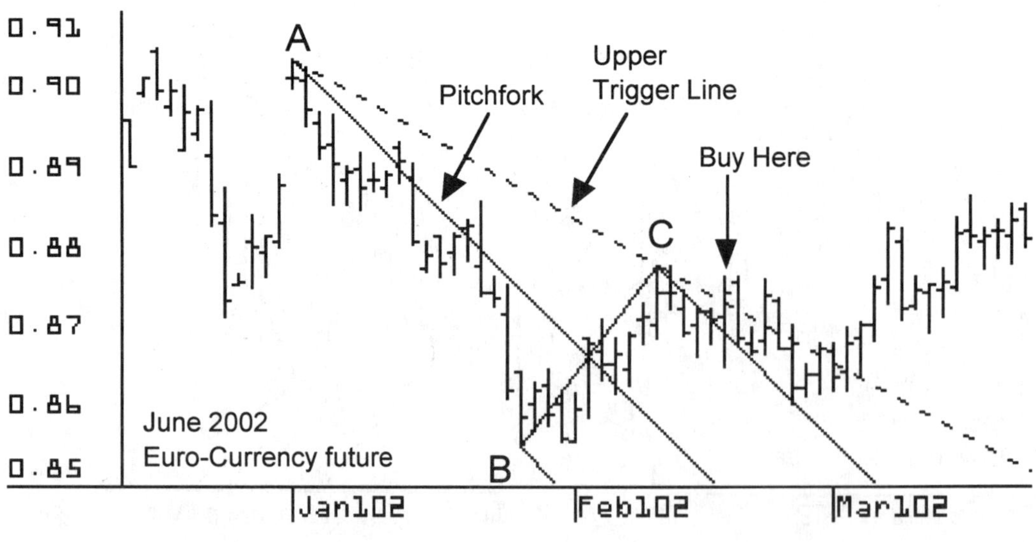

The chart below shows June 2002 Gold futures with a downward Pitchfork using pivots A, B, and C and an upper Trigger Line. After pivot C, the price falls but is unable to reach the Median Line. When the price moves above the Pitchfork upper parallel line, it indicates a buy signal may be coming. When the price breaks above the Trigger Line the buy signal is present.

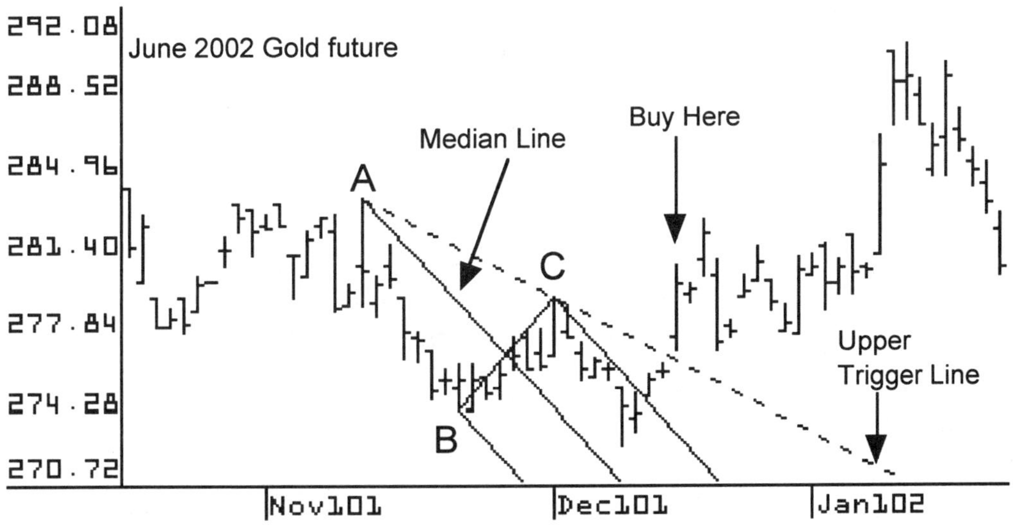

The chart below shows Intel, symbol INTC, with a downward Pitchfork and an upper Trigger Line drawn using pivots A, B, and C. After pivot C, the price falls but is unable to reach the Median Line. When the price moves above the Pitchfork upper parallel line, it indicates a coming buy signal. When the price breaks above the upper Trigger Line, the signal to buy is given.

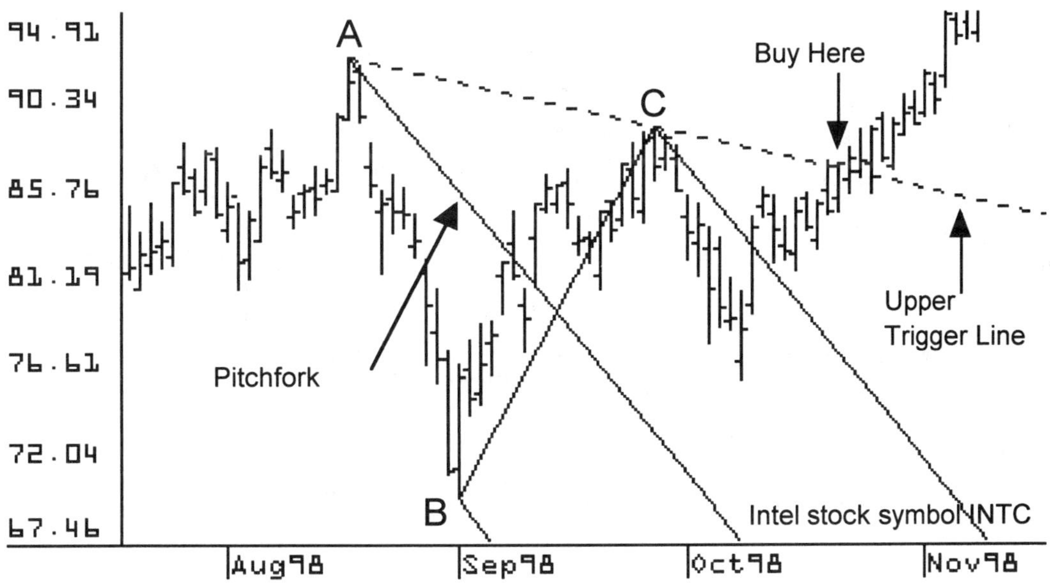

Mini-Median Line

The next Andrews trendline is the Mini-Median Line. This Median Line is drawn much the same way as a normal Median Line except it is drawn using very small pivots. The chart on this page shows a Mini-Median Line. The total number of bars used to draw this Mini-Median Line is only seven bars. The size of a price swing used to draw a Mini-Median Line is about two to five bars. The Mini-Median Line is applied to a chart to search for a signal from a larger Median Line. The Mini-Median Line often generates a signal before the larger Median Line. The signals generated by the Mini-Median Line can be used by themselves or as an early indication that a larger Median Line may be generating a signal soon.

Buy Rule: The Mini-Median Line buy rules are the same as the normal size Median Line buy rules.

Sell Rule: The Mini-Median Line sell rules are the same as for the normal size Median Line rules.

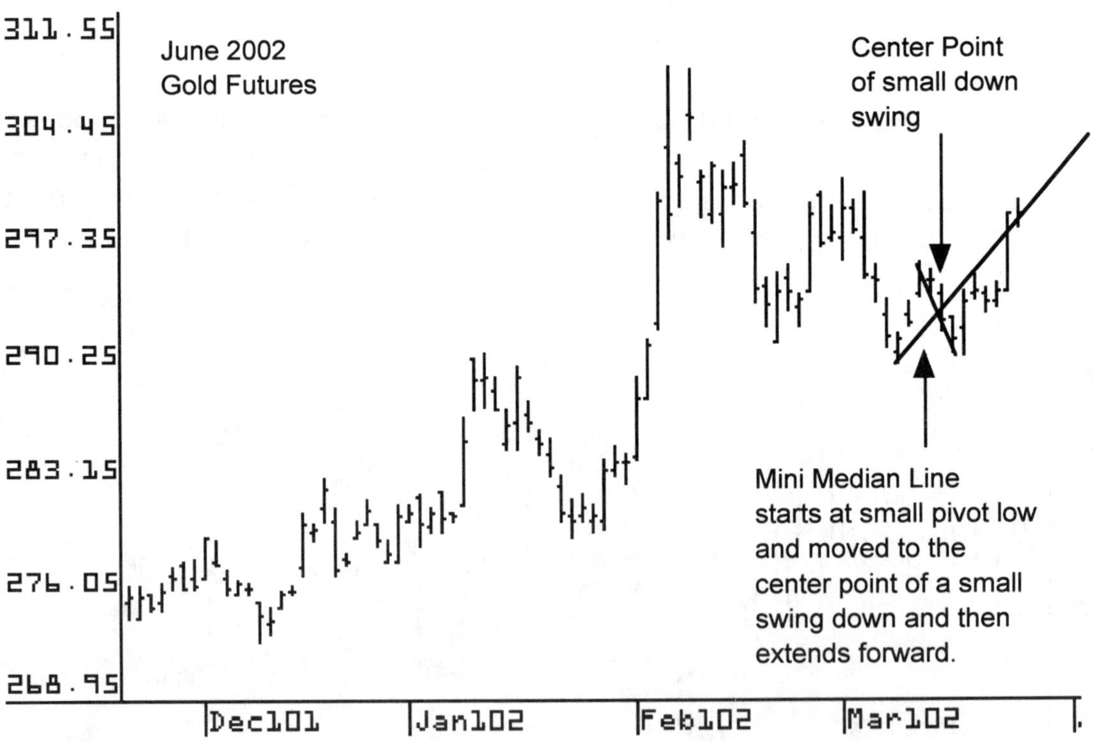

The chart on this page is for Micron Technology, symbol MU. A large Pitchfork is drawn using pivots A, B, and C and a Mini-Pitchfork is drawn using pivots C, D, and E. The Mini-Pitchfork is inside the larger normal size Pitchfork. The purpose of applying a Mini-Pitchfork is to search a for a signal from the larger Pitchfork. This means the Mini-Pitchfork usually is applied when the price is on one of the large Pitchfork lines or inside the larger Pitchfork. On the chart below, the price falls after pivot C, but can not reach the Median Line. This is a sign of strength and an indication to start looking for a buy signal. In this situation, a trader can draw the Mini-Pitchfork from the small swings to help locate the earliest indication of a buy signal. The arrow and text, "Mini Buy Signal," identifies where the price breaks above the Mini-Pitchfork upper parallel line and generates an early buy signal. The Mini-Pitchfork buy signals can be used to enter the market or as an indication the larger Pitchfork will soon give a signal. The arrow and text, "Large Buy Here," identify where the price breaks above the large Pitchfork upper parallel line and generates a buy signal.

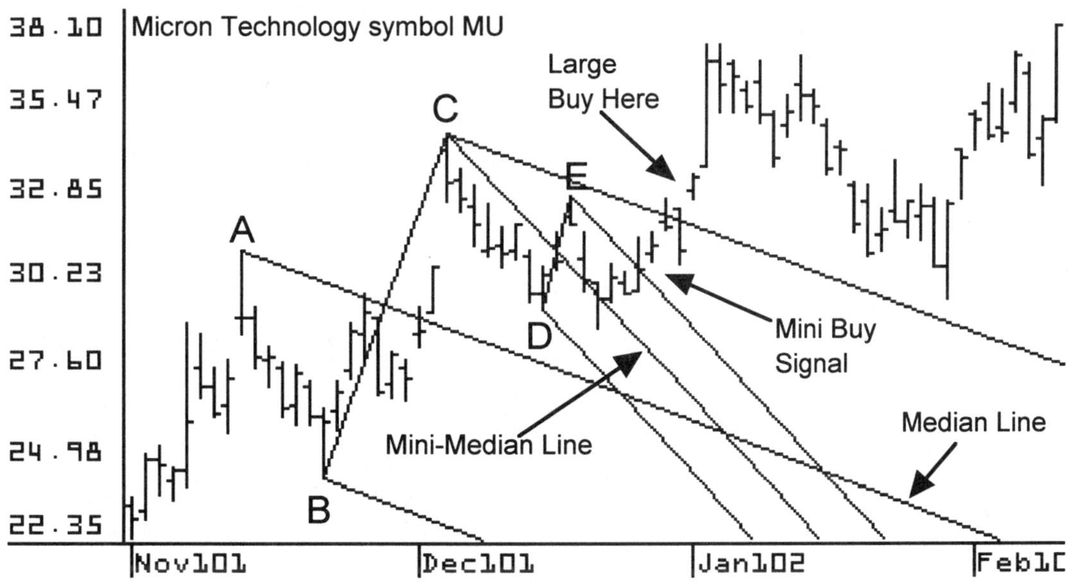

The chart below is for Solectron, symbol SLR and has large Pitchfork drawn using pivots A, B, and C and a Mini-Pitchfork drawn using pivots D, E and F. After pivot C, the price is unable to rise to the large Median Line. This indicates weakness. When the price starts to fall back towards the lower parallel line, the Mini-Pitchfork is drawn. The price moves up from pivot F to the Mini-Median Line and then quickly falls back below the Mini-Pitchfork lower parallel line. The arrow and text, "Mini-Sell Signal," identify where the price breaks below the Mini-Pitchfork lower parallel line and generates a sell signal. This sell signal from the Mini-Pitchfork can be used to enter the market or as an indication that the large Pitchfork may soon give a sell signal. The price continues to fall until it breaks below the lower parallel line of the large Pitchfork. This generates another sell signal. The arrow and text, "Sell Signal," identify where the price breaks below the large Pitchfork lower parallel line and generates a sell signal.

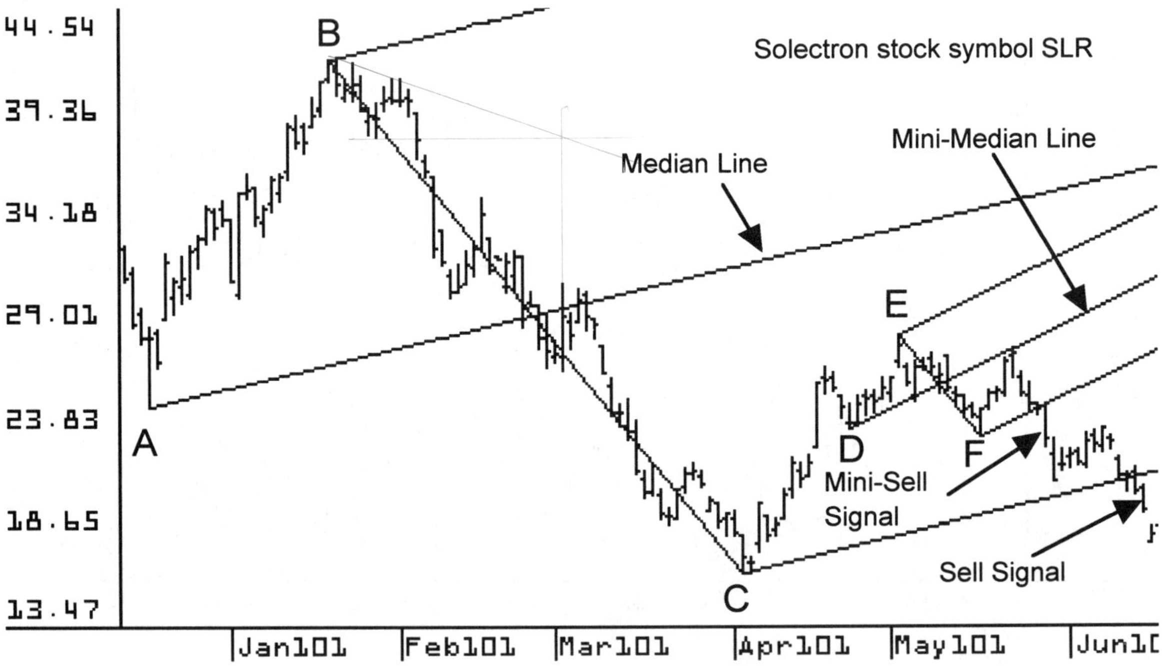

The chart on this page is for Solectron, symbol SLR. A large Pitchfork is drawn using pivots A, B, and C. After pivot C, the price moves up to the large Median Line and starts to make a sideways formation. At this time the Mini-Pitchfork is drawn to look for indications that the market is going to move to the large upper parallel line or move back downward. An upward sloping Mini-Pitchfork is drawn using pivots D, E and F. Also a lower mini-Trigger Line is drawn using pivots D and F. Notice that the price is unable to move up to the Mini-Median Line after pivot F and then falls and breaks below the lower mini-Trigger Line which is a sell signal. This mini sell signal can be used to enter the market or as an indication that a larger sell signal may soon occur.

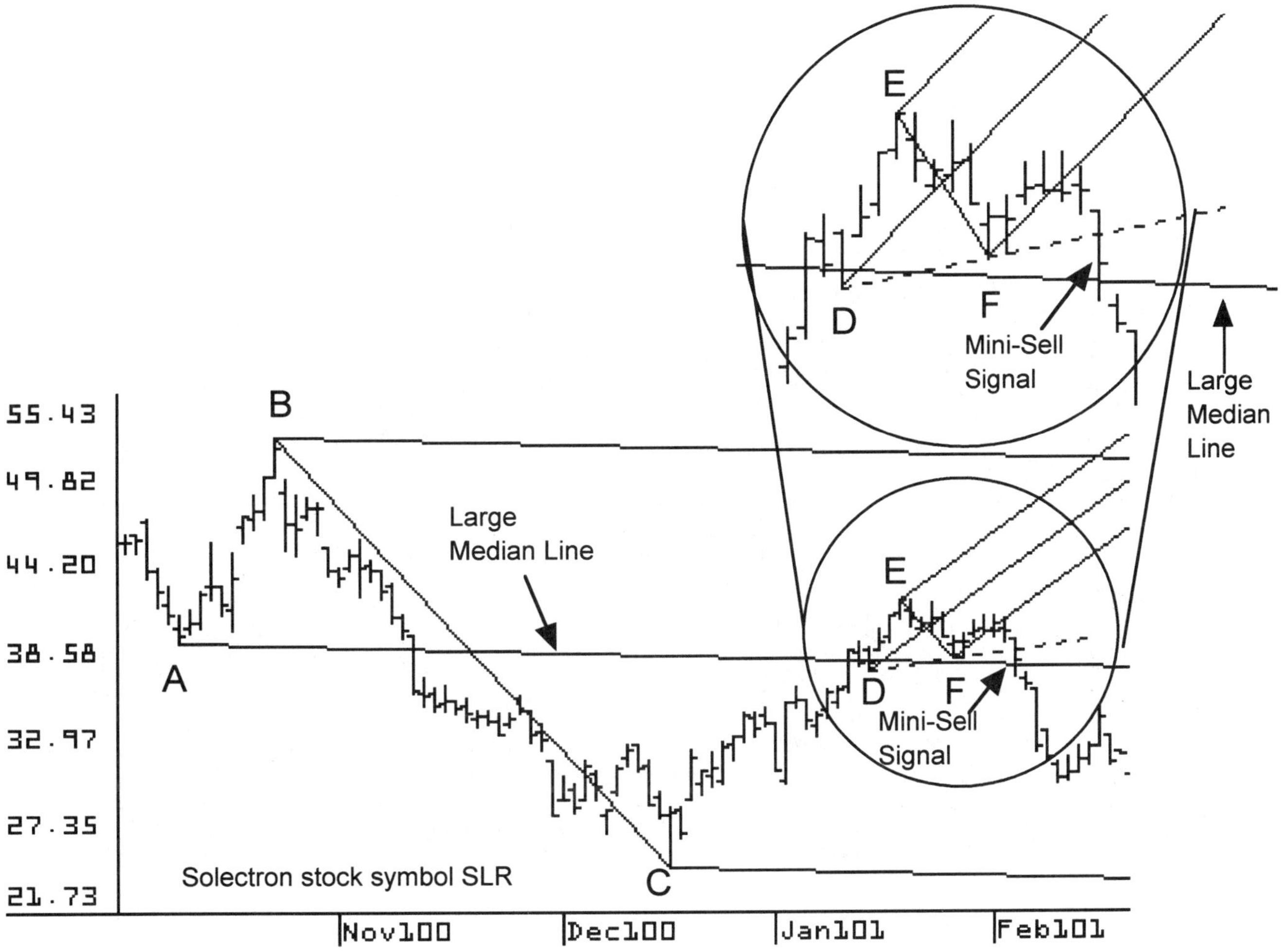

Warning Lines

After the upper and lower parallel lines are drawn to create the Pitchfork, Andrews added additional parallel lines above and below the Pitchfork. These lines are named Warning Lines. On the chart below, two dashed Warning Lines are added to the Pitchfork above the top parallel line and below the bottom parallel line. The position of the top Warning Lines is determined by the distance from the Median Line to the upper parallel line. This distance is measured upward from the upper parallel line and a Warning Line is drawn at each increment. The same is true for the bottom Warning Lines. The distance from the Median Line to the lower parallel line is measured and extended downward. At each increment a lower Warning Line is drawn.

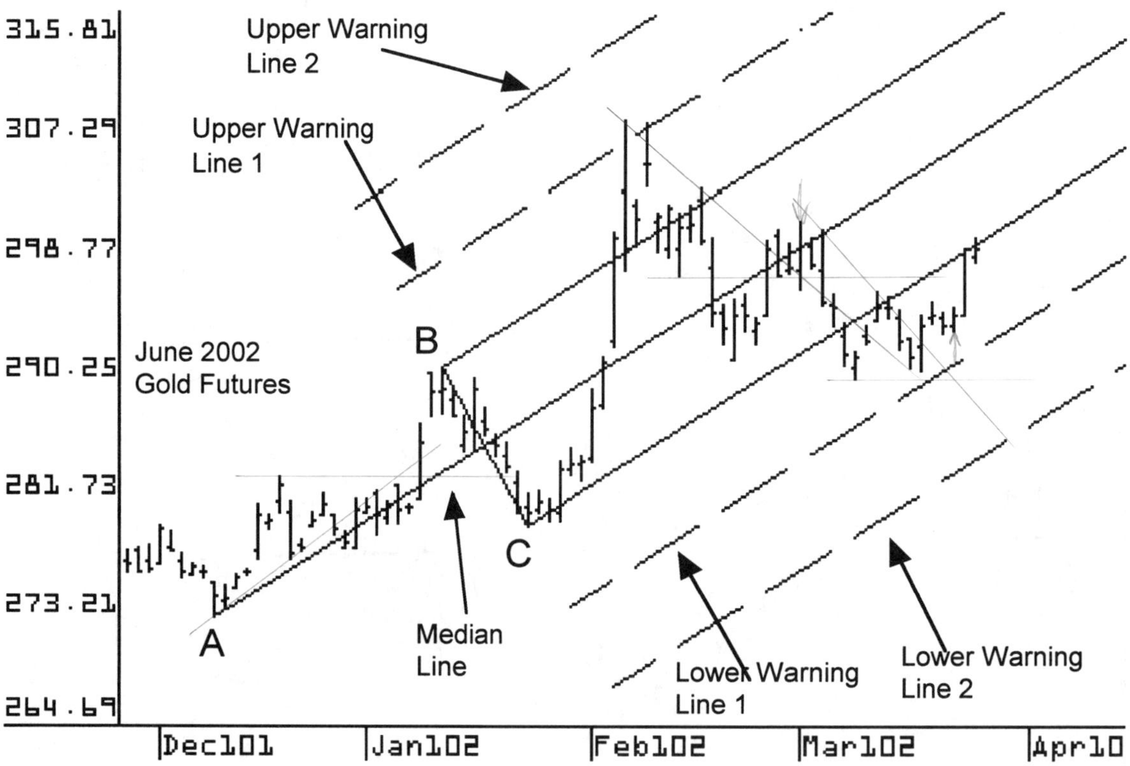

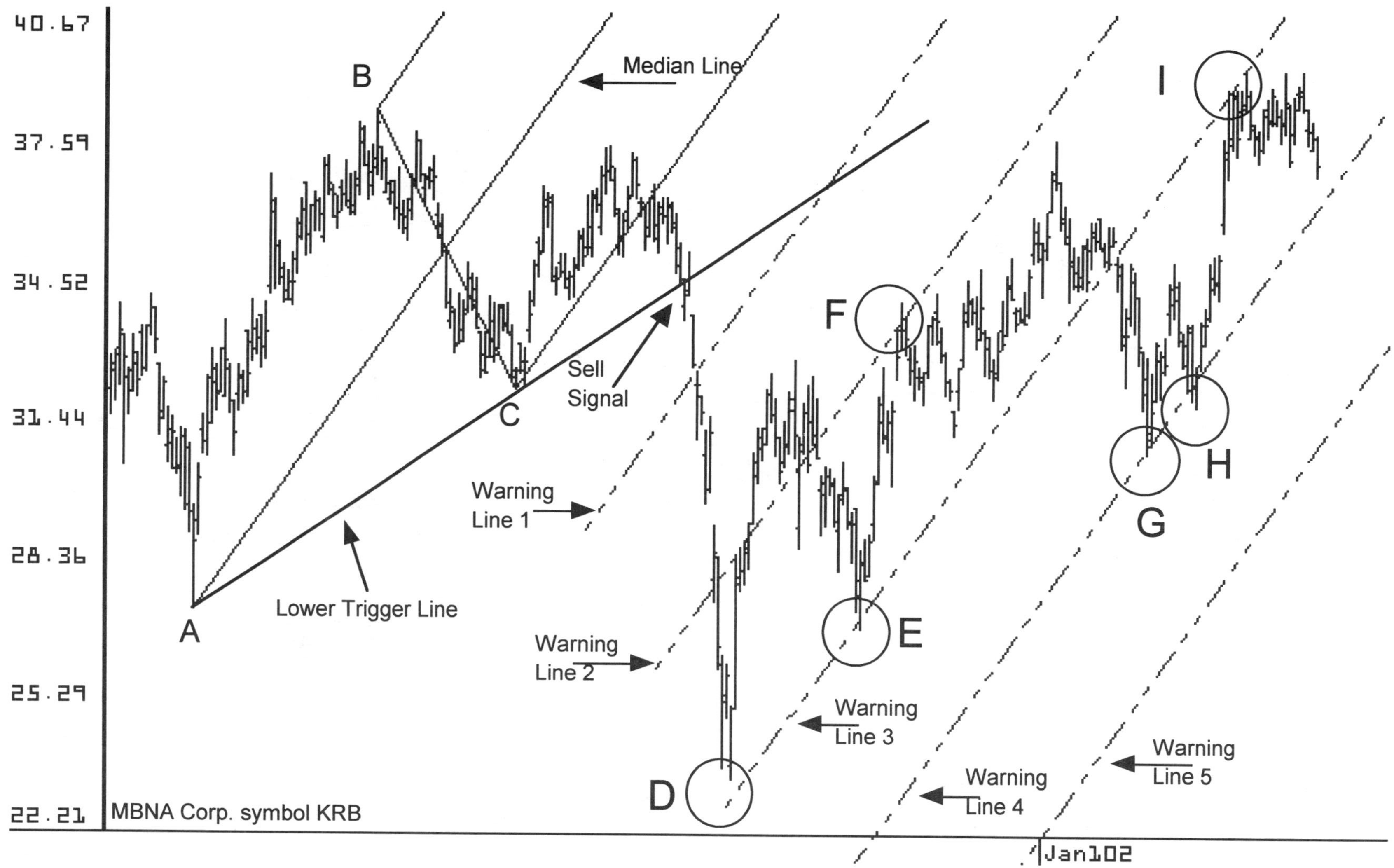

The chart on this page shows the stock for MBNA Corporation, symbol KRB. A Pitchfork and a lower Trigger Line are drawn using pivots A, B, and C. Notice after pivot C, the price does not move up and reach the Median Line. When the price falls and breaks below the lower Trigger Line, a sell signal is generated. After this sell signal, the price falls dramatically and makes a sharp bottom directly above Warning Line 3 at point D. As the price moves up from point D, the price makes bottoms against Warning Lines at points E, G, and H and makes tops against Warning Lines at points F and I. Notice after point D, Warning Line 2 and 3 work as a trendline channel until the price breaks below Warning Line 3 down to point G. Then Warning Lines 3 and 4 start working as a trendline channel.

Below is a long term weekly chart for Philip Morris, symbol MO. A Pitchfork and one Warning Line are drawn using pivots A, B, and C. After pivot C, the price moves down in two waves. The first wave moves down and makes a bottom at point D on the Pitchfork lower parallel line. The second wave moves down and makes a bottom on the Warning Line at point E. After making a bottom on this Warning Line, the price moves up for almost a year.

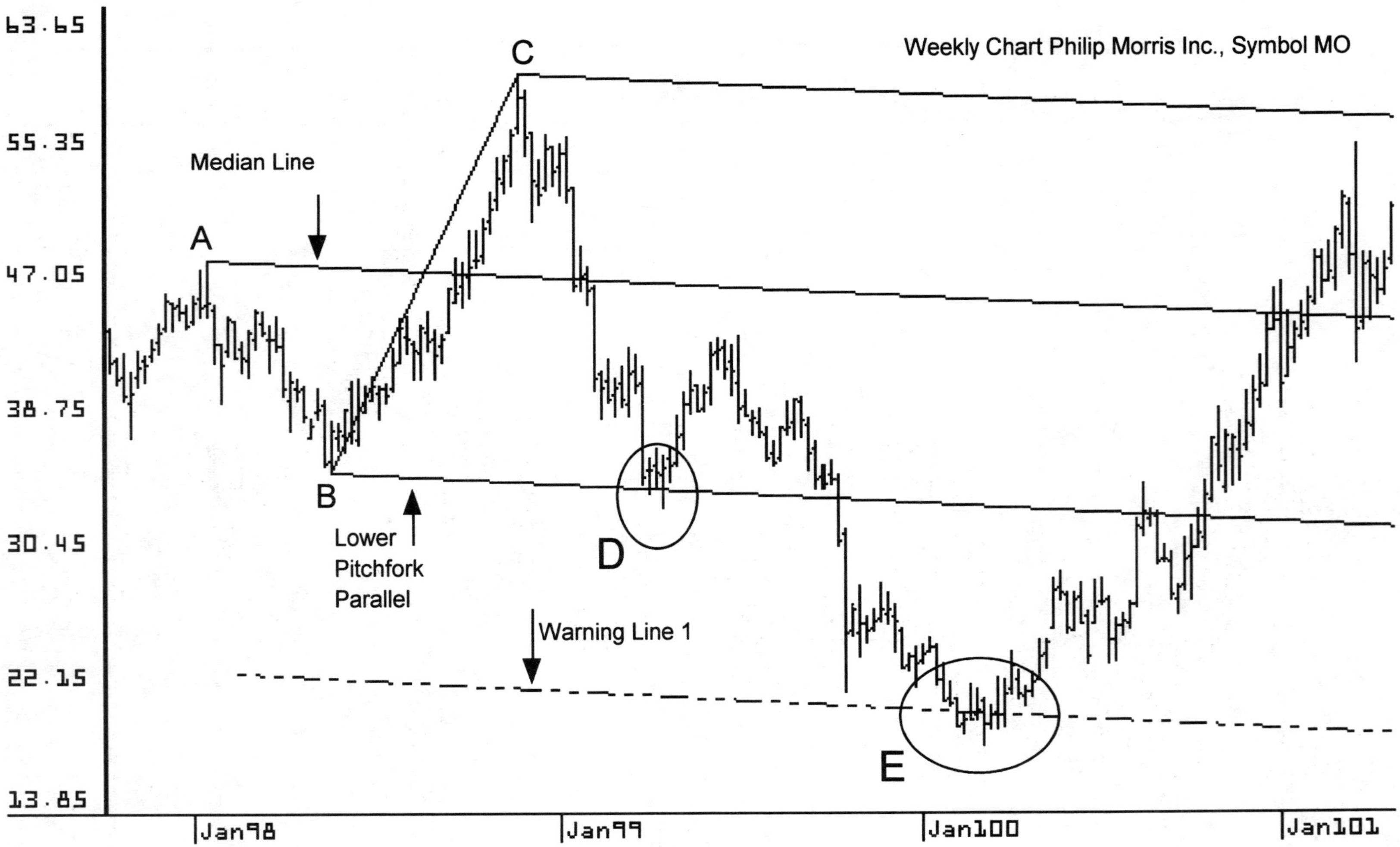

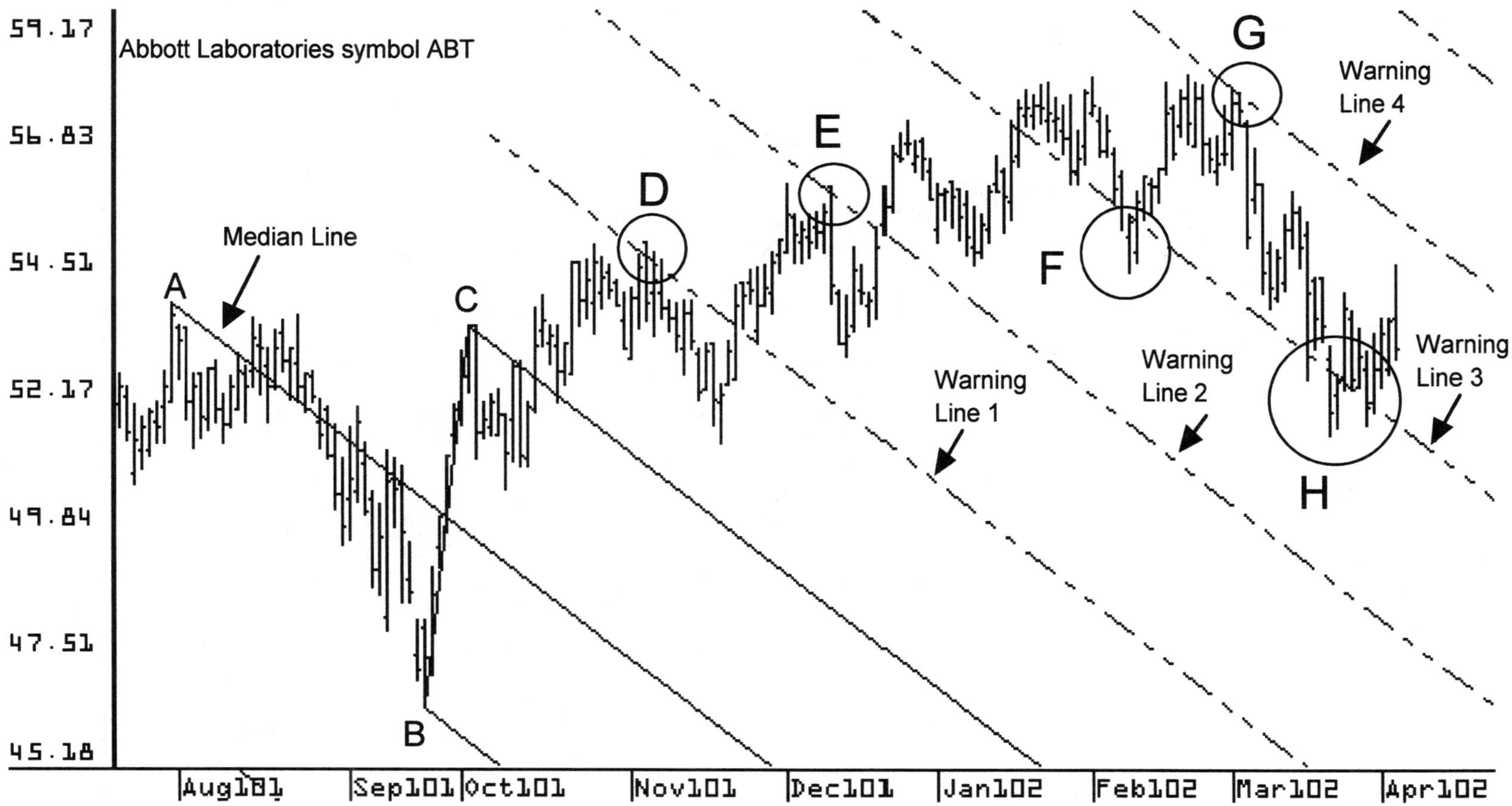

The chart above is for Abbott Laboratories, symbol ABT. A Pitchfork and four upper Warning Lines are drawn using pivots A, B, and, C. After pivot C, the price does not fall to the Median Line which is an indication of market strength. As the price moves up, it makes a swing top against Warning Line 1 at point D, also against Warning Line 2 at point E, and against Warning Line 4 at point G. This market also makes two bottoms against Warning Line 3 at points F and H.

Below is a chart for Comcast corporation, symbol CMCSK. On this chart a Pitchfork and two lower Warning Lines are drawn using pivots A, B, and C. After pivot C, the price moves up and makes a top at point D against the Median Line. The price then makes a second top against the Median Line at point E. After Point E, the price falls sharply and makes its next top against the Pitchfork lower parallel at point F. After point F, the price moves swiftly down to Warning Line 2 at point G. Finally the price moves up and makes a top against Warning Line 1 at point H. This shows that almost all the significant swing tops and bottoms are made against one of the Pitchfork lines or the Warning Lines.

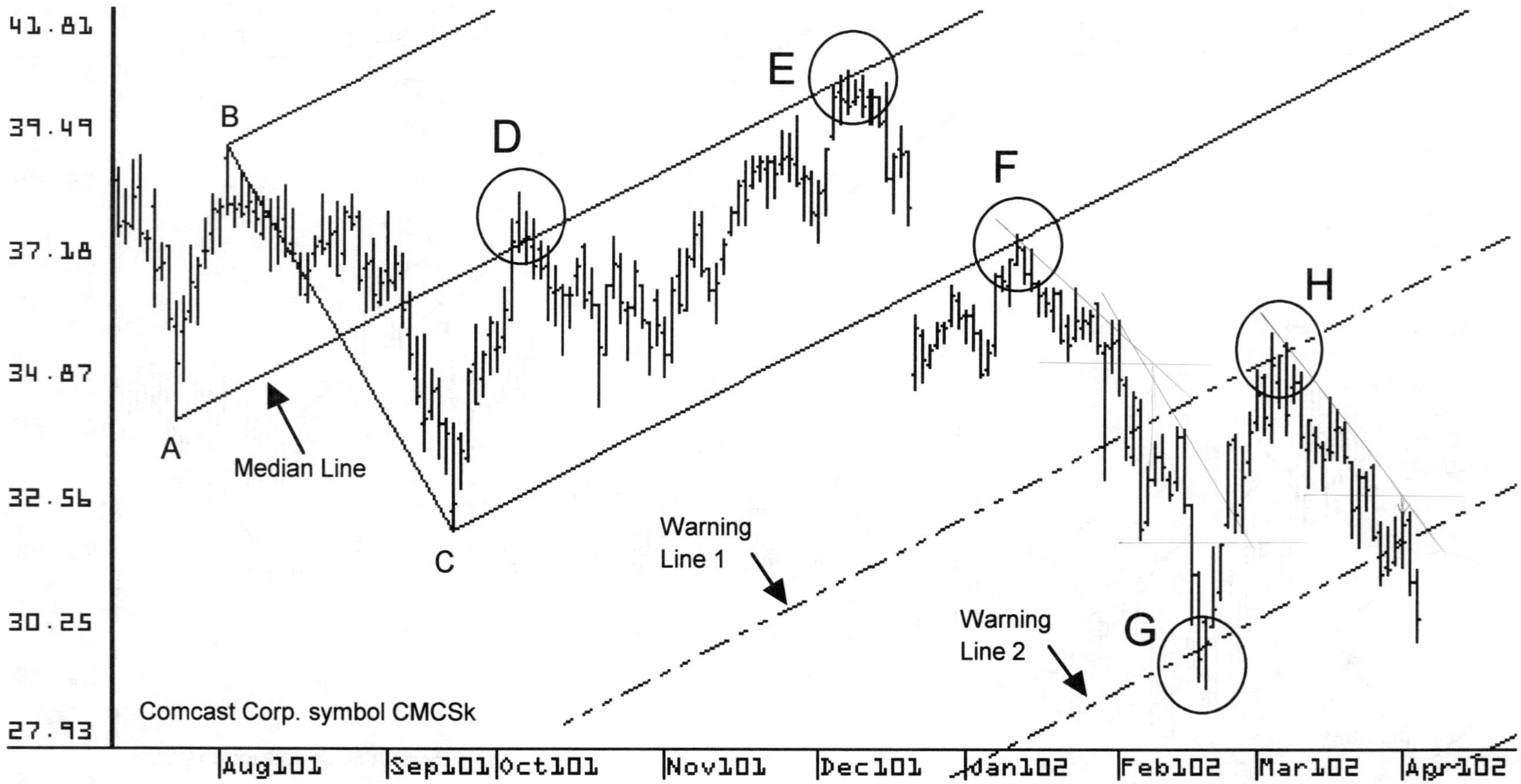

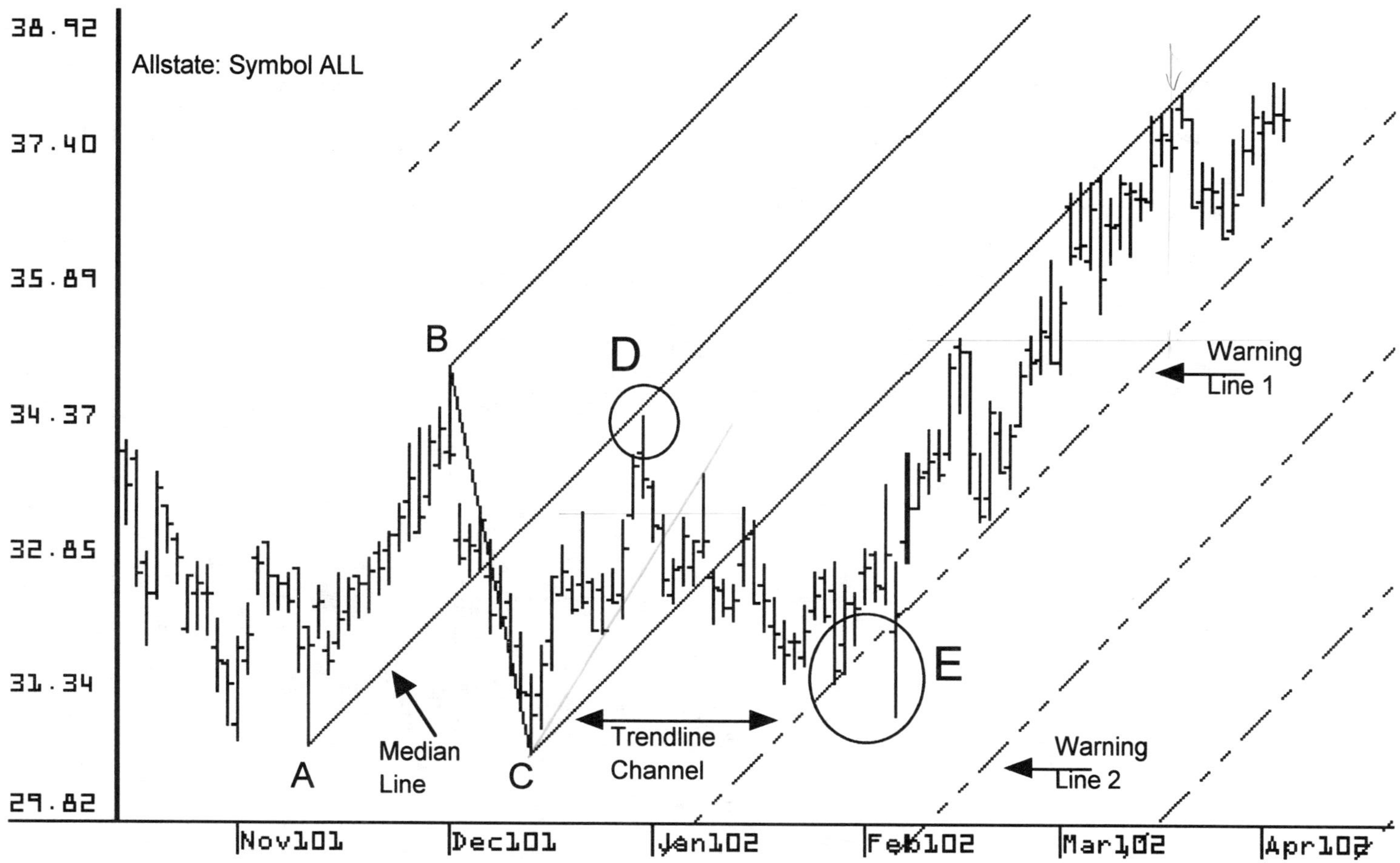

Above is a very simple example using the chart for Allstate, symbol ALL. A Pitchfork and several Warning Lines are drawn using pivots A, B, and C. After pivot C, the market moves up to the Median Line at point D. The price then falls to Warning Line 1 at point E and makes a bottom. After point E, the Pitchfork lower parallel line and Warning Line 1 work as a trendline channel for the upward trend which follows point E.

The next chart shows Boeing stock, symbol BA. A Pitchfork and four Warning Lines are drawn using pivots A, B, and C. After pivot C, the price moves up to a top just below the Pitchfork upper parallel line at point D. The price then falls and makes a sideways congestion area against the Pitchfork lower parallel line at point E. Finally from point E, the price collapses down to Warning Line 4 and makes a bottom at point F. This shows that the price levels set by the Pitchfork and the Warning Lines are a good estimation of the future swing sizes for Boeing.

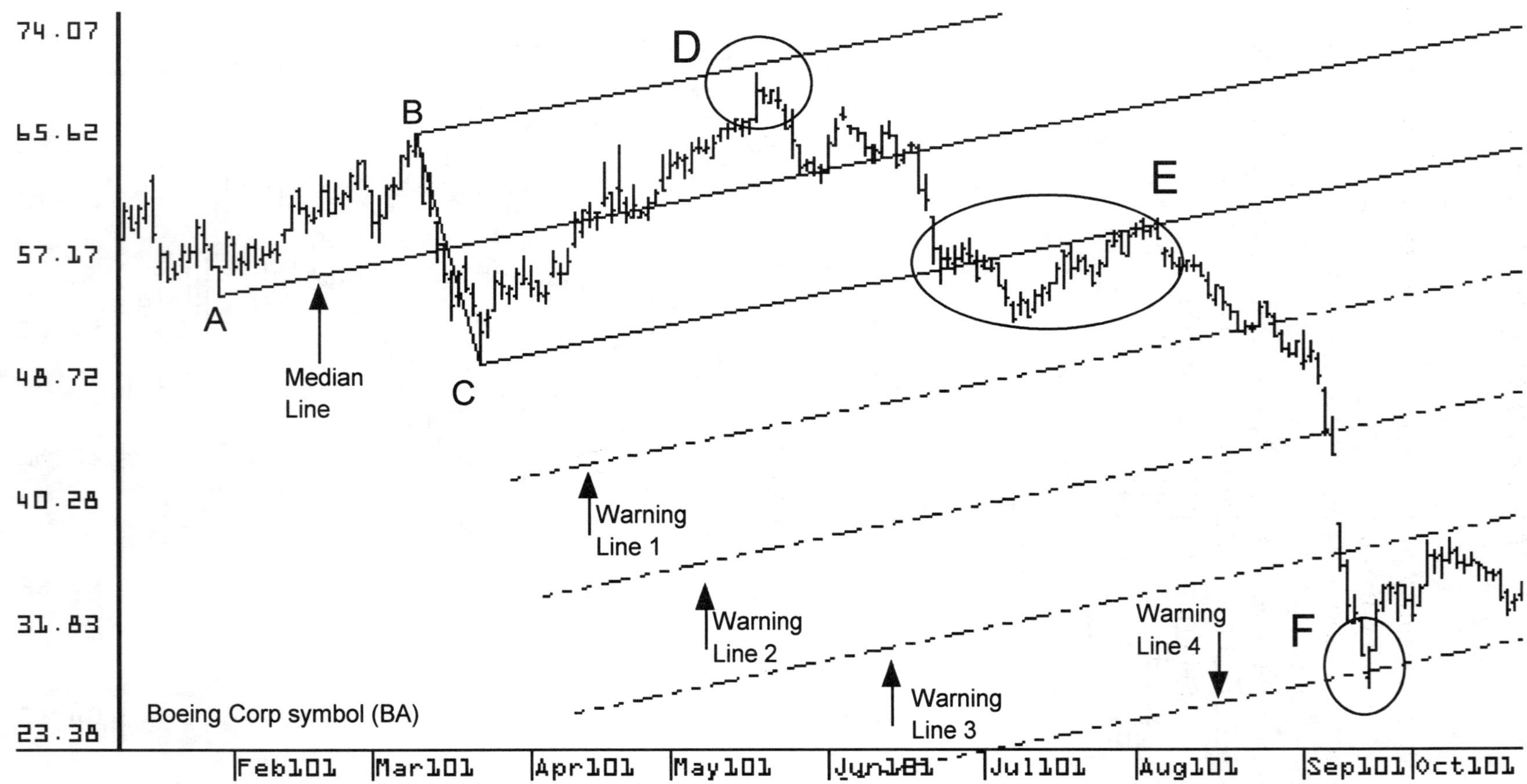

The Expanding Swings Pattern

There was only one pattern which Andrews considered important enough to include as part of his course. This is the expanding swings pattern which is shown in the diagram below. This pattern occurs when a series of price swings become increasingly larger. On the diagram below, the swing from B to C is larger than the swing from A to B. The swing from C to D is larger than the swings that precede it and the swing from D to E is the largest. Andrews believed that this pattern is formed in a market that is becoming unstable and would soon have a sharp break to the down side.

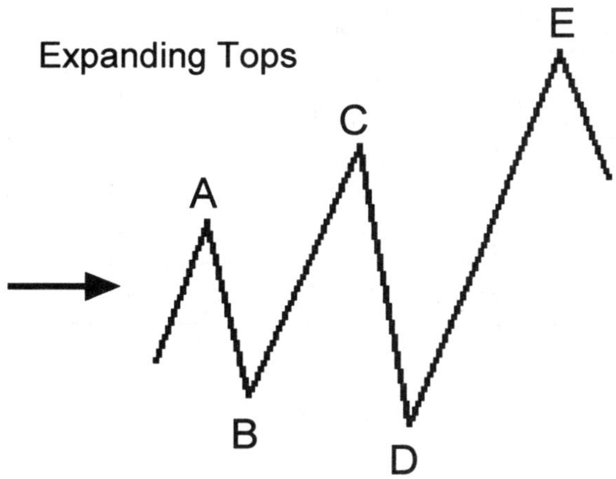

Below is an example of Andrews expanding swings patterns. This is a topping pattern and usually occurs when the market is more volatile than normal. This pattern indicates that the market is becoming unstable and a breakdown is coming. The heavy black line below the price bars identifies the up and down swings in the price bars which make up this pattern. Each up swing is greater than the previous up swing and each down swing is greater than the previous down swing. This specific pattern in this stock is considered extra important because it forms on a long term Median Line. After the pattern forms, the price does have a downward move.

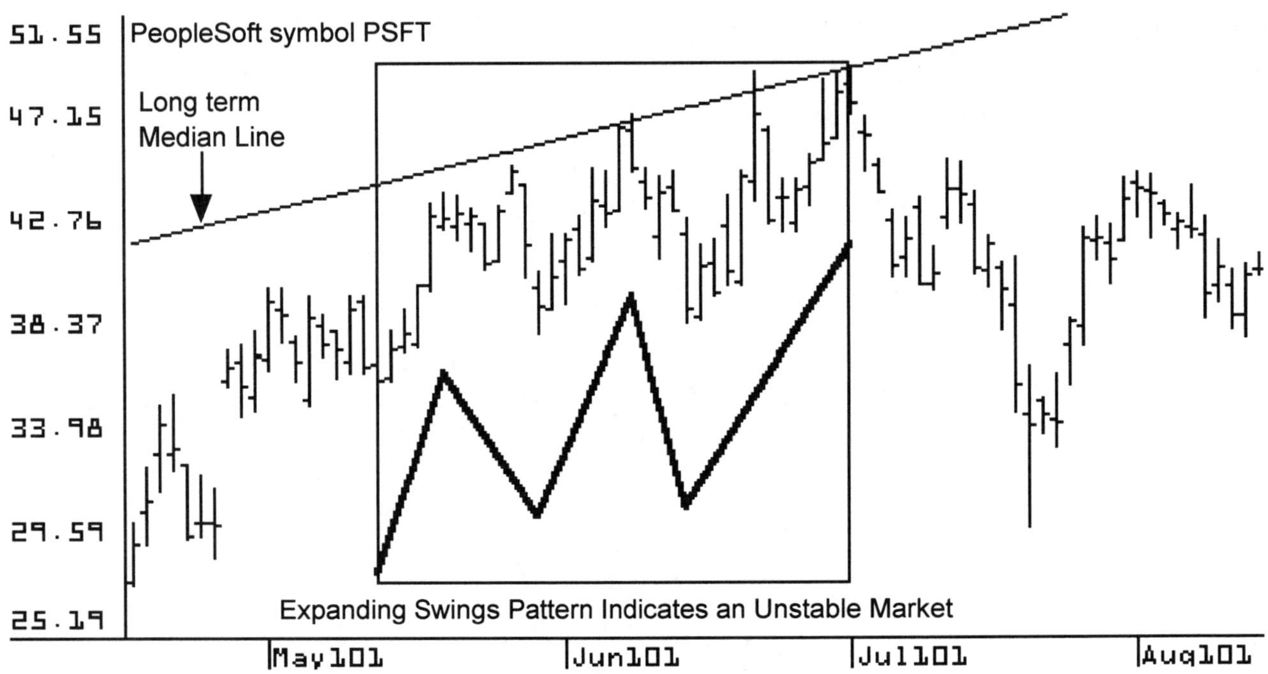

Action Reaction Method 1

In Andrews seminars and in his Action Reaction course, Andrews said if traders understood this one method they could make a million dollars.

Step 1: Center Line

Action Reaction Method 1 uses three different types of lines, the Center Line, the Action Lines, and the Reaction Lines. The first step in applying this method is to select a Center Line. A Center Line can be Median Line, a trendline or Multi-Pivot Line. The Center Line can not be one of the parallel lines such as the upper or lower parallel line on a Pitchfork or a Warning Line. The chart below is a weekly chart for Halliburton, symbol HAL. On this chart there is a simple trendline connecting pivots A and B. This A - B trendline is used as a Center Line. This method is explained further on the next few pages.

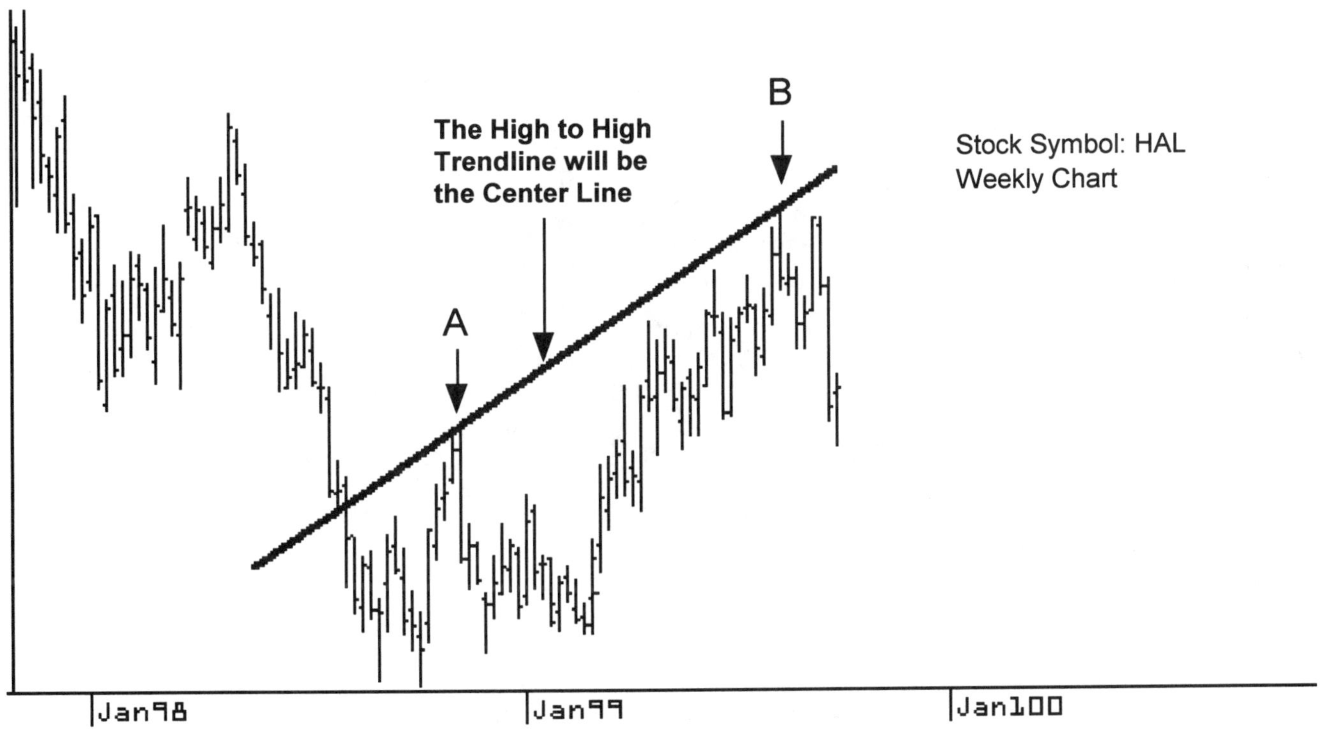

Step 2: Action Lines

The chart below is the same chart for HAL seen on the previous page. The A - B trendline is the Center Line for the Action Reaction Method. Andrews' principle of action reaction in the financial markets is simply that for every action there is a reaction. Action is the historical part of the chart to the left of the Center Line and reaction is the future part of the chart on the right side of the Center Line. According to Andrews the historical market cycles and pivots to the left of the Center Line should correlate with a reaction in the future on the right side of the Center Line.

The Action Lines are drawn with the same slope as the Center Line. The Action Lines are drawn to the left of the Center Line on the historical part of the chart and are positioned so they touch a high or low pivot. On the chart below, Action Line 1 is positioned so it touches a low pivot. Action Line 2 is positioned so it touches a high pivot. This is marked clearly on the chart below.

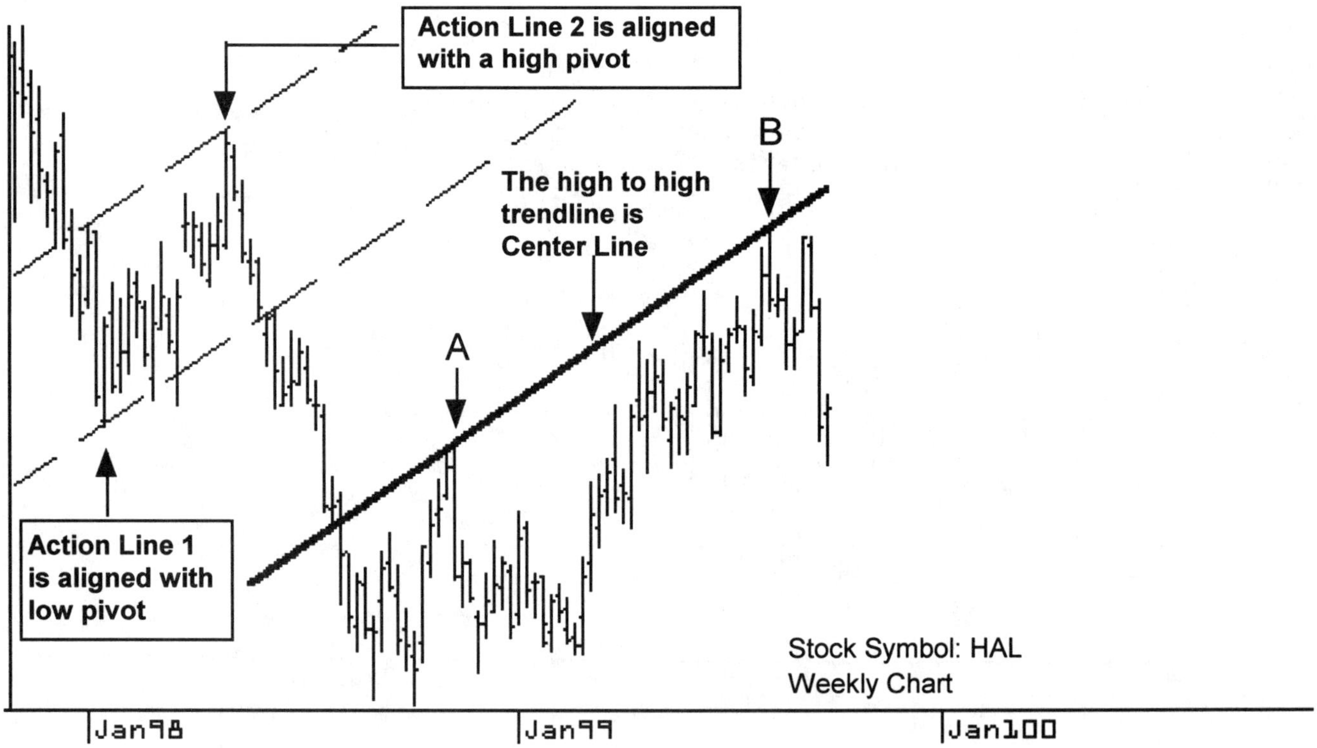

Step 3: Reaction Lines

Action is the historical chart movement and reaction is the future price movement. To draw a Reaction Line, the distance from the Center Line to the Action Line 1 is measured. A Reaction Line is drawn an equal distance into the future from the Center Line. The distance from the Center Line will be the same for Action Line 1 and Reaction Line 1 with Action Line 1 on the left and Reaction Line 1 on the right. This procedure is repeated for Action Line 2. It is obvious how the Center Line earns its name. The Center Line is in the center of the Action Lines and the Reaction Lines. The chart below shows the Center Line with two Action Lines and two corresponding Reaction Lines. The Reaction Lines have the same slope as the Center Line and the Action Lines.

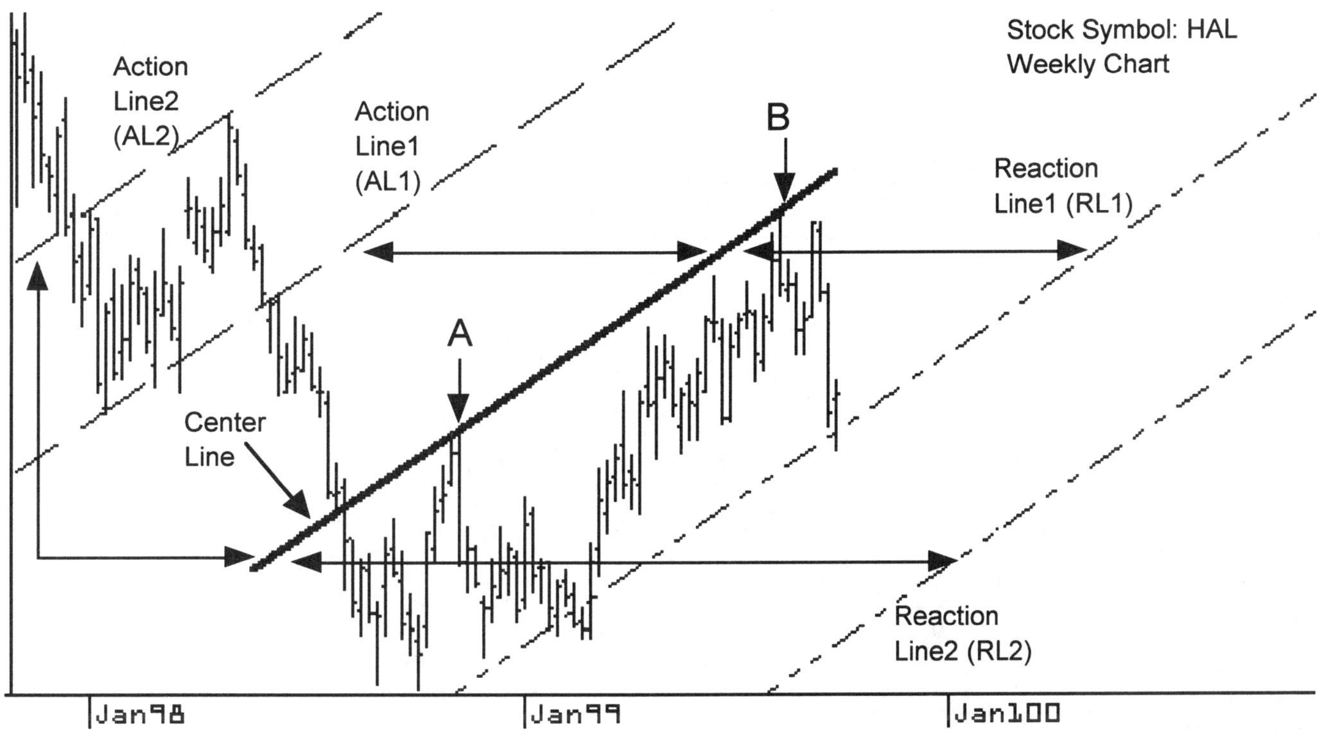

The chart on this page is a continuation of the HAL chart seen on the previous page. The price bars are filled in through the end of the chart. Along Reaction Line 1, there are three swing top pivots at points A, C, and E. For the action of the historical pivot used to create Action Line 1, there is a reaction of three pivots along Reaction Line 1. There are also two bottom pivots along Reaction Line 2. For the action of the historical pivot used to draw Action Line 2, there is a reaction of two pivots on Reaction Line 2. Andrews' action-reaction concept is that each historical pivot is an action for which there will be a future reaction pivot. Using this method a trader is looking for pivots to occur on Reaction Lines.

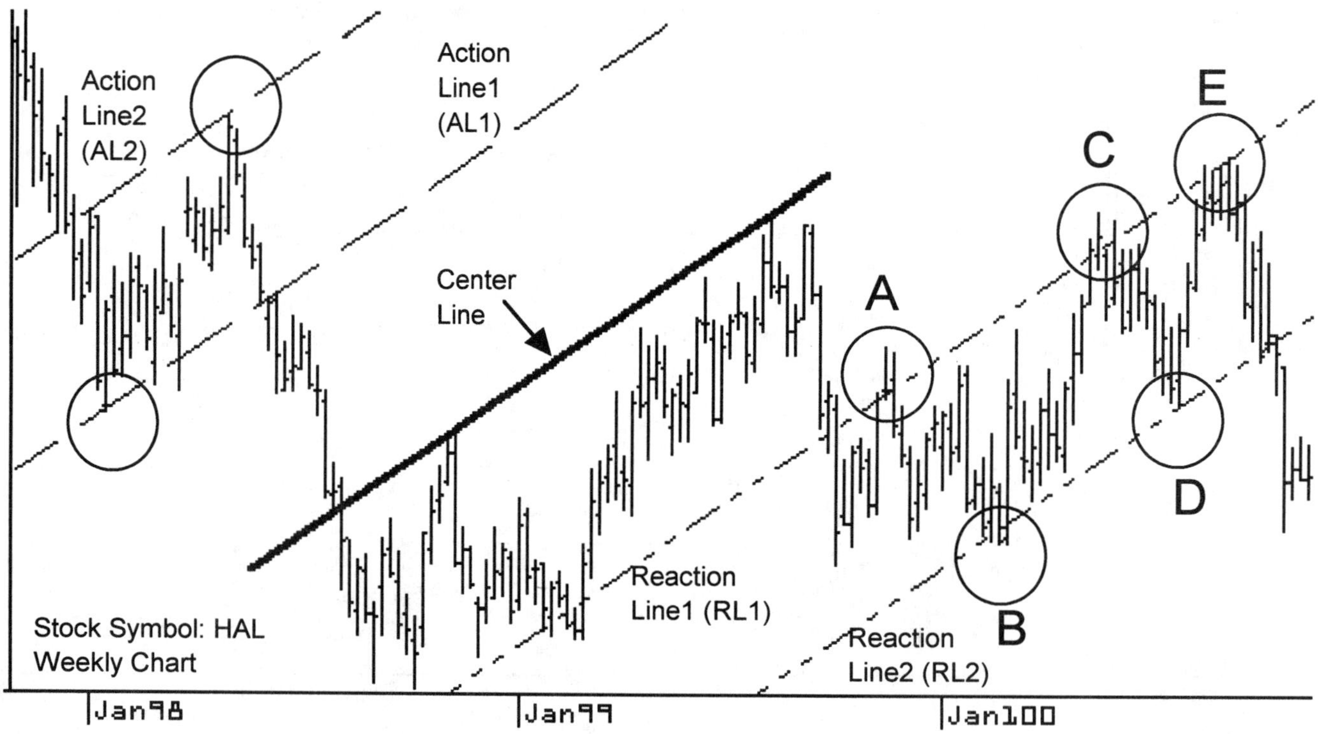

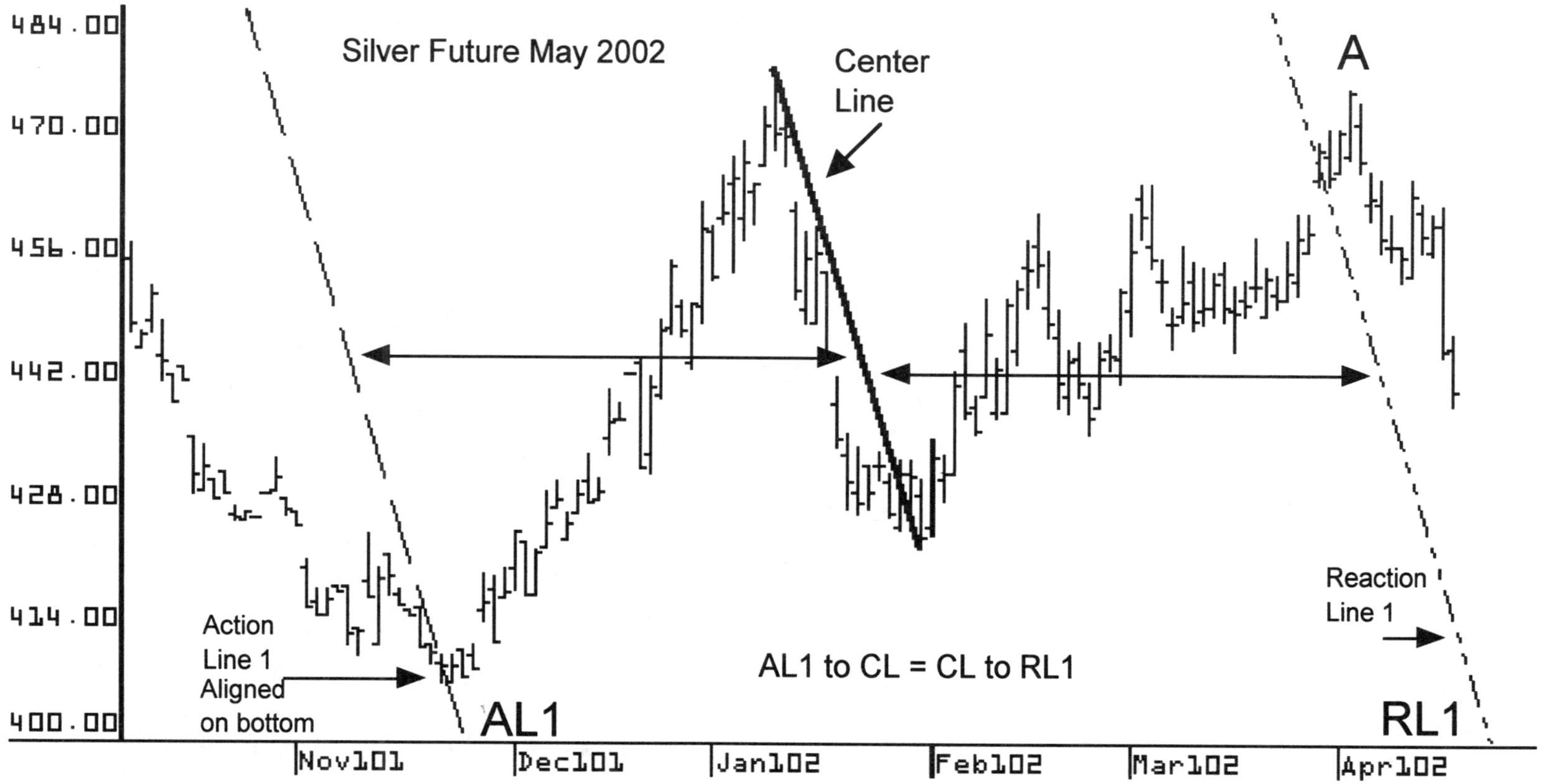

The chart on this page shows a simple example of Action Reaction Method 1. This is a May 2002 Silver futures chart. A high to low trendline is used for the Center Line. The Action Line is the same slope as the Center Line. The Action Line is aligned to start on the first significant swing bottom before the Center Line. The Reaction Line also has the same slope as the Center Line and is drawn the same distance away from the Center Line as the Action Line. The Action Line represents the historical cycle action and the Reaction Line represents future cycle reaction. A top in this market occurrs just after the price reachs the Reaction Line. This top is marked with the letter A.

The chart on this page shows an example of Action Reaction Method 1 using May 2002 Copper futures. The first step when using this method is to select a Center Line. In this case a high to low trendline is used for the Center Line. The four Action Lines on this chart have the same slope as the Center Line and are aligned with previous swing tops or bottoms. The Action Lines must all come before the Center Line and represent historical market action. The Reaction Lines are the same distance from the Center Line as their corresponding Action Lines and have the same slope as the Center Line. On this chart, the market makes a swing top against Reaction Line 1 at point A. The market makes a swing bottom against Reaction Line 2 at point B and makes another top against Reaction Line 4 at point C.

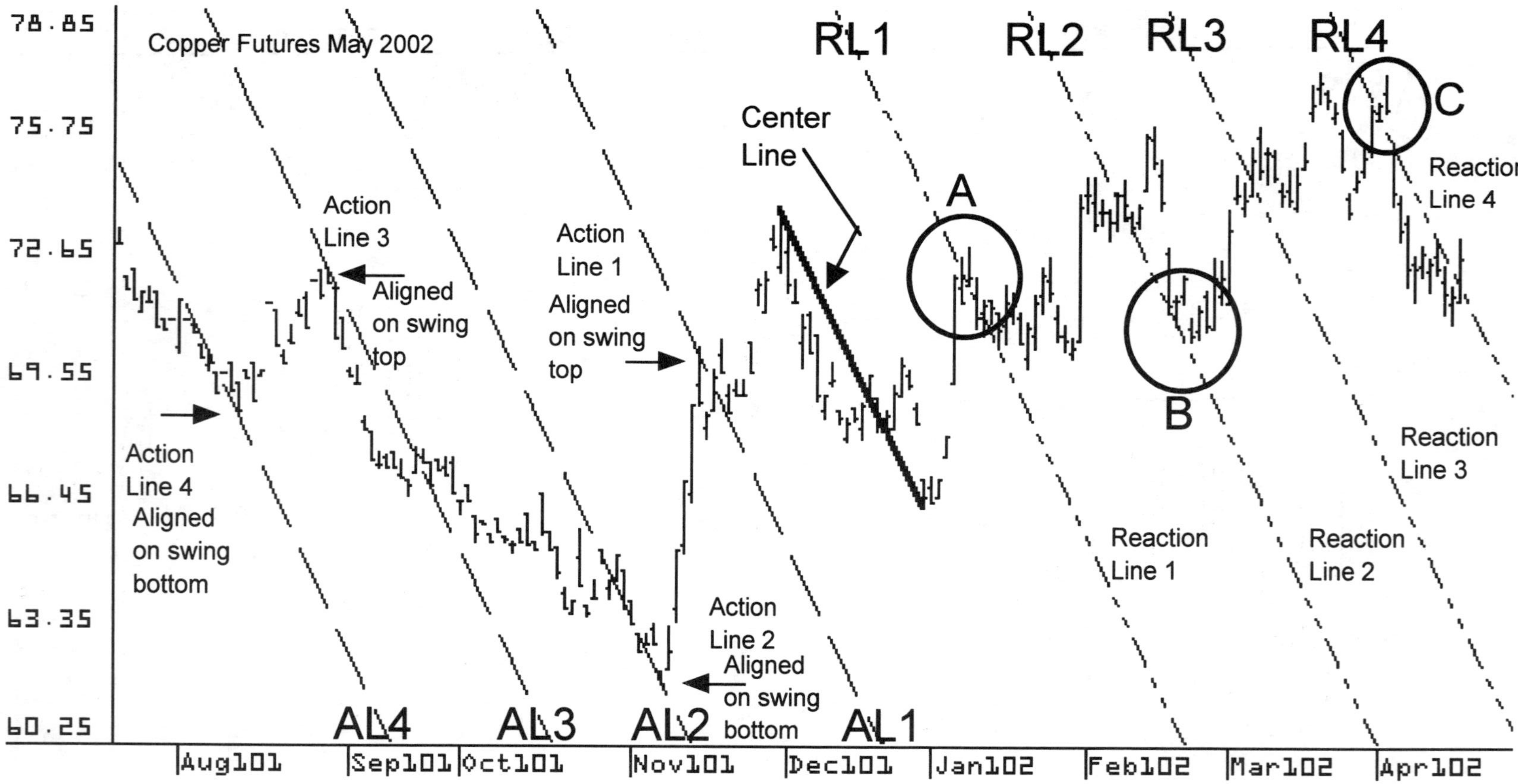

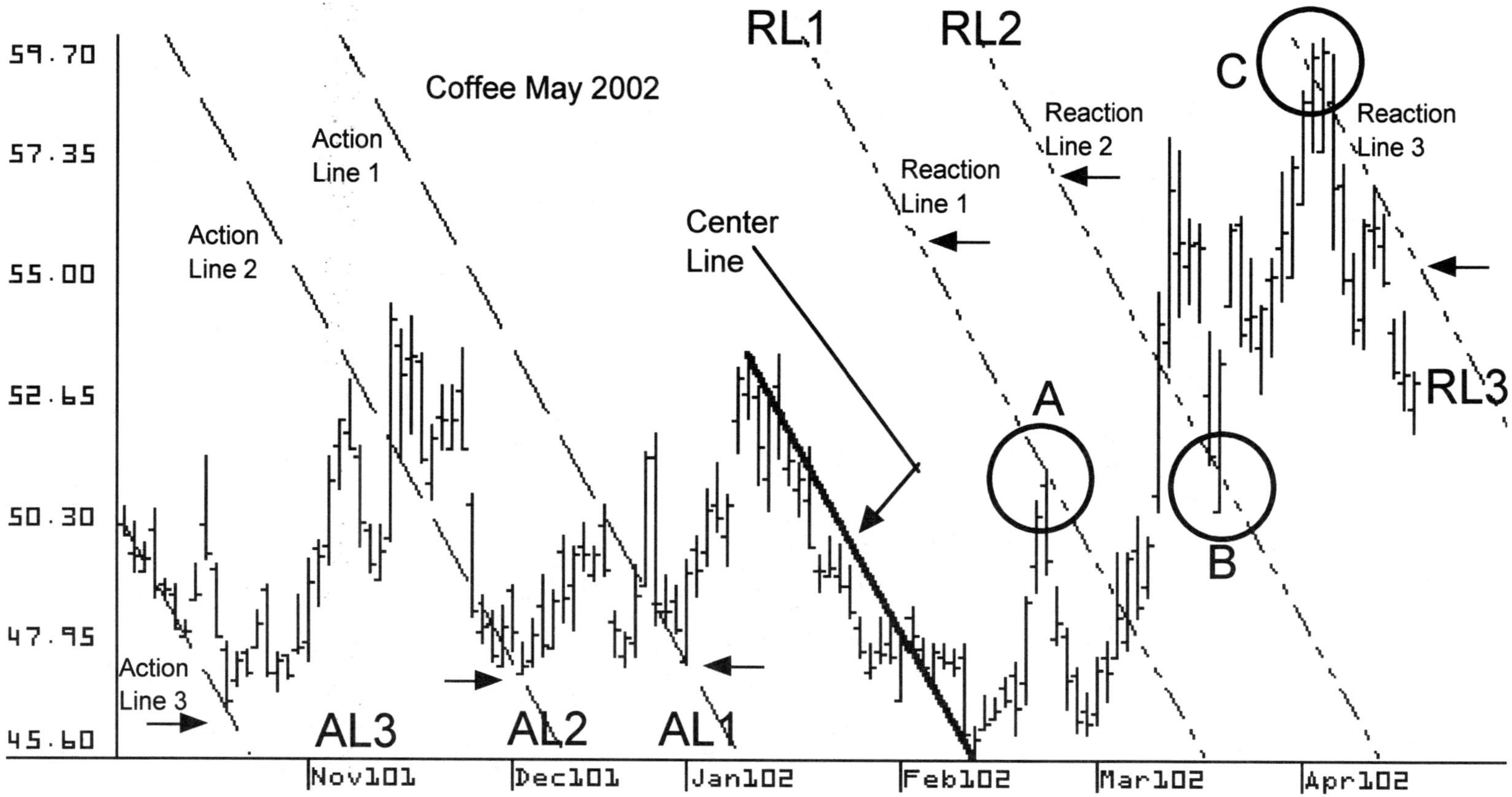

This page shows a chart for May 2002 Coffee futures. The Center Line is selected as a high to low trendline. Each of the three Action Lines on this chart are aligned with swing bottoms which occurred prior to the Center Line. The three Reaction Lines on this chart correspond to the three Action Lines. The Reaction Lines have the same slope as the Center Line and are the same distance from the Center Line as their corresponding Action Line. Reaction Line 1 is the same distance from the Center Line as Action Line 1 and so on. Notice that the market makes a top when it reaches Reaction Line 1 at point A. The market also makes a bottom on Reaction Line 2 at point B. Finally, the market makes a top on reaction Line 3 at point C.

This page shows a chart for Sun MicroSystems, symbol SUNW. A low to high trendline is selected to be the Center Line. On this chart there is only one Action Line which is labeled AL1. This Action Line is aligned against a swing bottom. There is only one Reaction Line on this chart and it is labeled RL1. This reaction line has the same slope as both the Center Line and the Action Line. The position of the Reaction Line is set by measuring the distance from the Center Line to the Action Line. The Reaction Line is an equal distance from the Center Line and the Action Line. On the chart below, a market bottom occurs right after the price falls below the Reaction Line.

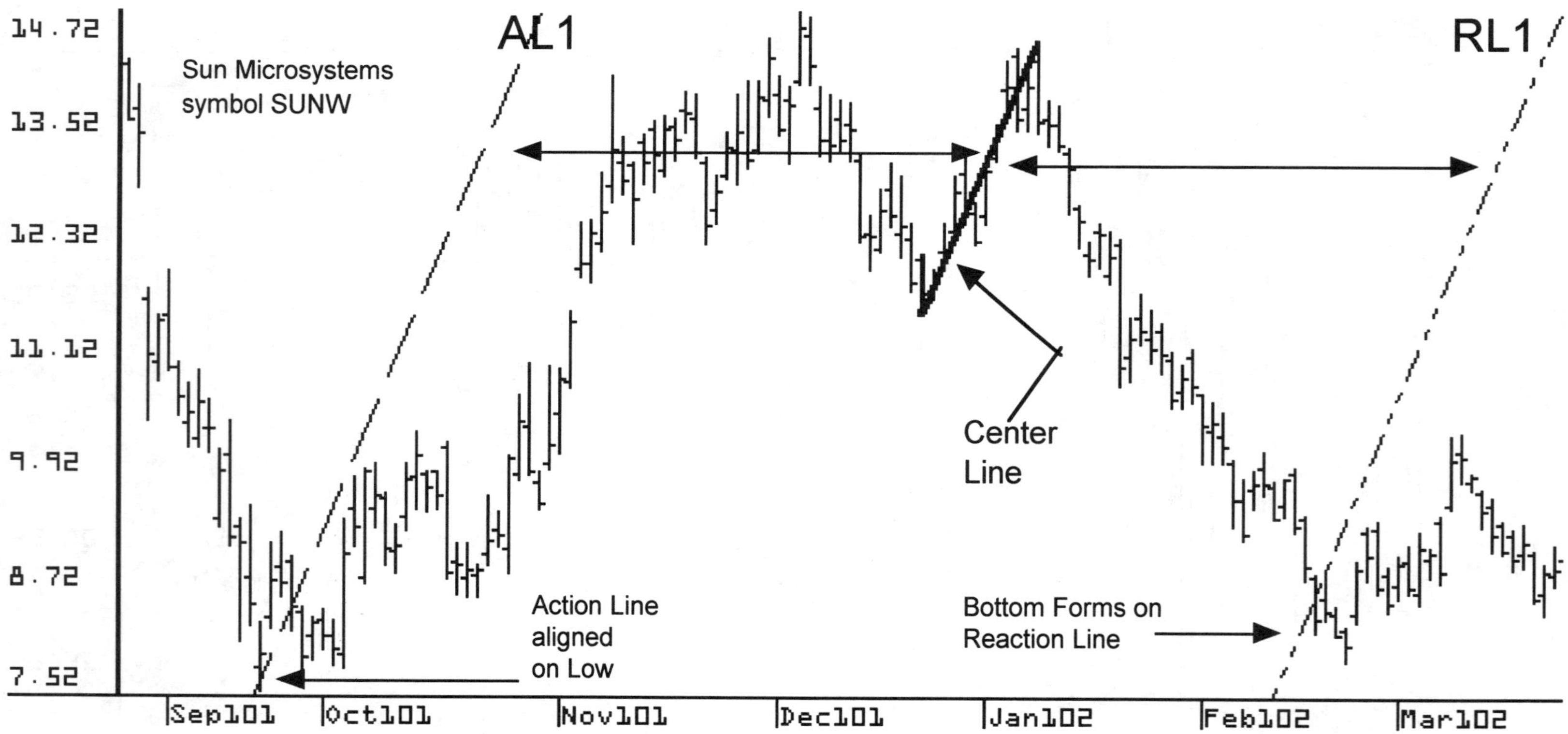

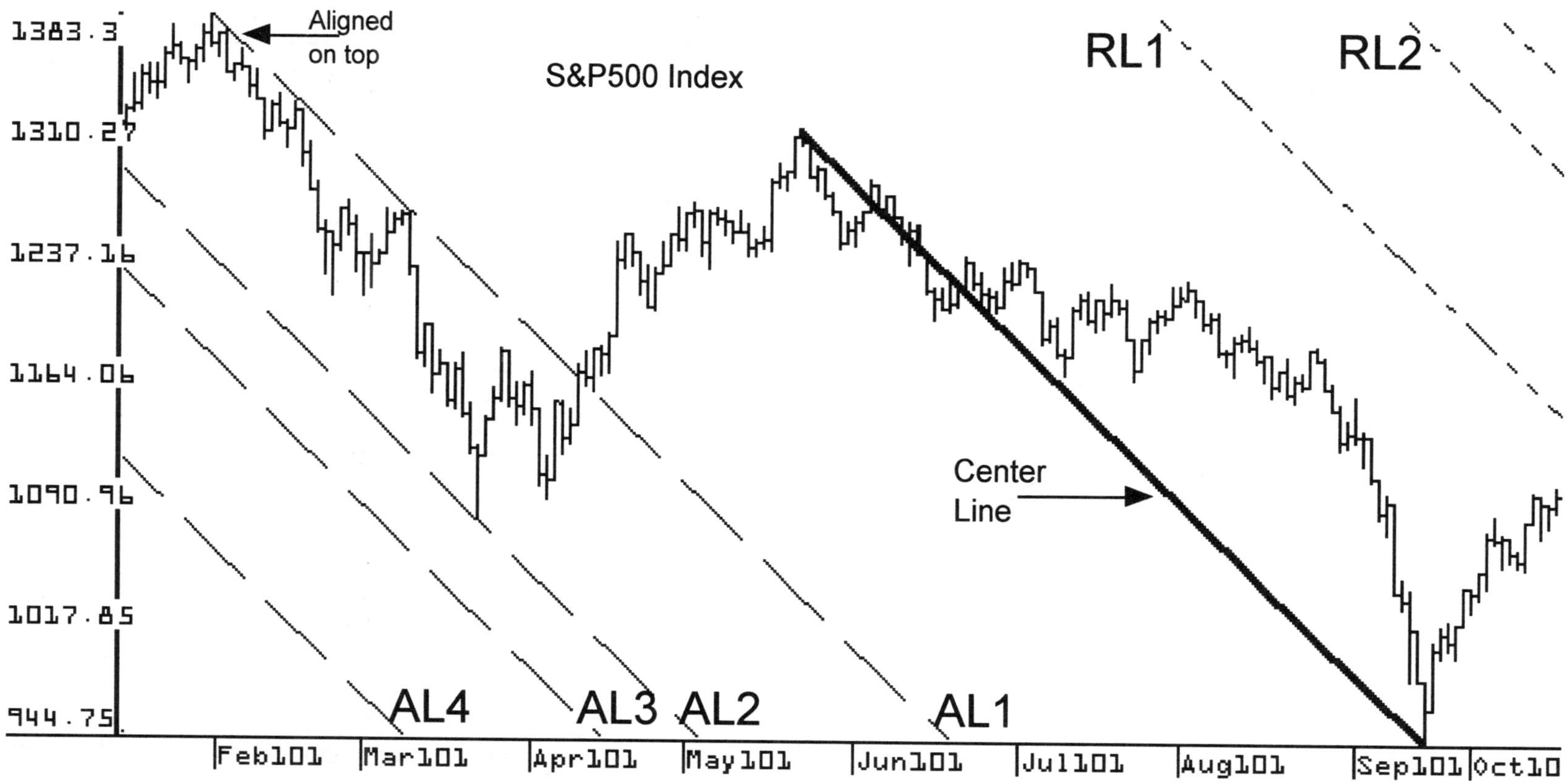

This page shows the first of three charts for the S&P500 Index. The first step in applying the Action Reaction Method is to select the Center Line. On the chart above, the Center Line is the high to low swing from the last swing top before the September 11 terrorist attack on the World Trade Center, down to the post attack low. This is a major high to low swing which almost every stock made. The Action Lines are on the next chart.

The chart on this page is the second of three charts showing Action Reaction Method 1 on the S&P500 index. The second step when applying the Action Reaction Method is to select the placement of the Action Lines. On this chart five Action Lines are aligned with the five swing tops which occurred before the Center Line. See the next chart to view the corresponding Reaction Lines.

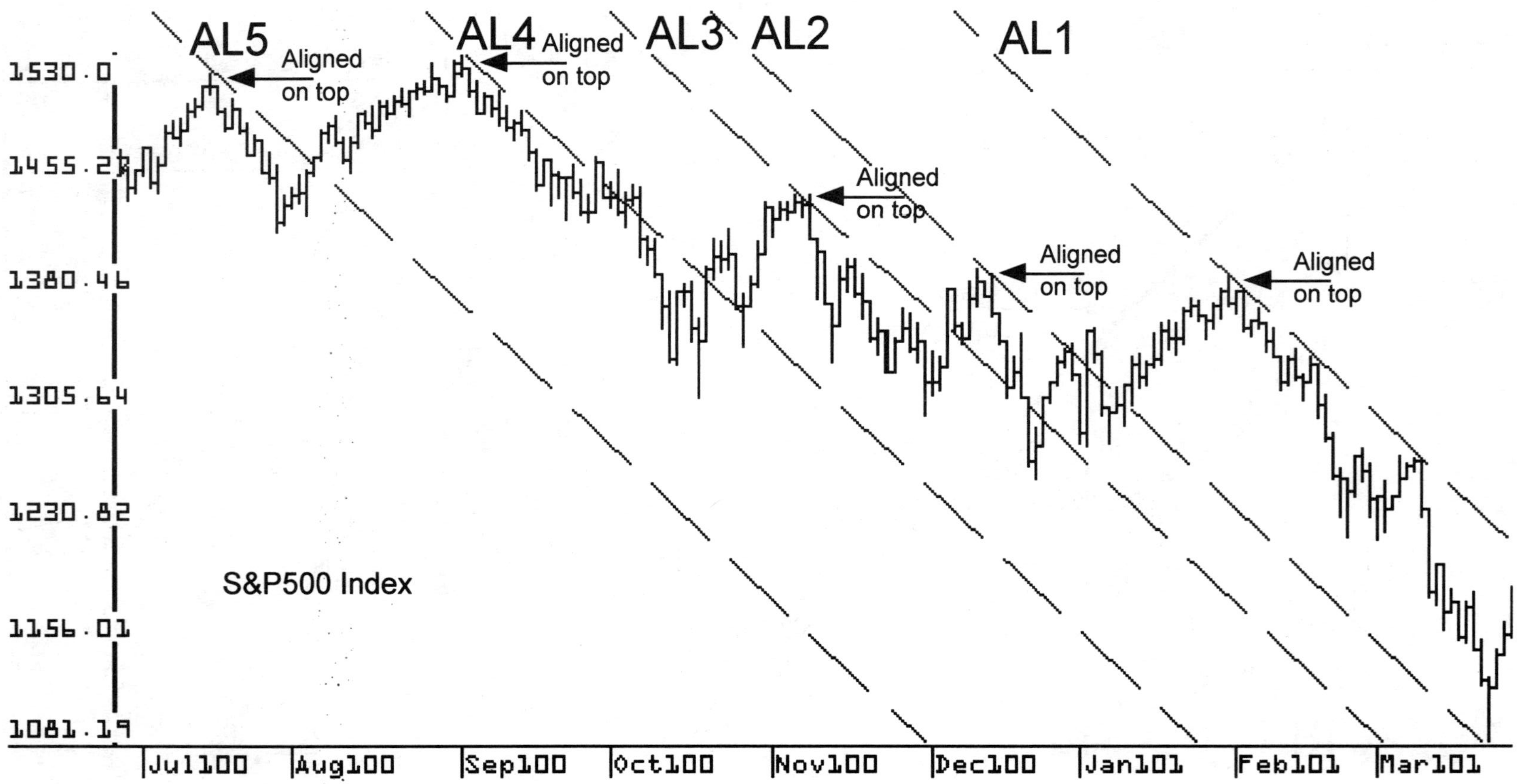

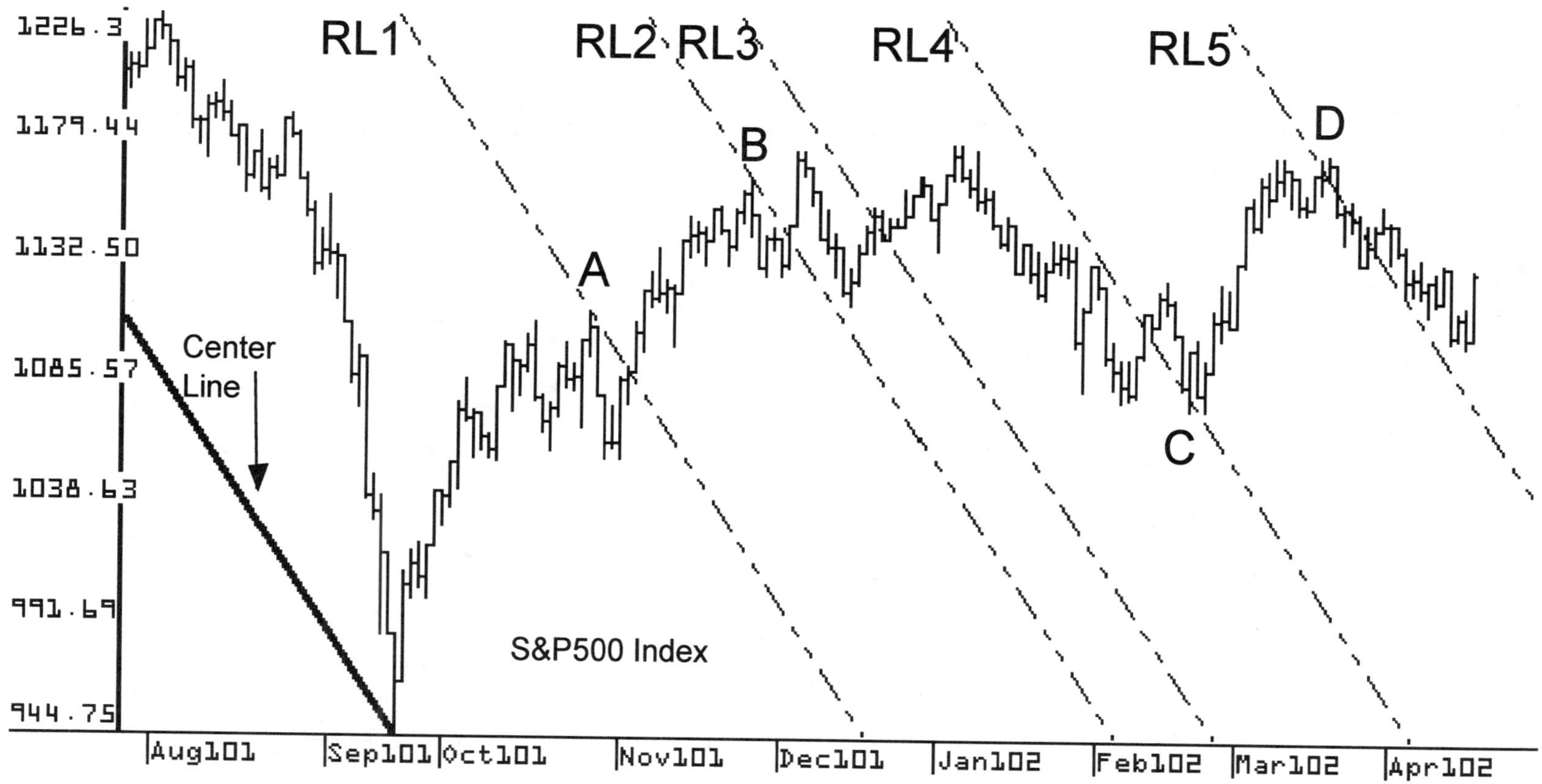

The chart on this page is the third and final chart for this S&P500 Action Reaction example. The five Reaction Lines on this chart correspond to the five Action Lines on the previous chart. Each Reaction Line has the same slope as the Center Line and is the same distance from the Center Line as the corresponding Action Line. The market makes a small top when it reaches Reaction Line 1 at point A. The market makes another small top when it reaches Reaction Line 2 at point B. The market makes a swing bottom when it reaches Reaction Line 4 at point C and finally the S&P500 Index makes a swing top when it reaches Reaction Line 5 at point D.

Below is a chart for Gap Inc., symbol GPS. On this chart there is a Median Line used as a Center Line. The first step in applying the Action Reaction Method is to select a Center Line. When using a Median Line as the Center Line, select a Median Line against which the market makes a reversal.

On the chart below, notice the price moves up and touches the Median Line at point B and makes a swing top against the Median Line. When the price makes a reversal against a Median Line, it indicates that the Median Line should work well as a Center Line.

The second step in applying the Action Reaction Method, is to draw the Action Lines. There is only one Action Line on the chart below. The Action Line is aligned against the swing top at point A and has the same slope as the Median Line.

The final step is to draw the Reaction Lines which correspond to the Action Lines. The distance from the Action Line to the Center Line, is the same as the distance from the Center Line to the Reaction Line. Notice that the market falls quickly from the Median Line at point B down to the Reaction Line at point C where the market makes a bottom.

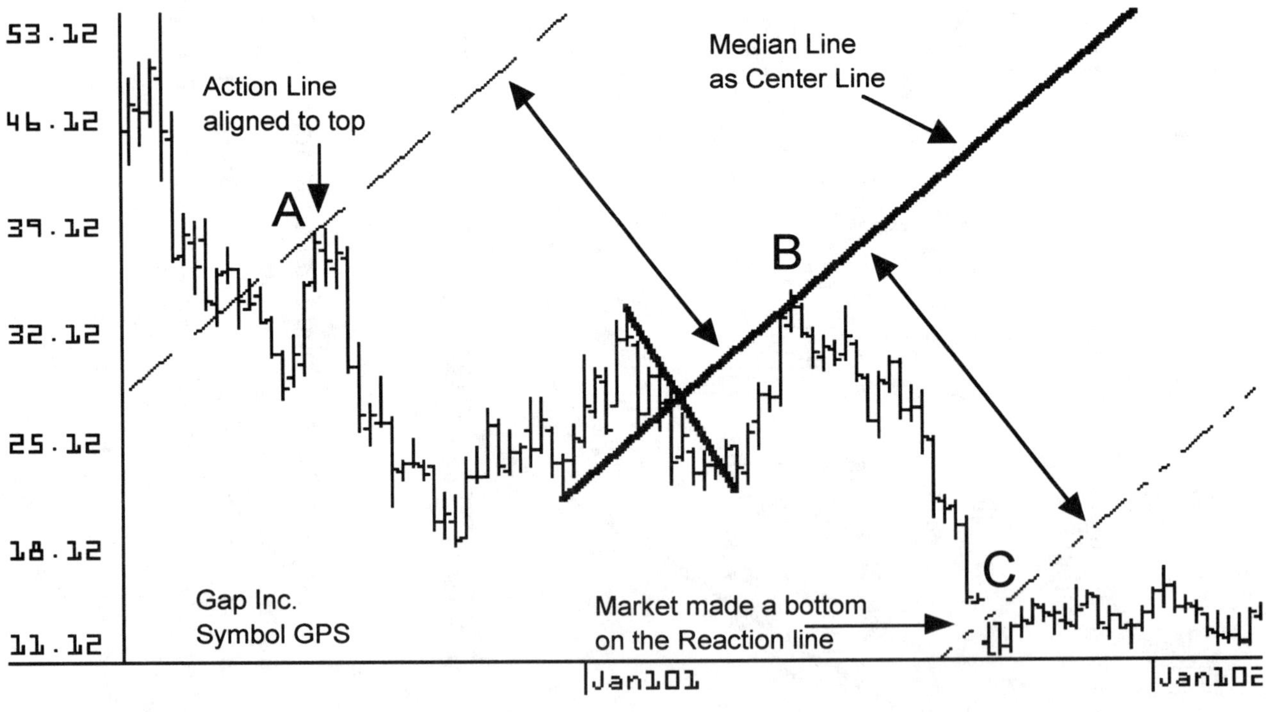

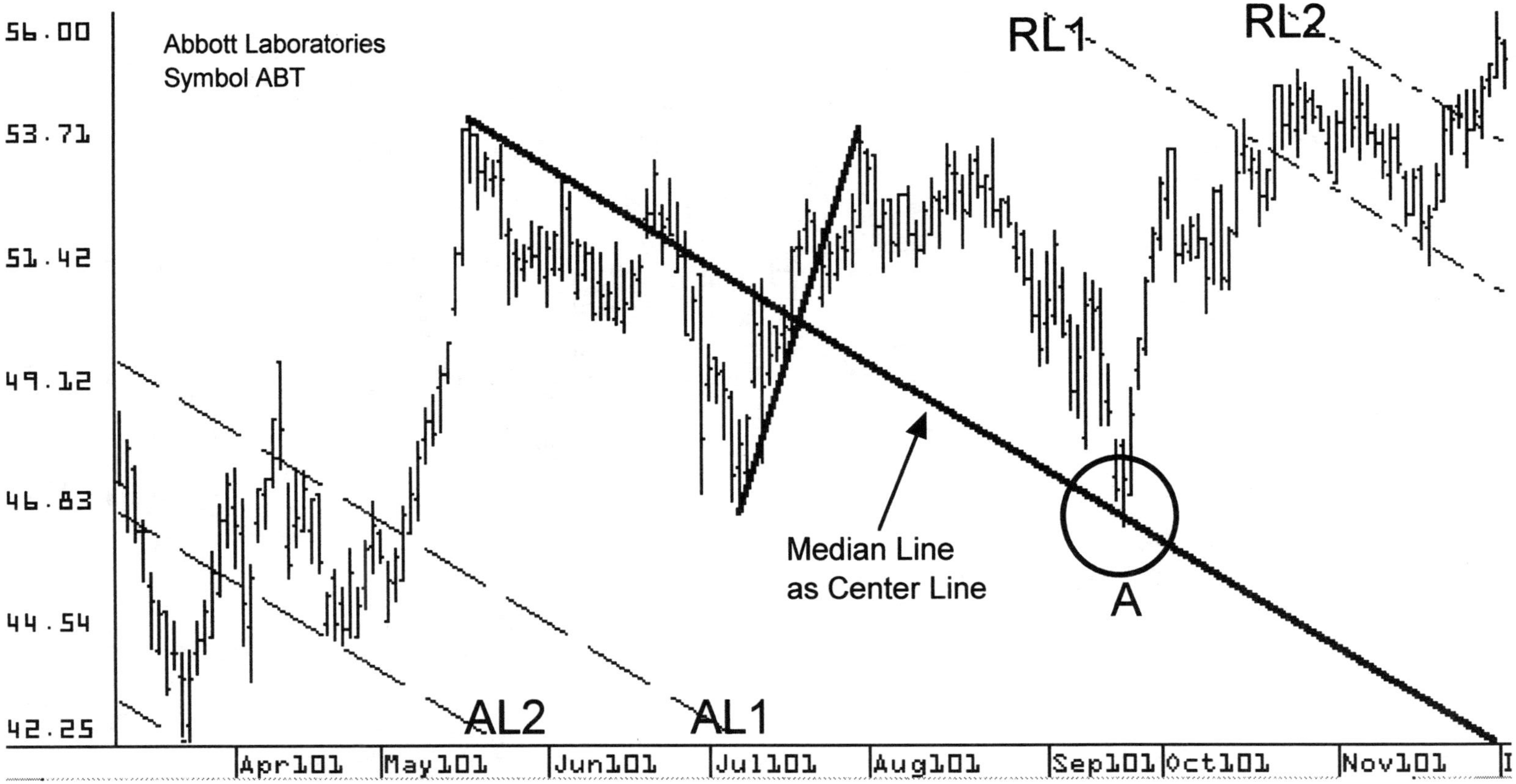

The chart on this page is the first of three price charts for Abbott Laboratories, symbol ABT. Each of these three charts shows part of a long term example for Action Reaction Method 1 using a Median Line as a Center Line. The chart above shows a Median Line which is selected to be the Center Line. This Median Line is selected because the market makes a pivot against this Median Line at point A. The chart on the next page shows the placement of the Action Lines.

Below is the second of three charts for Abbott Laboratories. After selecting a Center Line, the second step in applying the Action Reaction Method is to draw the Action Lines to the left of the Center Line. The Action Lines use the same slope as the Center Line and are aligned against a high or low pivot. On the chart below, Action Line 1 (AL1) is aligned against a swing top, Action Line 2 (AL2) is aligned against a swing bottom, Action Line 3 (AL3) is aligned against a swing bottom and finally Action Line 4 (AL4) is aligned against a swing bottom. The distance from each Action Line to the Center Line is a historical cycle measurement and is used to draw a corresponding Reaction Line into the future. The chart on the next page shows the placement of the Reaction Lines.

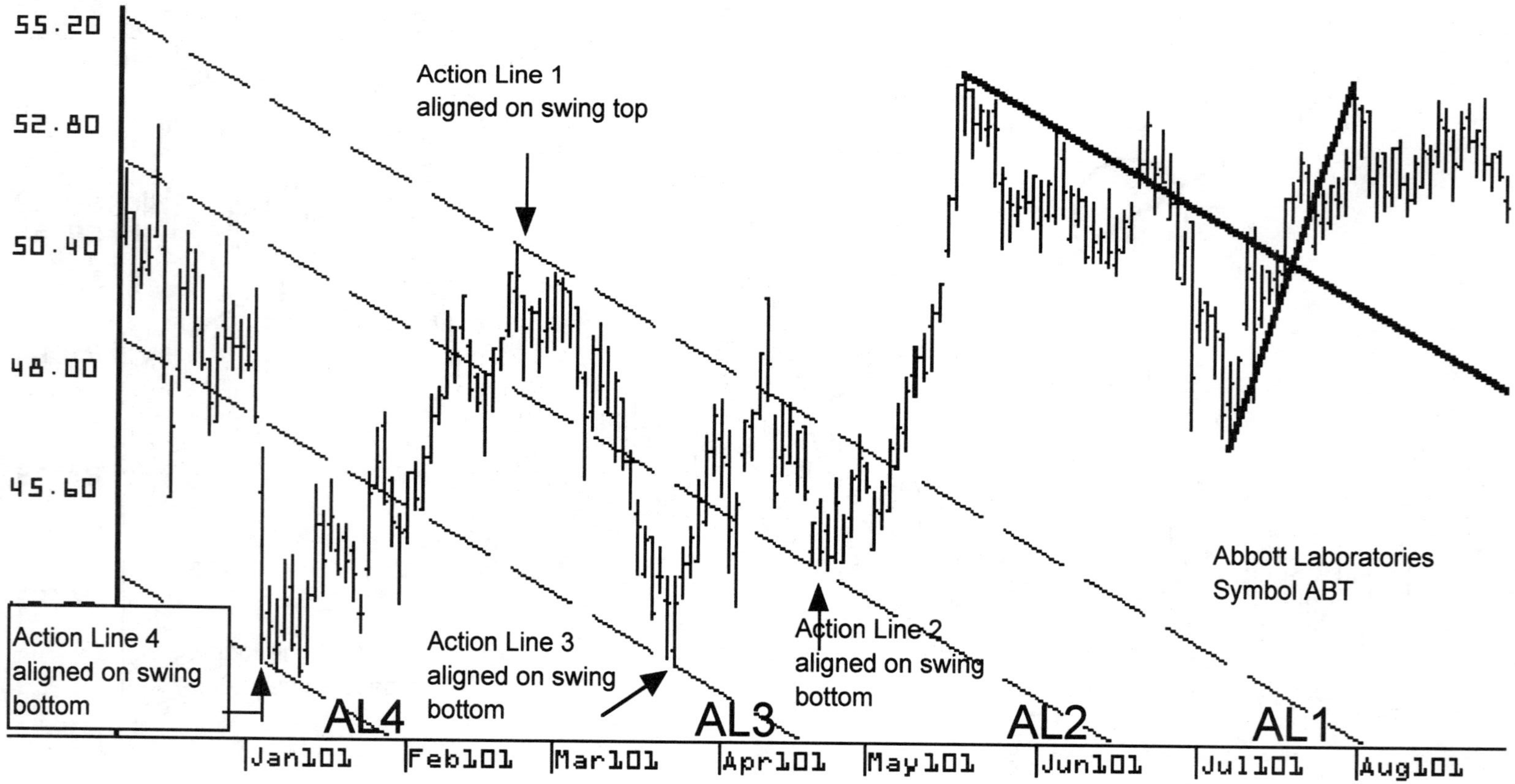

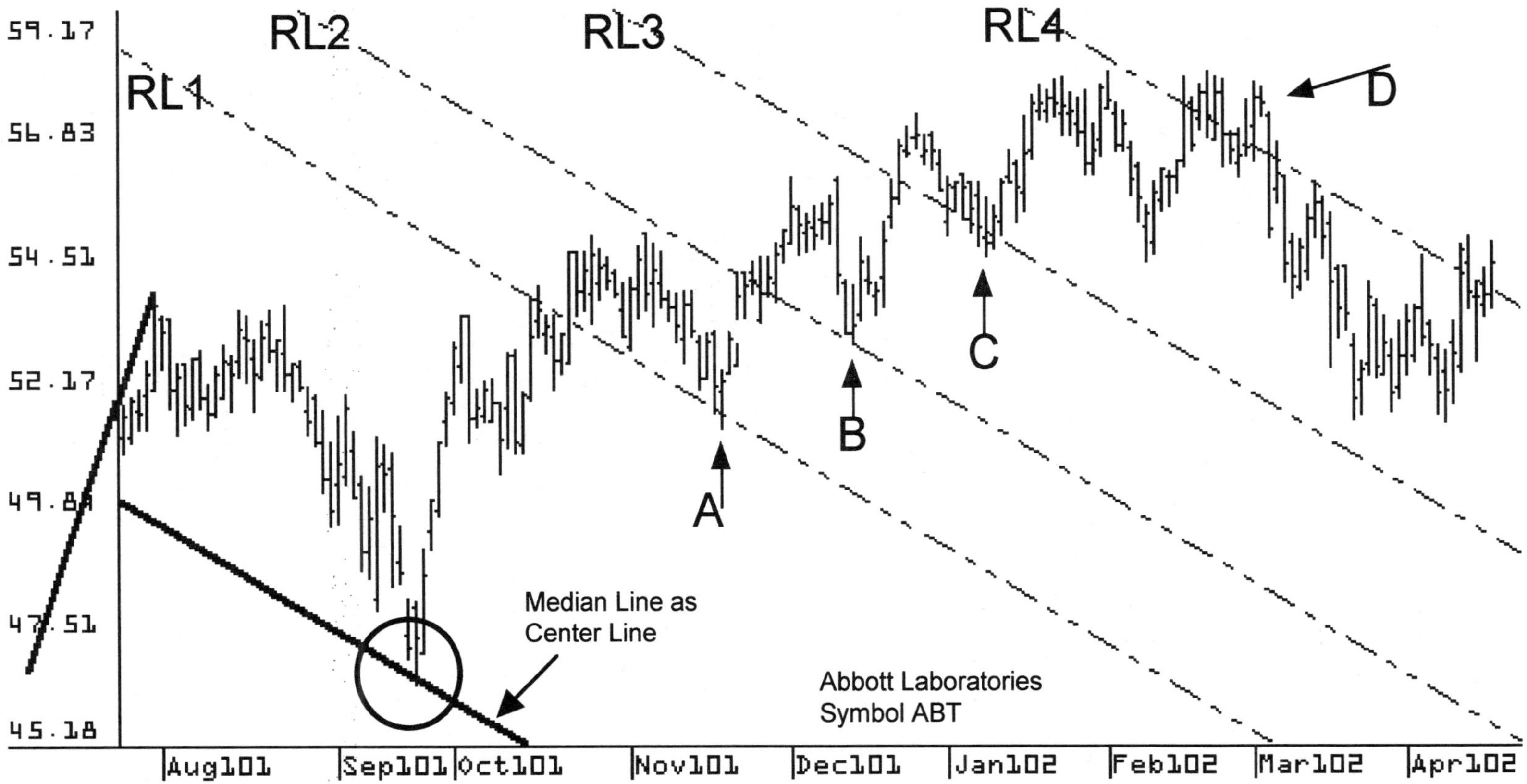

The chart on this page is the third and final chart for this Abbott Laboratories example. The Reaction Lines on this chart correspond to the Action Lines on the previous chart. Reaction Line 1 (RL1) is the same distance from the Center Line as Action Line 1. Reaction Line 2, 3, and 4 are the same distance from the Center Line as Action Line 2, 3, and 4. The Reaction Lines all have the same slope as the Center Line. The price makes a swing bottom against Reaction Line 1 at point A. The price makes another bottom against Reaction Line 2 at point B. The price makes a third bottom against Reaction Line 3 at point C and finally the market makes a swing top against Reaction Line 4 at point D.

Action Reaction Method 2

Step 1: Center Line

The difference between Action Reaction Method 1 and 2 has to do with the number of Action Lines each method uses and the calculation of the Reaction Line location. The Action Line and Reaction Lines will be discussed on the next two pages. On this page we will discuss the Center Line.

The first step in applying Action Reaction Method 2 is to select a Center Line. Rules for selecting the Center Line for Action Reaction Method 1 and 2 are the same. A Center Line can be Median Line, a trendline or Multi-Pivot Line. The Center Line can not be one of the parallel lines such as the upper or lower parallel line on a Pitchfork or a Warning Line. The chart below uses Walgreen stock, symbol WAG, as an example. On this chart there is a high to low trendline. This trendline is used as the Center Line to explain Action Reaction Method 2 on the next three pages.

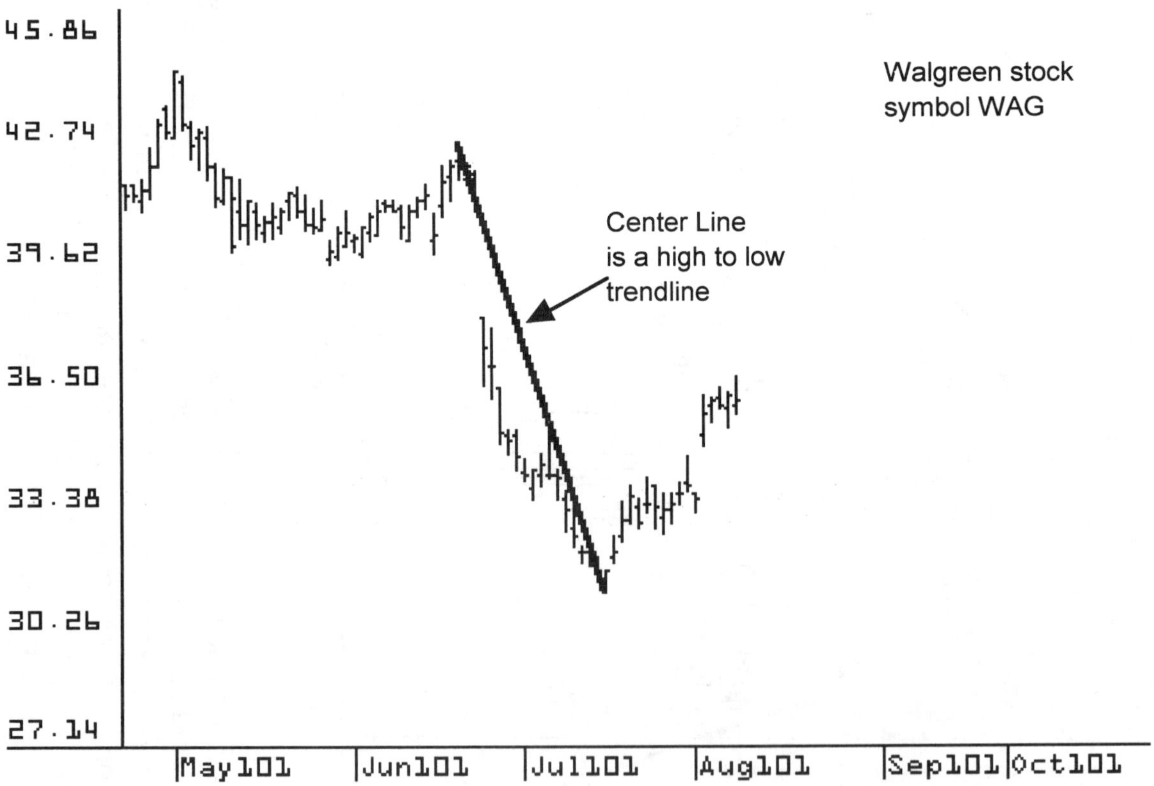

Step 2: Action Line

Action Reaction Method 2 uses only one Action Line which is used to calculate the position of all the Reaction Lines. The Action Line must be drawn to the left of the Center Line and must use the same slope as the Center Line. The Action Line must be aligned with a previous swing top or bottom. The distance between the Action Line and the Center Line is the historical cycle measurement which is used to draw the Reaction Lines into the future. The Walgreen chart below shows one Action Line which is aligned with a swing top.

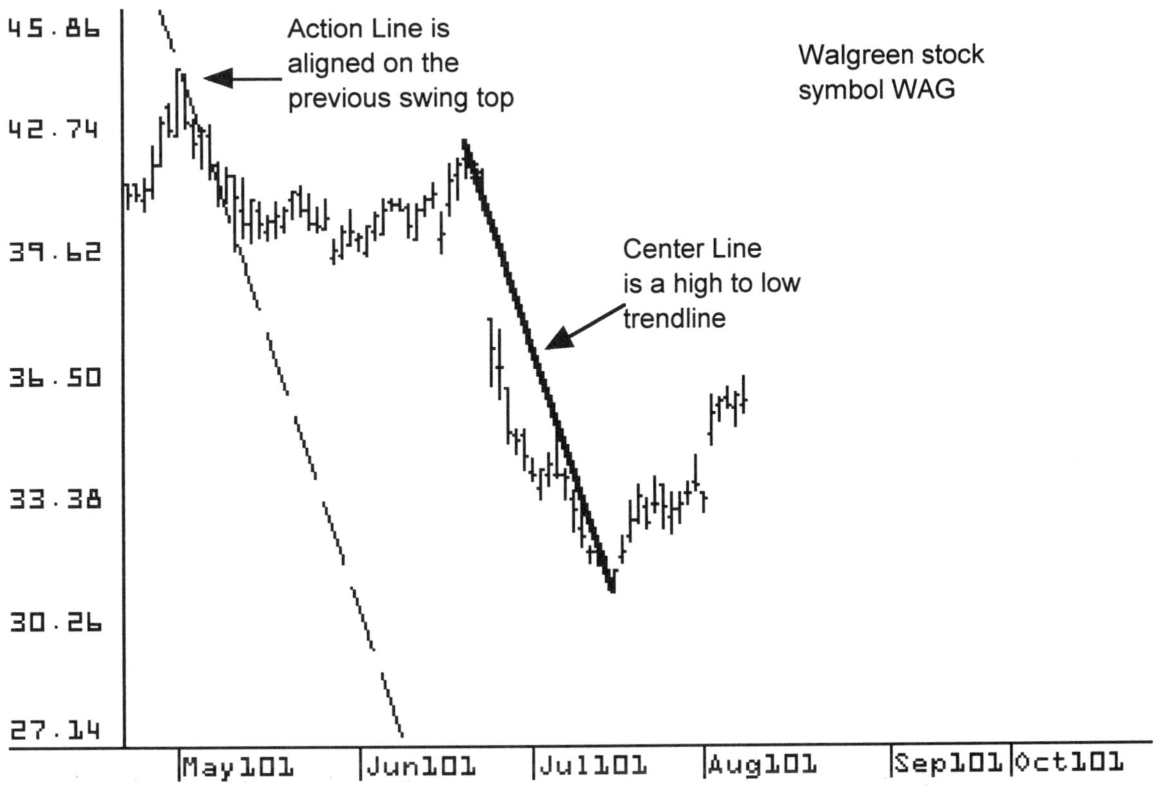

Step 3: Reaction Lines

Using Action Reaction Method 2, there is only one Action Line which is used to calculate the location for all the Reaction Lines. The distance from the Action Line to the Center Line is used to determine the location of all the Reaction Lines. Reaction Line 1 is drawn an equal distance from the Center Line as the Action Line. The Reaction Line 2 is drawn twice as far from the Center Line as the Action Line. Reaction Line 3 is drawn three time as far from the Center Line as the Action Line. The distance between the Action Line and the Center Line is the distance between each Reaction Line. On the chart below the distance between the Action Line and the Center Line is the same as the distance between Reaction Line 2 and Reaction Line 3 or Reaction Line 2 and Reaction Line 1 or Reaction Line 1 and the Center Line. Using this version of the Action Reaction Method, an unlimited number of Reaction Lines can be drawn into the future. All are the same distance apart.

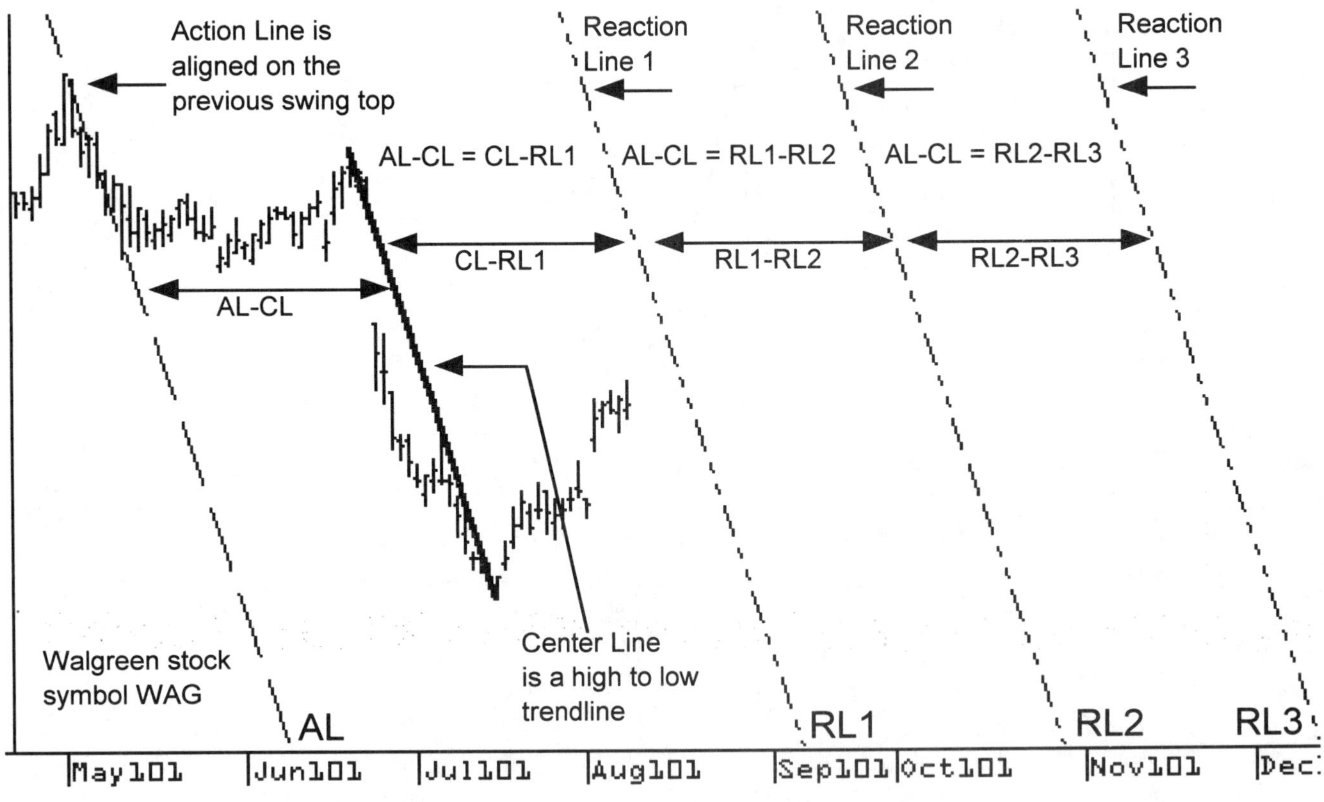

The chart on this page is a continuation of the chart on the previous page. In this example, the price bars are filled in through the end of the chart. Action Reaction Method 2 focuses attention on the market when the price reaches the Reaction Lines. The price makes a top just before reaching Reaction Line 1 at point A and then declines. The price makes a sideways top when it touches Reaction Line 2 at point B and then declines. Finally, when the price arrives at Reaction Line 3 at point C, it makes a top and declines. This shows that the distance between Action Line 1 and the Center Line proves to be a good measurement for judging future cycles.

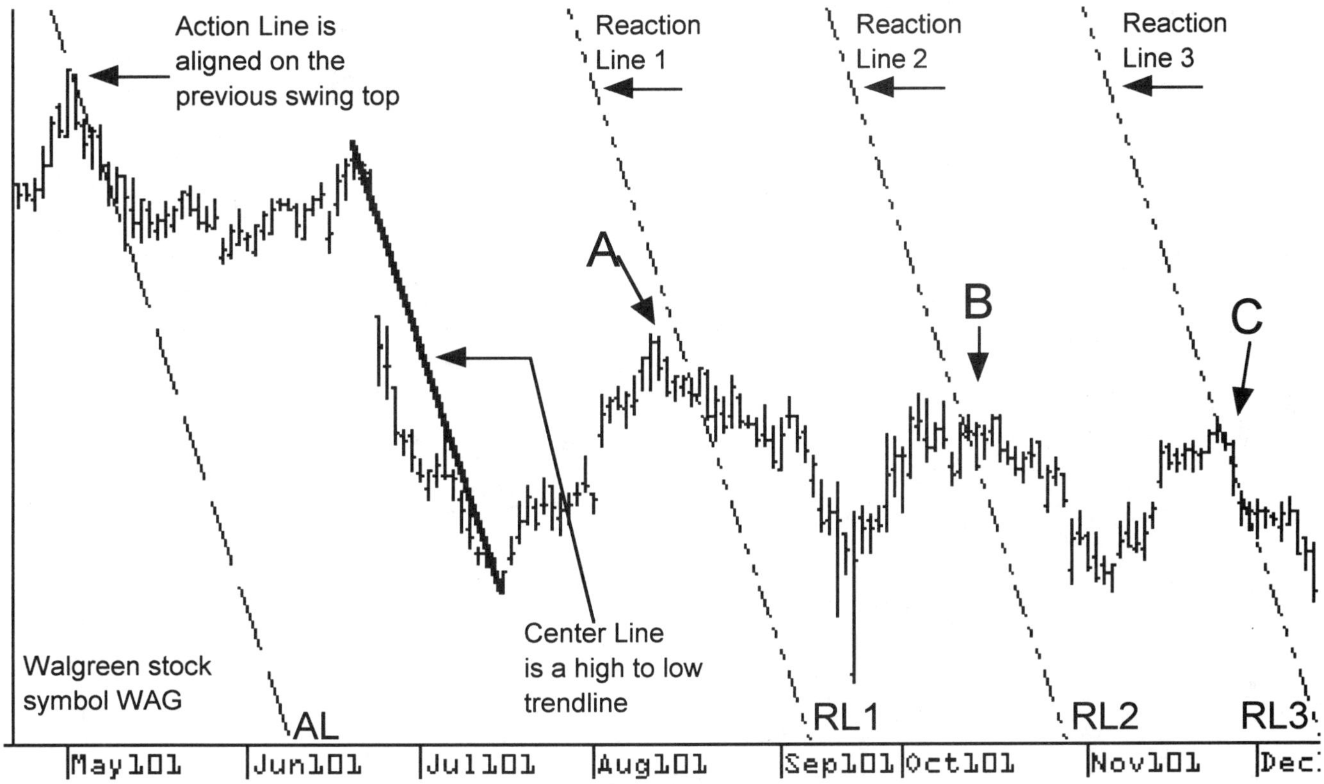

The chart on this page is a long term daily chart for Teradyne, symbol TER. On this chart Action Reaction Method 2 is applied. The Center Line is a low to high trendline on the left side of this chart. There is only one Action Line used with this method. The Action Line is on the left edge of the chart and is aligned with a swing top at point A. The Action Line is labeled “AL”. Using the distance between the Action Line and the Center Line, three Reaction Lines are drawn. The Reaction Lines are the same distance apart. When the price reaches Reaction Line 1, (RL1), it makes a bottom at point B and a top at point C. When the price contacts Reaction Line 2, (RL2), it makes a bottom at point D. The price moves sideways into RL3 at point E where it makes a small bottom and a fast move upward. The price again reaches RL3 at point F where the up swing ends.

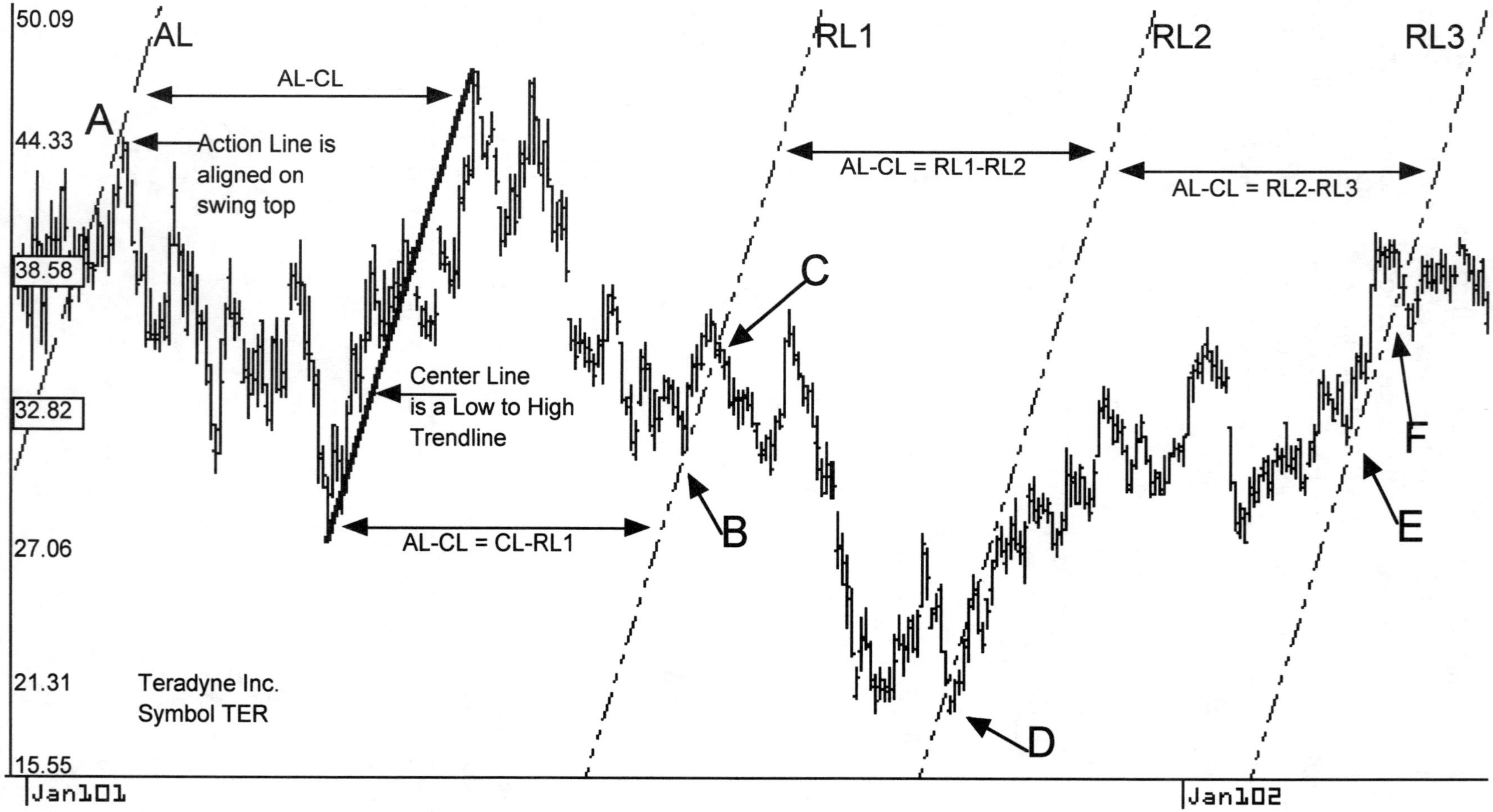

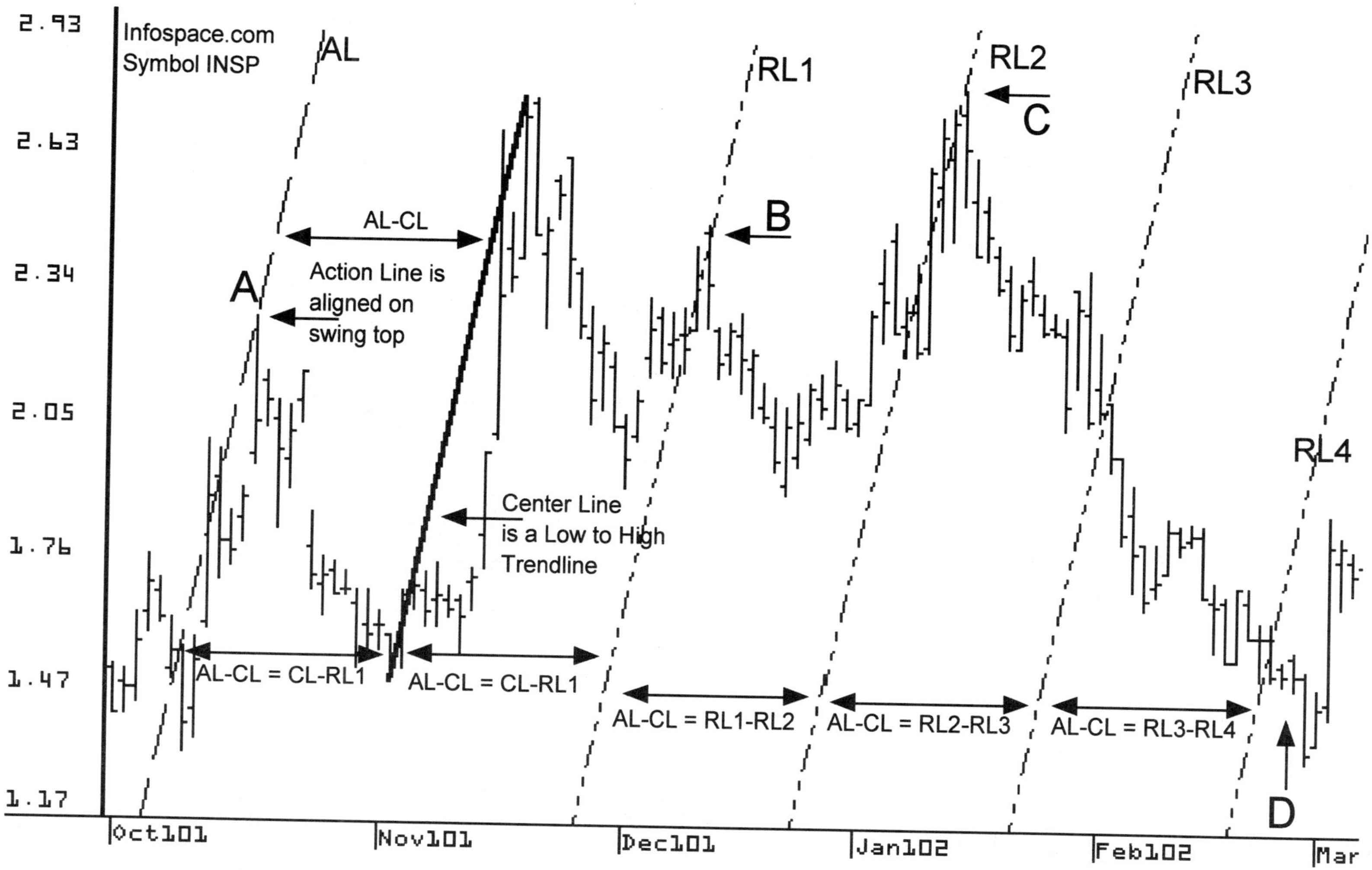

The chart on this page is for Infospace.com, symbol INSP. On this chart, Action Reaction Method 2 is applied. The Center Line is a low to high trendline which can be found on the left portion of this chart. There is only one Action Line used with this method. The Action Line, “AL”, is on the left edge of the chart and is aligned with a swing top at point A. Using the distance between the Action Line and the Center Line, four Reaction Lines are drawn on this chart. All the Reaction Lines are an equal distance apart. When the price reaches Reaction Line 1 (RL1) it produces a top at point B. When the price touches Reaction Line 2 (RL2) the price makes a top at point C. Right after Reaction Line 4 (RL4) the price executes a bottom at point D.

Sliding Trendline

The sliding trendline is unique among Andrews' trendline methods because it is not drawn based on a fixed pivot but rather is a movable trendline. A Sliding Trendline starts with Multi-Pivot Line or a Median Line or a simple trendline and then duplicates the starting trendline. This duplicate line is the Sliding Trendline and it can be moved so it becomes a movable line parallel to the starting line. The Sliding Trendline is used to create a trendline channel. The Sliding Trendline is moved to resize the trendline channel. The Sliding Trendline is employed to set a top and bottom boundary of a up trend or down trend.

The chart below is for Advanced Micro Devices, symbol AMD. The heavy black line is a Multi-Pivot Line and is the starting trendline. The Second line on this chart is a duplicate trendline and is used as a Sliding Trendline to create a trendline channel for the market down trend. The Sliding Trendline is positioned so it creates a top boundary for the swing tops in this down trend. As long as prices stay inside this trendline channel, the trend is still down.

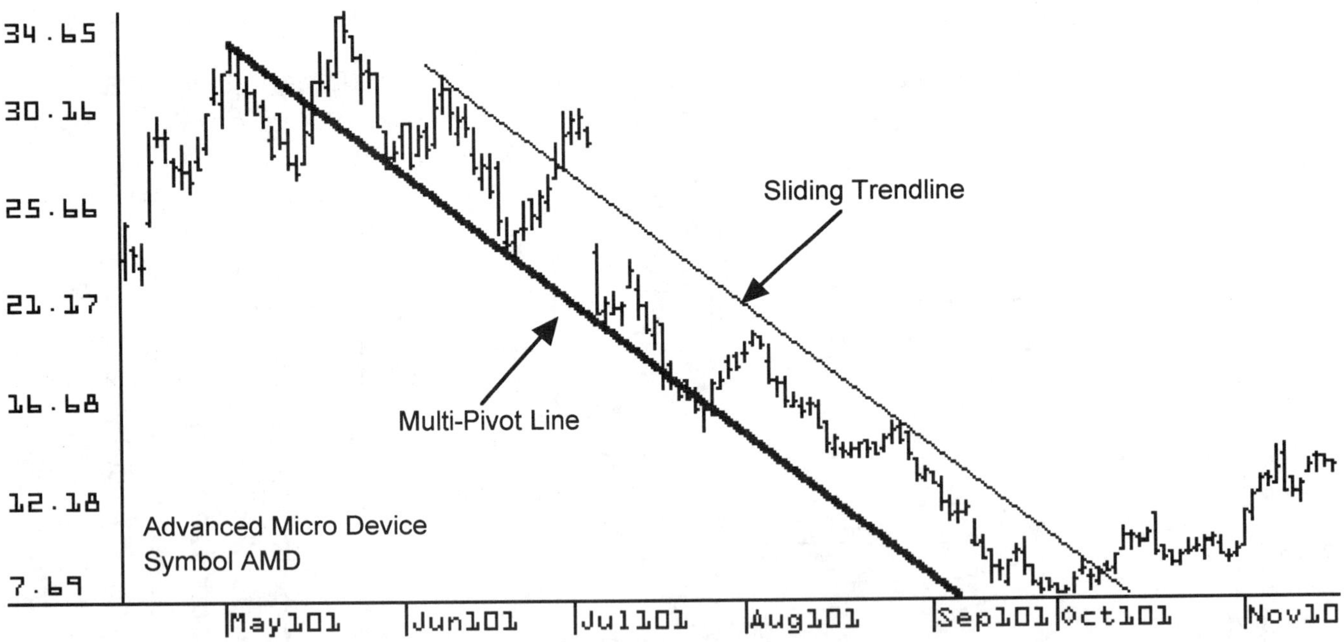

The top chart on this page shows Amazon.com, symbol AMZN. The heavy black line is a Multi-Pivot Line. The other two trendlines on this chart are duplicates of the Multi-Pivot Line which are being used as Sliding Trendlines. The Sliding Trendlines are positioned so they represent the bottom boundary for the swings in a down trend. As long as the price swings stay inside this trendline channel, the trend is still downward.

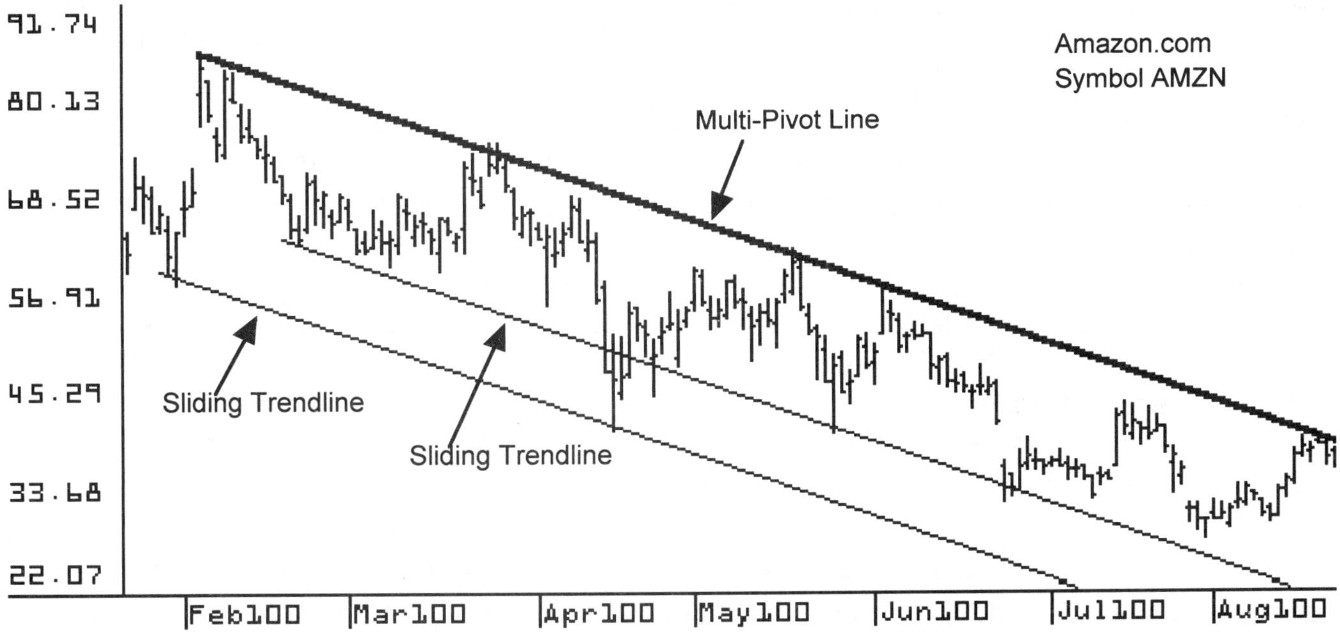

The chart below shows KLA Instruments, symbol KLAC. The heavy black line is a Multi-Pivot Line. The other two trendlines are duplicates of the Multi-Pivot Line which are being used as Sliding Trendlines. The Sliding Trendlines are positioned so they represent the top and bottom boundary for the swings in an uptrend. As long as the price swings stay inside this trendline channel, the trend is still upward.

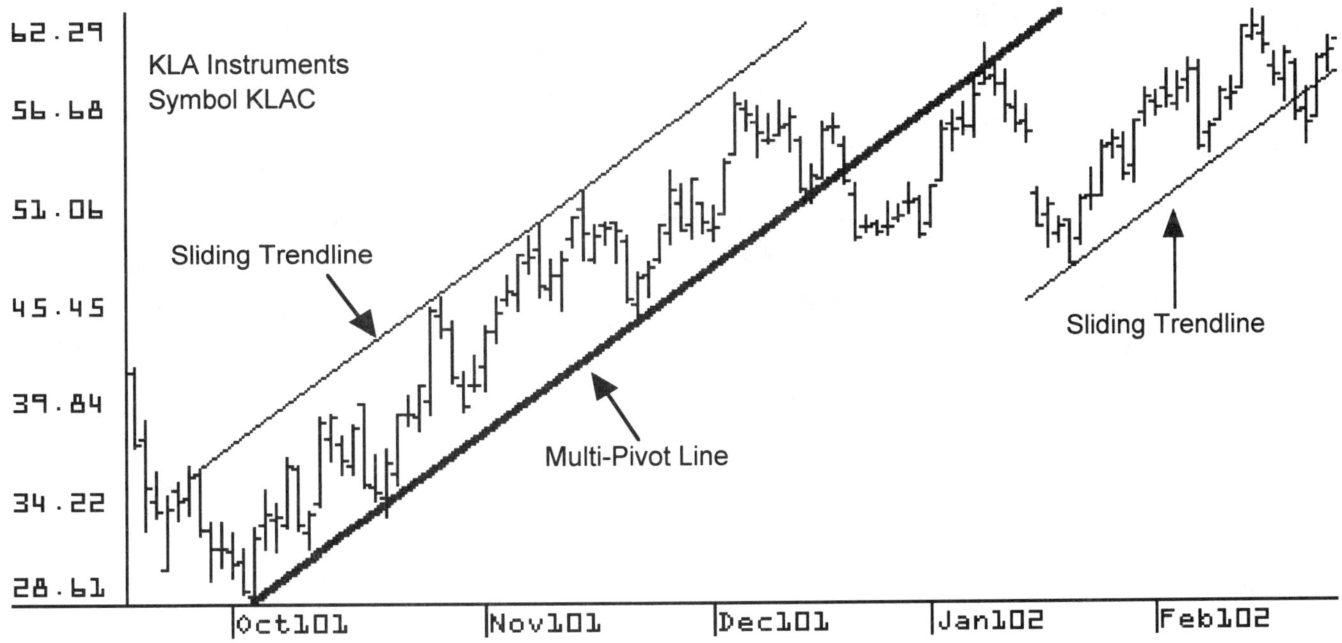

Trading The Elliott Wave Pattern

The Elliott Wave Principle was popular during the latter part of Andrews' career and he was aware of this method. Andrews used trendlines to try and take advantage of the Elliott Wave pivot predictions. This book does not provide an in depth discussion of the Elliott Wave Theory which can fill a book all its own. The Elliott Wave Theory teaches that market trends move in five waves. An example of an up trend moving up in five waves is seen in the diagram below. The price swings 1, 2, 3, 4, 5 make up Elliott's five wave pattern. The Elliott Wave Theory then teaches that a market correction will move in three waves in the opposite direction. On the diagram below the price swings labeled a, b, c are the three counter trend swings. The same pattern also occurs in a down trend with five waves down and three counter trend waves.

Andrews taught that this pattern does not form in every trend but does occur frequently enough that traders should be aware of it. The strategy Andrews showed for trading this pattern is to draw a trendline connecting pivots 0 and 4. In an uptrend, the price must fall below the 0 - 4 trendline as the trend turns down after the wave 5 top. A trader sells when the price falls below the 0 - 4 trendline.

In a down trend when the five wave pattern forms Andrews drew a downward 0 - 4 trendline. After the final wave 5 bottom, the price must progress above the 0 - 4 trendline to form the upward a, b, c counter trend move. When the price breaks above the 0 - 4 trendline, Andrews' strategy maintains that this is a time to buy.

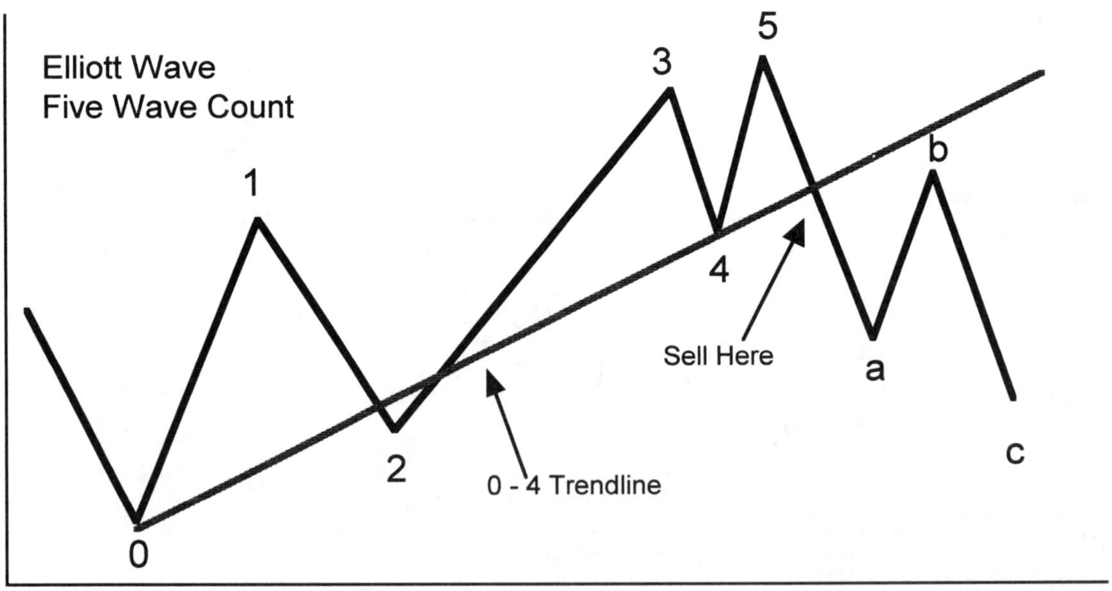

The top chart on this page shows May 2002 Coffee futures. This coffee contract makes a five wave pattern upward. This pattern is labeled 0 to 5 and a trendline is drawn connecting pivots 0 and 4. When the price breaks below this 0 - 4 trendline, a sell signal is given.

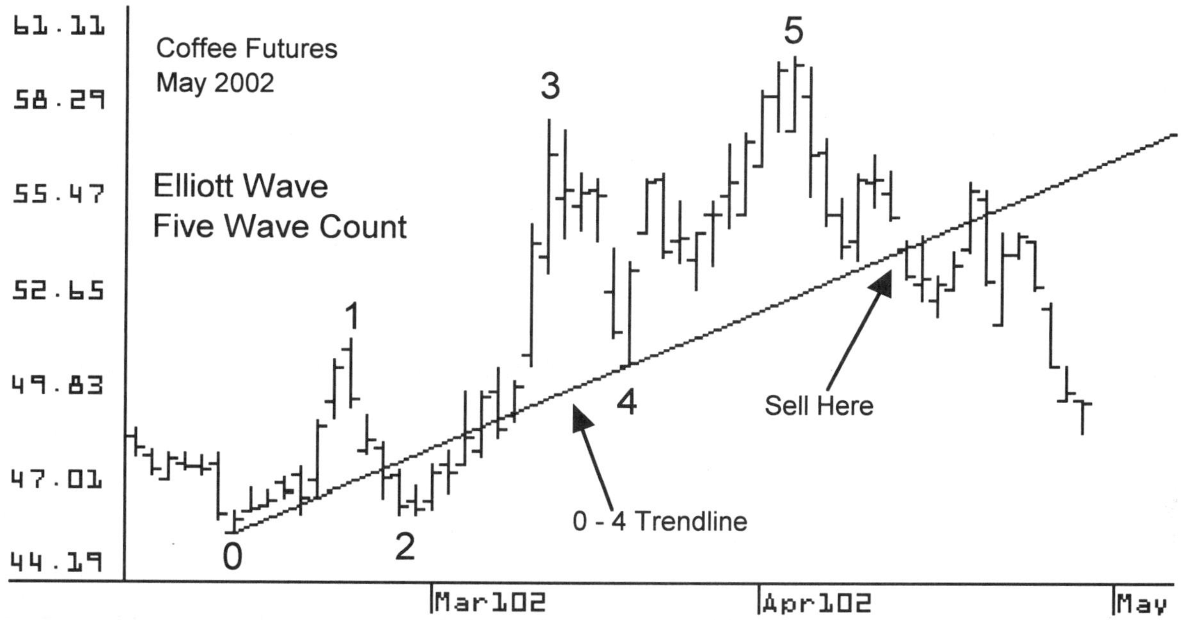

The chart below shows 3Com, symbol COMS. This stock makes a five wave pattern upward which is labeled 0 to 5. A trendline is drawn connecting pivots 0 and 4. When the price breaks below this 0 - 4 trendline, a sell signal is triggered.

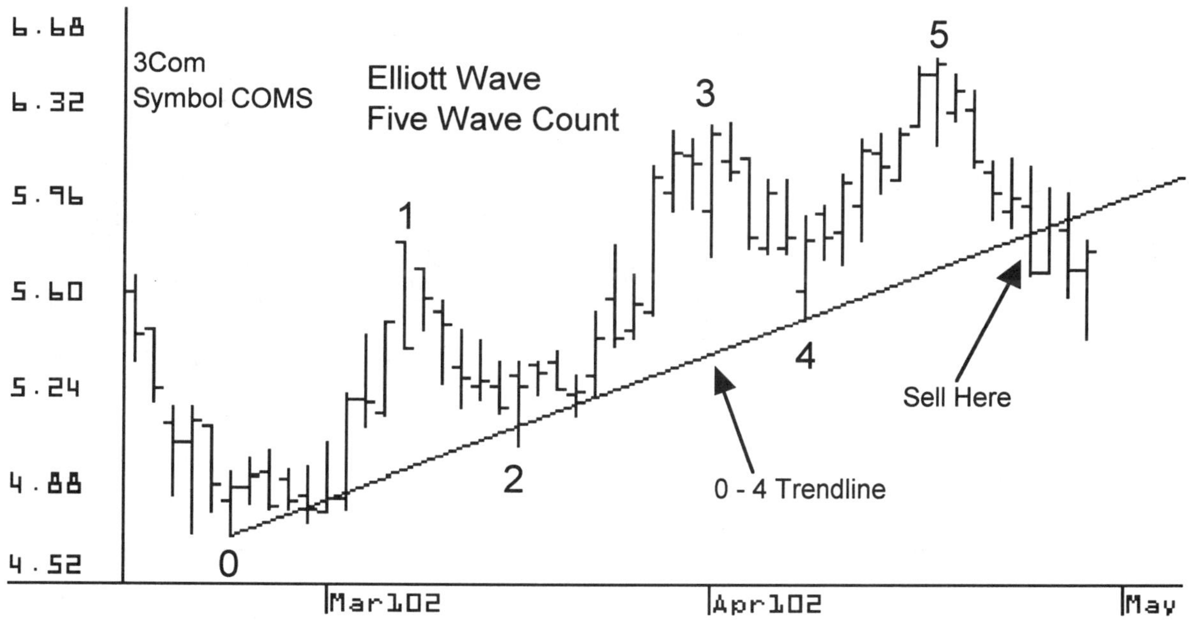

The top chart on this page shows November 2002 Soybean futures. This soybean contract makes a five wave pattern upward. This pattern is labeled 0 to 5 and a trendline is drawn connecting pivots 0 and 4. When the price breaks below this 0 - 4 trendline, it indicates the start of the a, b, c counter trend down move.

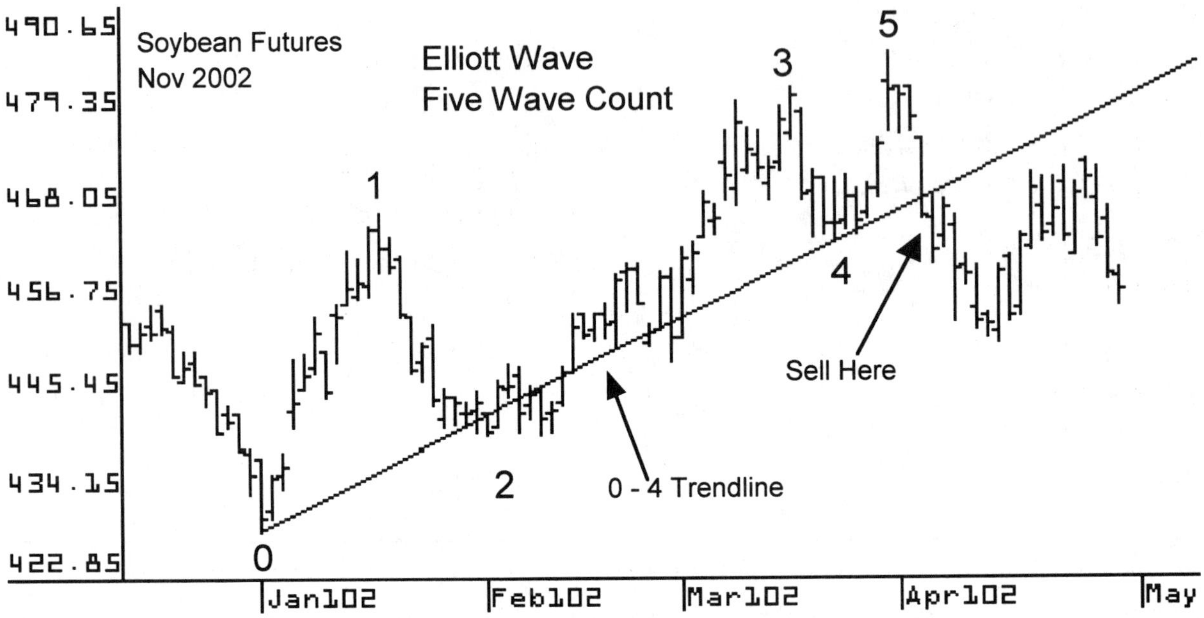

The chart below shows Double Click, symbol DCLK. This stock makes a five wave pattern upward which is labeled 0 to 5. A trendline is drawn connecting pivots 0 and 4. When the price breaks below this 0 - 4 trendline, the start of a downward counter trend move is indicated and it is time to sell.

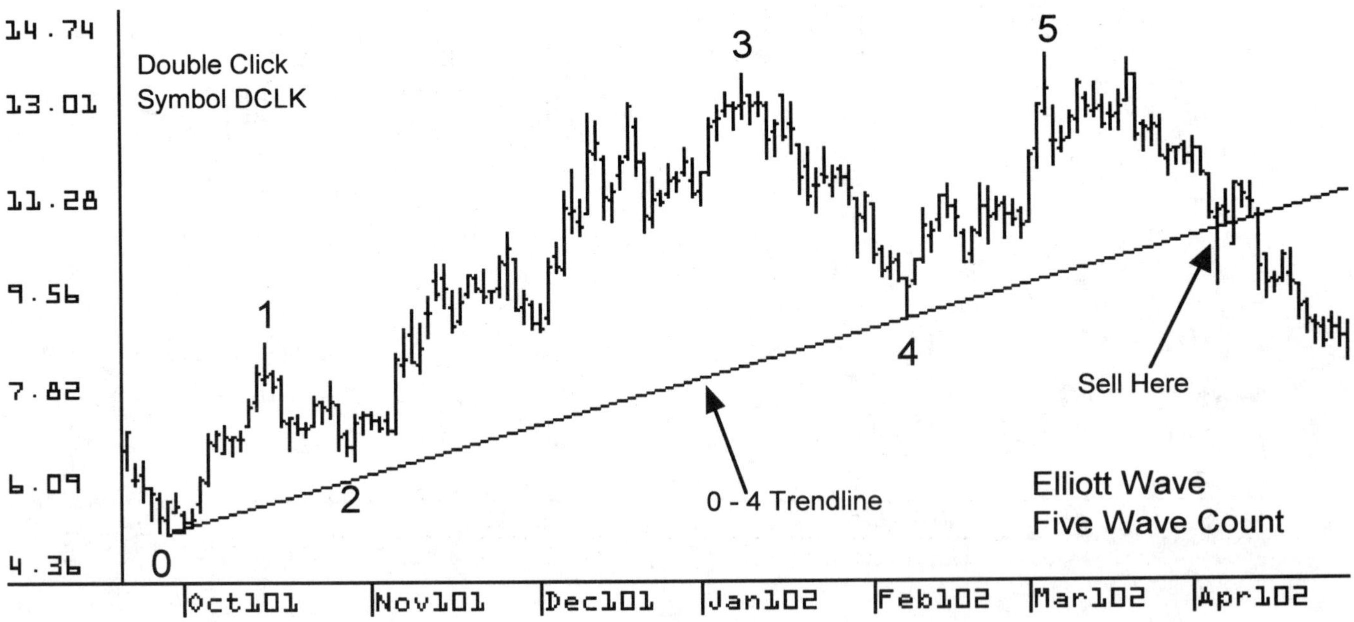

The top chart on this page is a weekly chart for Gillette, symbol G. This stock makes a five wave pattern upward which is labeled 0 to 5. A trendline is drawn connecting pivots 0 and 4. When the price breaks below this 0 - 4 trendline, Andrews' rules indicate a downward counter trend move is under way.

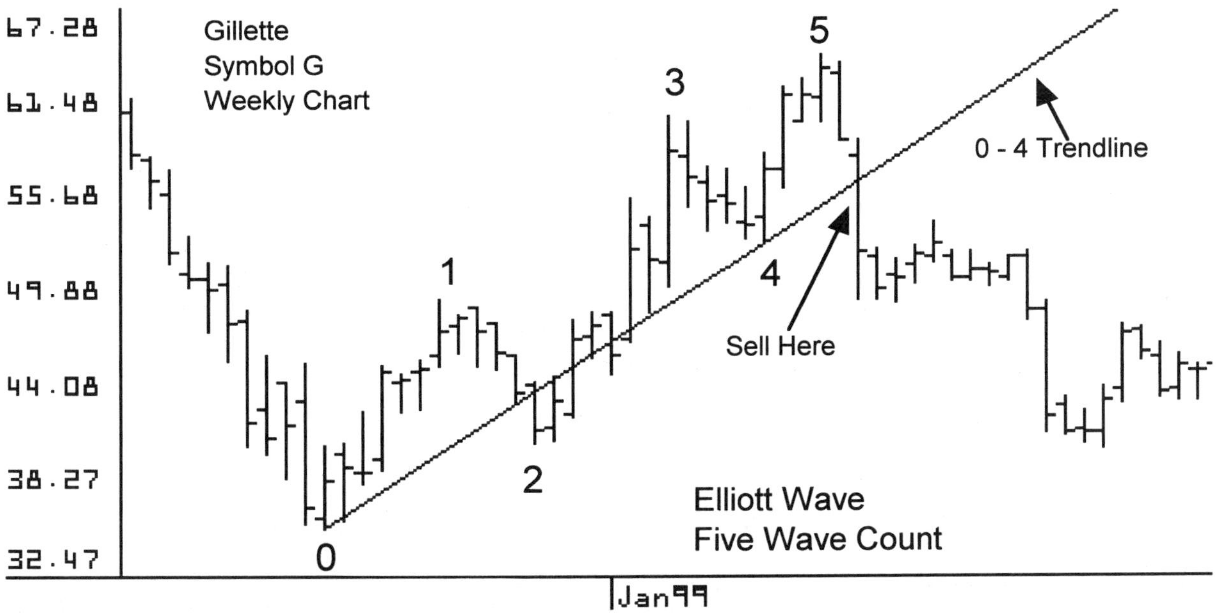

The chart below shows Knight Trading, symbol NITE. This stock makes a five wave pattern upward which is labeled 0 to 5. A trendline is drawn connecting pivots 0 and 4. When the price breaks below this 0 - 4 trendline, a trader can sell the down move with confidence knowing the counter trend down move is under way.

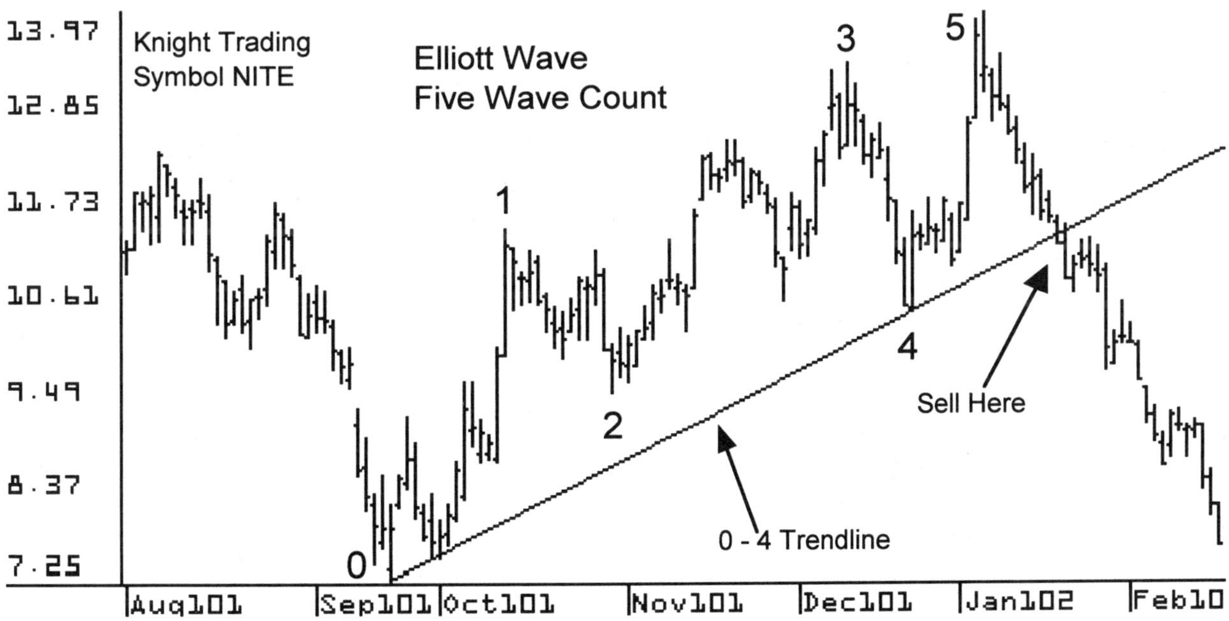

Section 2:
Five New Trendline Techniques

New Pitchfork Trading Rule 1

Pitchfork Buy Rule 1: Draw a downward sloping Pitchfork. If the price moves along the Pitchfork upper parallel and never dips very much into the Pitchfork, it is a sign of market strength. When a full price bar moves above the upper parallel, it is an sign to buy.

Pitchfork Sell Rule 1: Draw an upward sloping Pitchfork. If the price moves along the Pitchfork lower parallel, never rising very much into the Pitchfork, it is a sign of market weakness. When a full price bar moves below the lower parallel, it is an indication to sell.

The chart on this page is for Dell, symbol DELL. A Pitchfork is drawn using pivots A, B, and C. After pivot C, the price moves along the Pitchfork upper parallel line. The price does not move even half way down to the Median Line which is a show of strength in this market. When a full price bar moves above the upper parallel line, a buy signal is given. The arrow labeled, "Buy Here," identifies the exact signal bar.

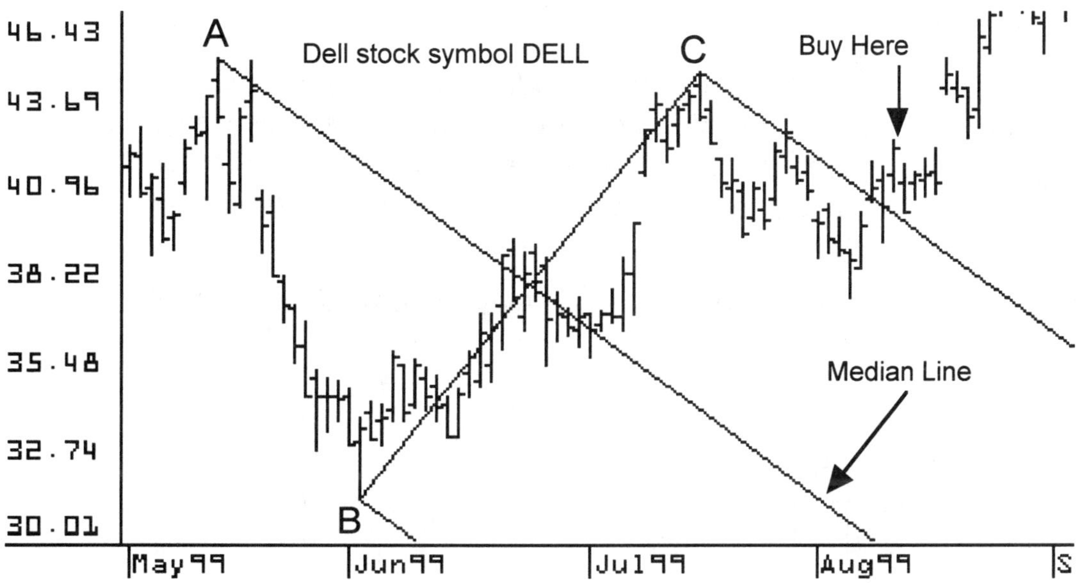

The top chart on this page is for Solectron, symbol SLR. A Pitchfork is drawn using pivots A, B, and C. After pivot C, the price moves along the lower parallel line. The price does not move even half way up to the Median Line which is a show of weakness in this market. When a full price bar moves below the lower parallel line, a sell signal is given. The arrow labeled, "Sell Here," identifies the exact signal bar.

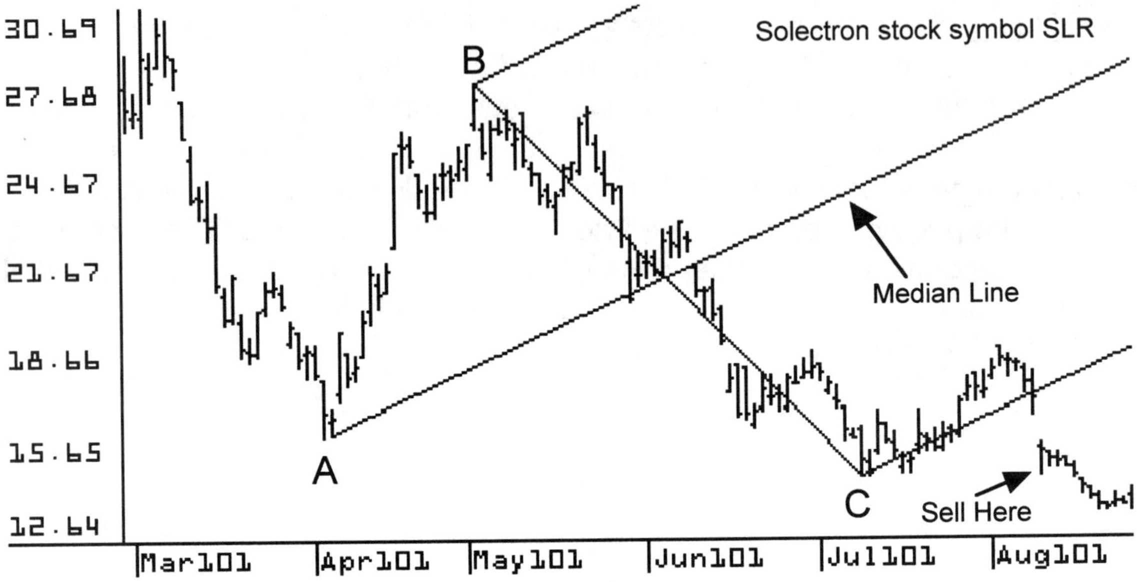

The chart below is for Real Networks, symbol RNWK. A Pitchfork is drawn using pivots A, B, and C. After pivot C, the price moves along the lower parallel line which is a show of weakness in this market. When a full price bar moves below the Pitchfork lower parallel line, a sell signal is present. The arrow labeled, "Sell Here," shows the signal bar.

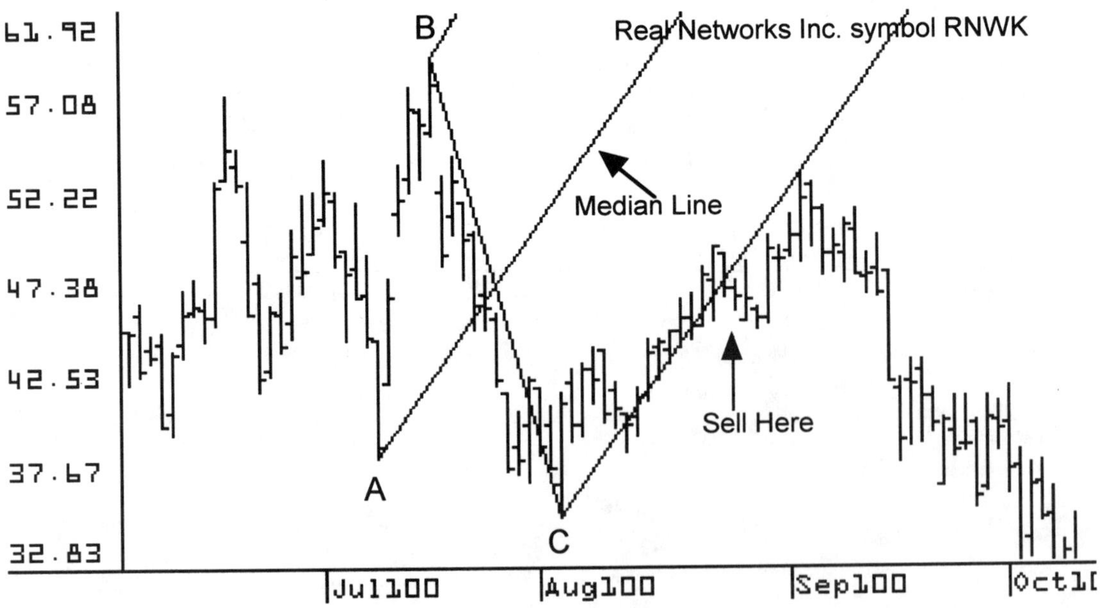

New Pitchfork Trading Rule 2

There are several patterns which work very well to signal trades when they form in relation to the Median Line. Rule 2 and Rule 3 are both based on price action around the Median Line.

Pitchfork Buy Rule 2: If the price moves down to the Median Line, and then makes a gap up or a long range day up away from the Median Line, it is a signal to buy.

Pitchfork Sell Rule 2: If the price moves up to the Median Line, and then makes a gap down or long range day down away from the Median Line, there is a signal to sell.

The chart on this page is for Solectron, symbol SLR and shows this Median Line pattern. The Pitchfork is drawn using pivots A, B, and C. After pivot C, the price moves up to the Median Line and moves sideways. Finally the price makes a large gap down and long range day down away from the Median Line. This strong move down from the Median Line is a sell signal and a good indication the price is going to fall at least to the lower parallel and probably lower.

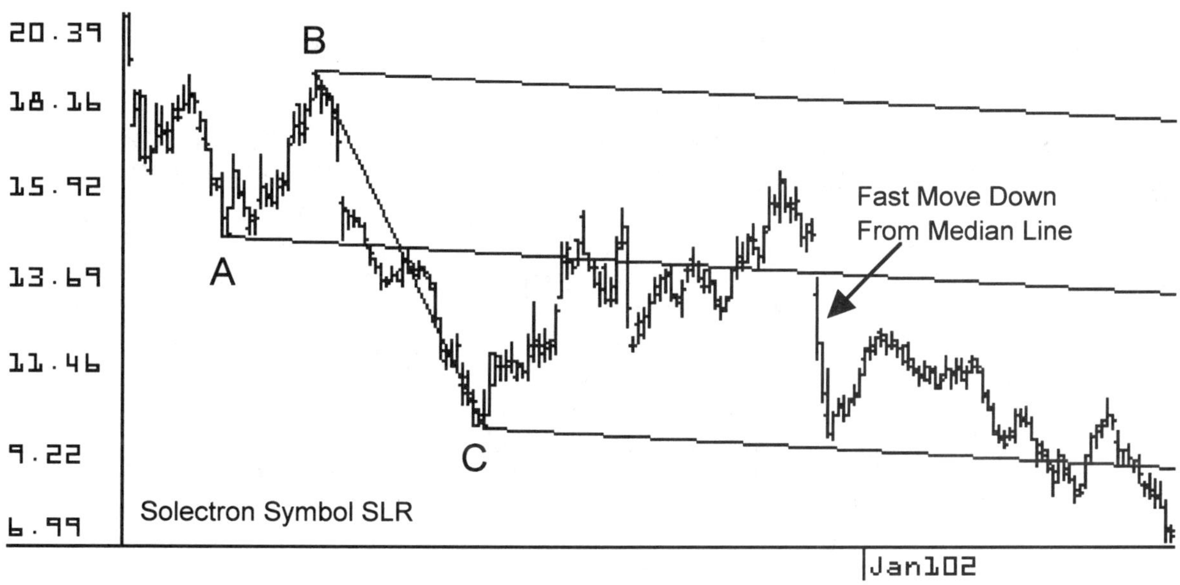

New Pitchfork Trading Rule 3

Pitchfork Buy Rule 3: Draw an upward sloping Median Line. If the price makes a spike top against the Median Line, it is a signal to sell.

Pitchfork Sell Rule 3: Draw an downward sloping Median Line. If the price makes a spike bottom against the Median Line, it is a signal to buy.

The chart on this page shows Yahoo, symbol YHOO. A Pitchfork is drawn using pivots A, B, and C with pivot A being off the screen. After pivot C, the price moves up toward the Median Line. The price reaches the Median Line with a fast contact top and then falls back. This is an indication that the move to touch the Median Line is a price exhaustion. When this type of contact occurs, it is an indication that the price is moving lower and is a signal to sell.

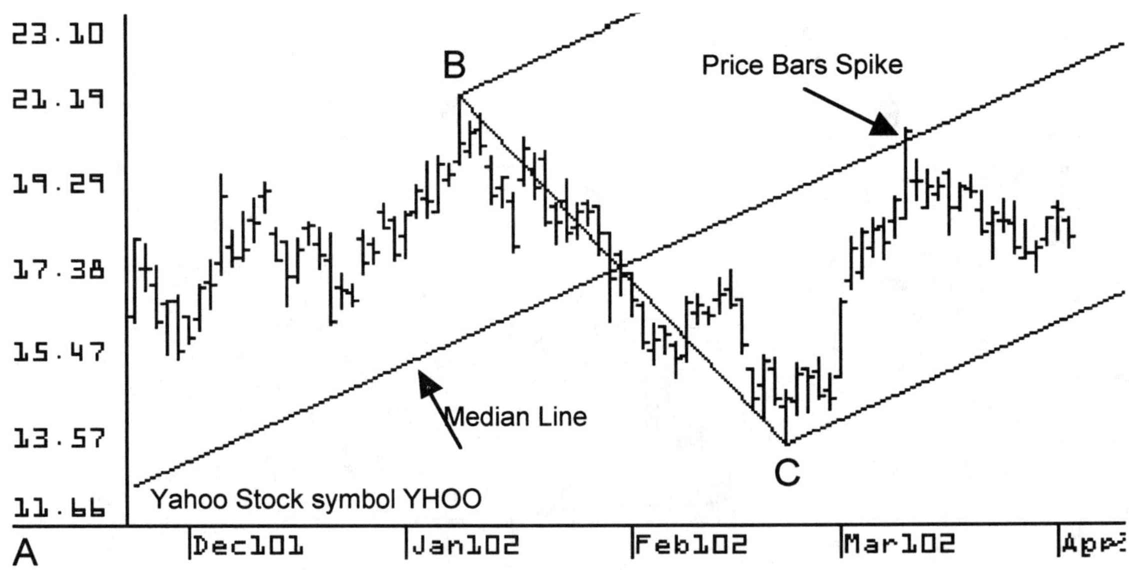

The chart on this page shows Royal Dutch Petroleum, symbol RD. A downward Pitchfork is drawn from pivots A, B, and C. After pivot C, the price moves down toward the Median Line. The price touches the Median Line with a fast spike bottom then turns and moves back up. This is an indication that the price is moving higher and is a signal to buy.

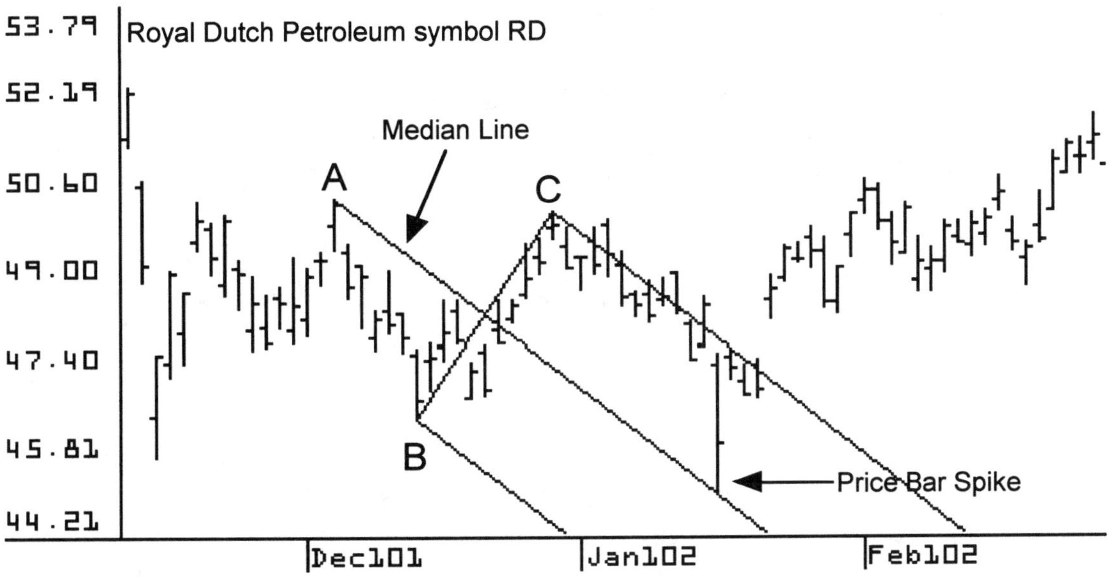

The Median Line - Momentum Swing Trading Strategy

The following strategy is a swing trading method developed at Austin Financial Group. This method combines the Median Line and the Slow Stochastic indicator. The Stochastic indicator is the most widely used momentum indicator in financial analysis. In this book it is assumed that the reader knows about the Stochastic indicator and a basic discussion of this indicator's formulae is not presesented. The settings for the Slow Stochastic indicator used with this method are a 14 bar look-back period, an oversold level of 20 and an overbought level of 80.

Median Line theory states that a Median Line drawn from the most recent pivots will see the price reach the Median Line about 80% of the time.

Stochastic theory holds that when a market is moving in a cyclical mode and the Slow Stochastic moves below the oversold line, a bottom is forming. If the Slow Stochastic moves above the overbought line, a top is forming. This is not true in trending markets.

Using the two market theories mentioned above it is possible to find high probability pivots to trade by watching for the price to reach the Median Line when the Stochastic is oversold or overbought.

The Buy Setup

Step 1: Draw a downward sloping Median Line from the most recent pivots.
Step 2: Apply a Slow Stochastic to the chart.
Step 3: Watch for the price to move down to the Median Line and the Slow Stochastic to become oversold at the same time.
Step 4: If the conditions in Step 3 are met, buy long on any observation that the market has turned upward.

The Sell Setup

Step 1: Draw an upward sloping Median Line from the most recent pivots.
Step 2: Apply a Slow Stochastic to the chart.
Step 3: Watch for the price to move up to the Median Line and the Slow Stochastic to become overbought at the same time.
Step 4: If the conditions in Step 3 are met, sell short on any observation that the market has turned downward.

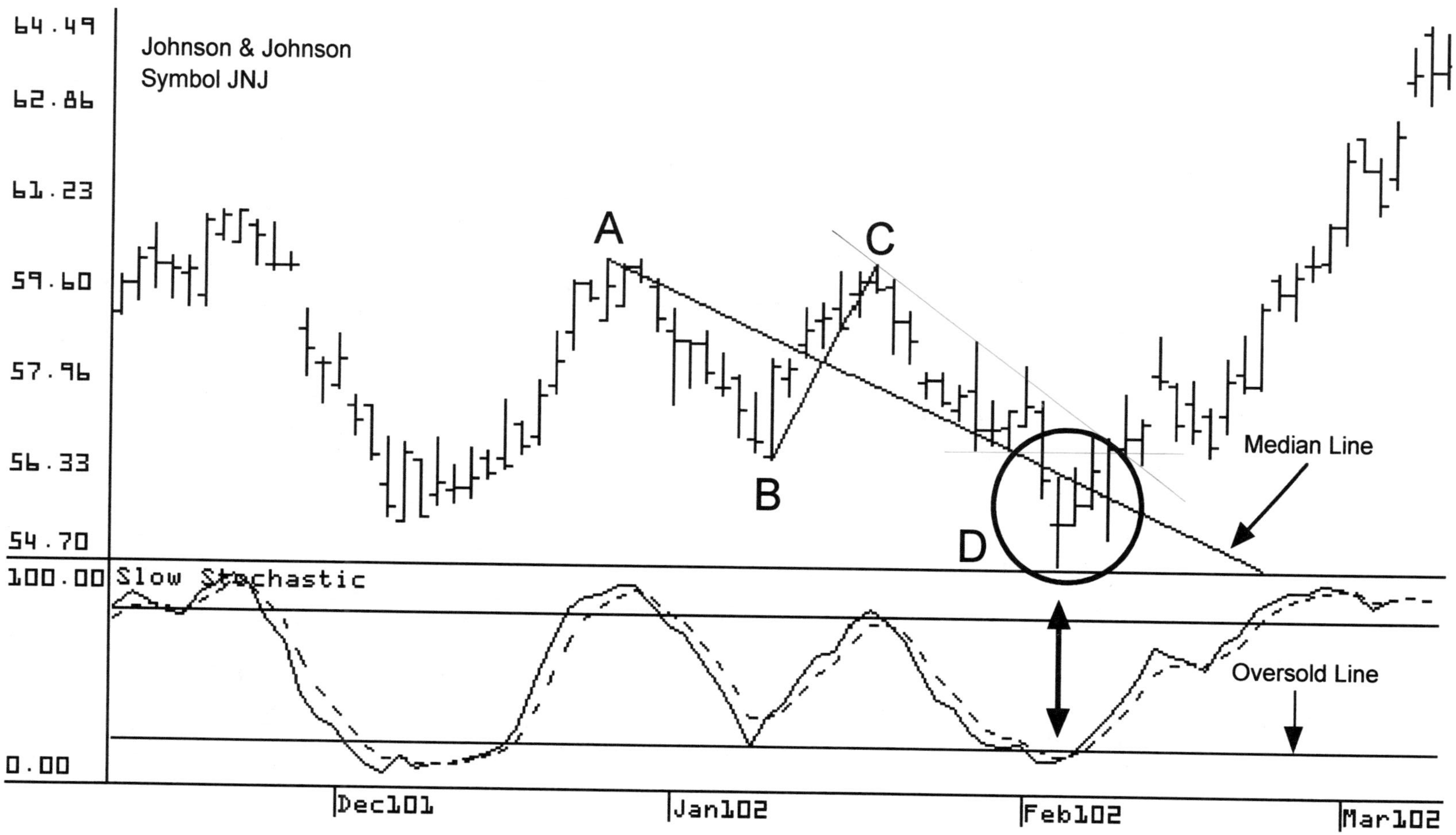

The chart on this page shows Johnson and Johnson, symbol JNJ. A downward sloping Median Line is drawn using pivots A, B, and C. The Slow Stochastic is applied to this chart. The price falls to the Median Line at point D and the Slow Stochastic is also below the oversold line. This is a high probability swing trade setup at which a trader buys long the swing bottom at point D and holds for the next up swing.

The chart on this page uses data on J.P. Morgan, symbol JPM. An upward sloping Median Line is drawn using pivots A, B, and C and a Slow Stochastic is added to the chart. The price increases to the Median Line at point D and the Slow Stochastic is also above the overbought line. This is a high probability swing trade setup. A trader would sell short the swing top at point D and hold for the next down swing.

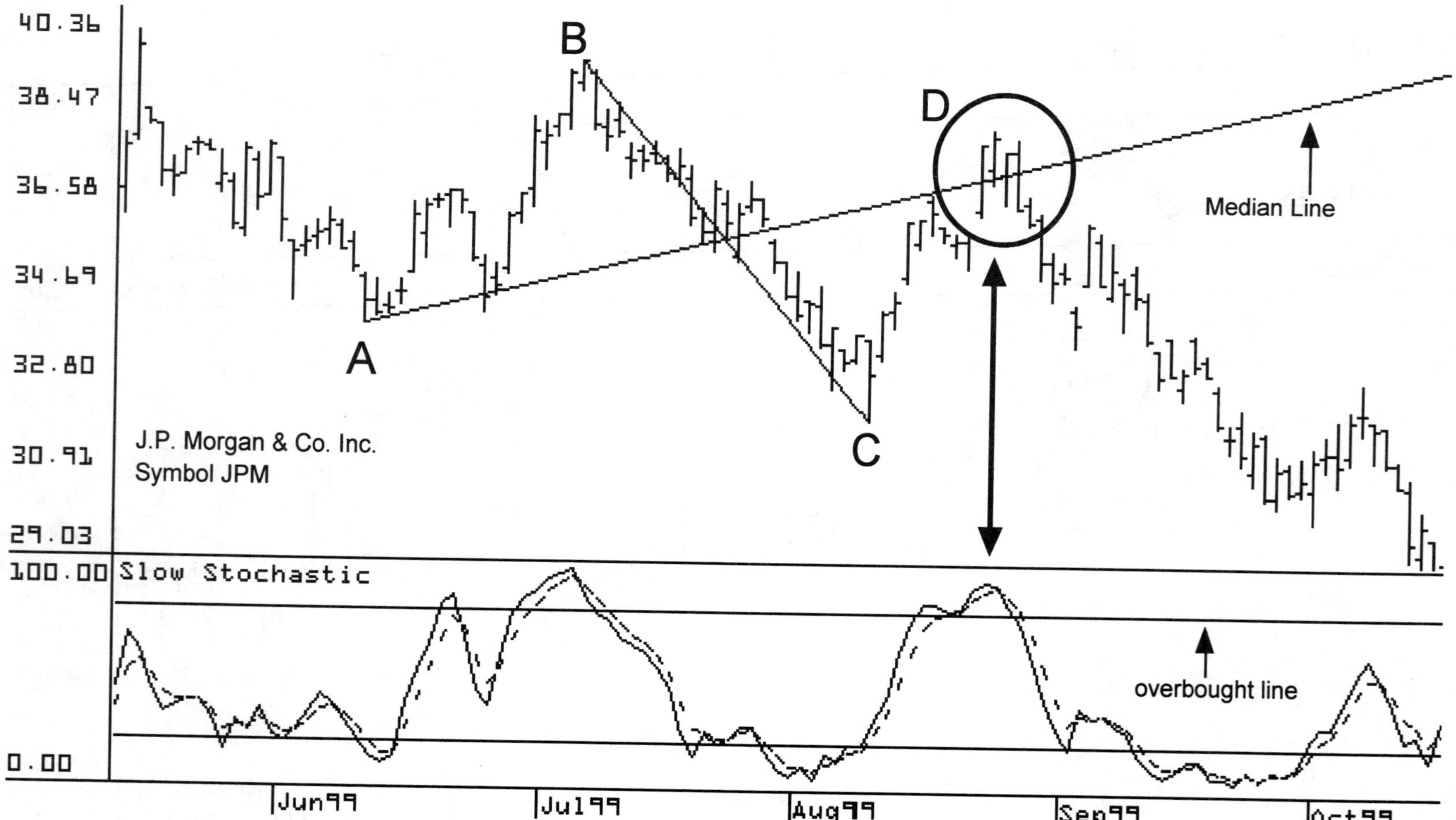

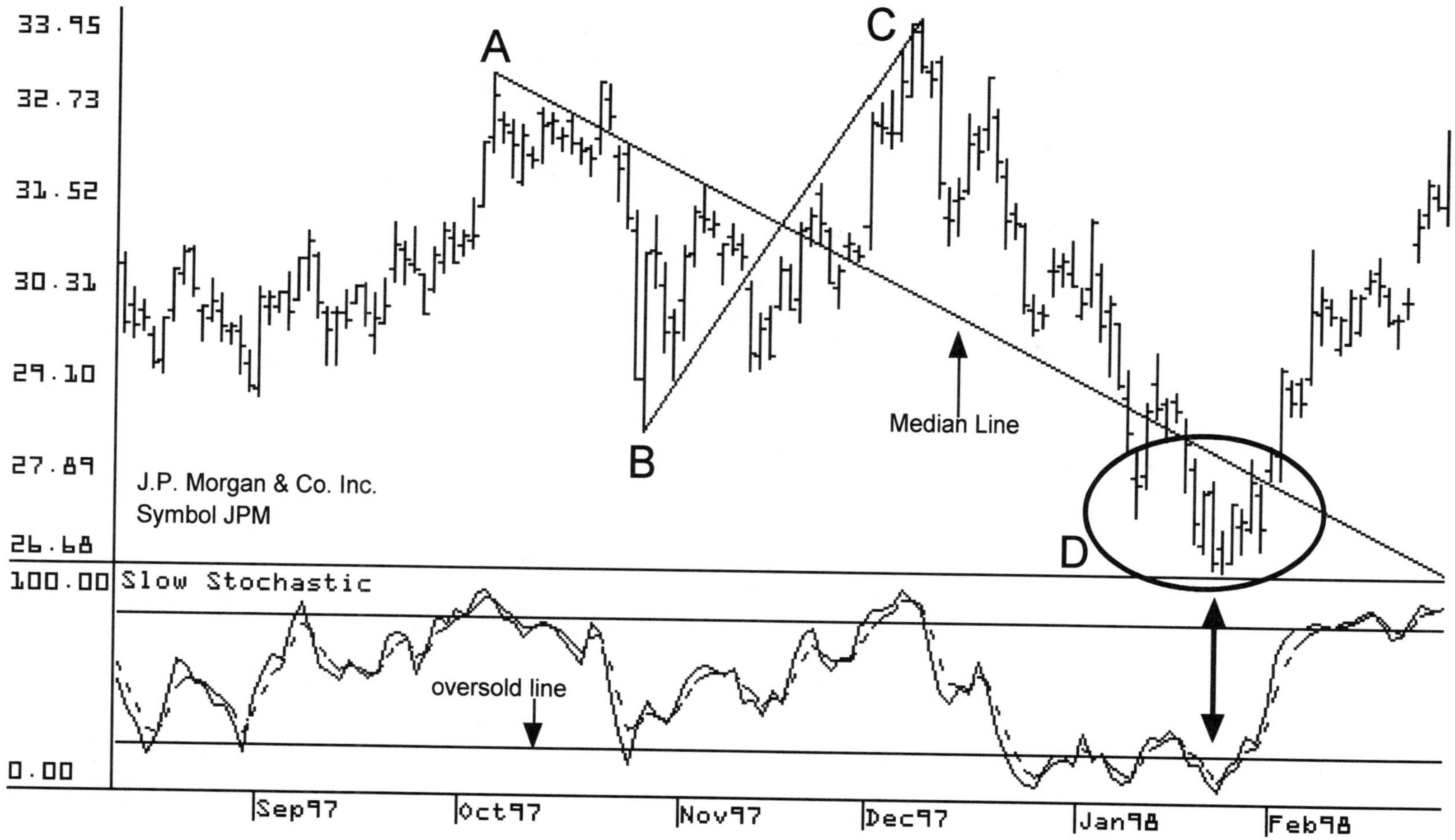

This page shows a second chart for J.P. Morgan, symbol JPM. A downward sloping Median Line is drawn using pivots A, B, and C and a Slow Stochastic is added to the chart. On this chart the price falls to the Median Line at point D and the Slow Stochastic is also below the oversold line. This is a high probability swing trade setup where a trader buys long the swing bottom at point D and holds for the next up swing.

On this page there is a chart for Merrill Lynch, symbol MER. A downward sloping Median Line is drawn using pivots A, B, and C and a Slow Stochastic indicator is added to the chart. On this chart, the price falls to the Median Line at point D and the Slow Stochastic is also below the oversold line. This is a high probability swing trade setup. A trader buys long the swing bottom at point D and holds for the next up swing.

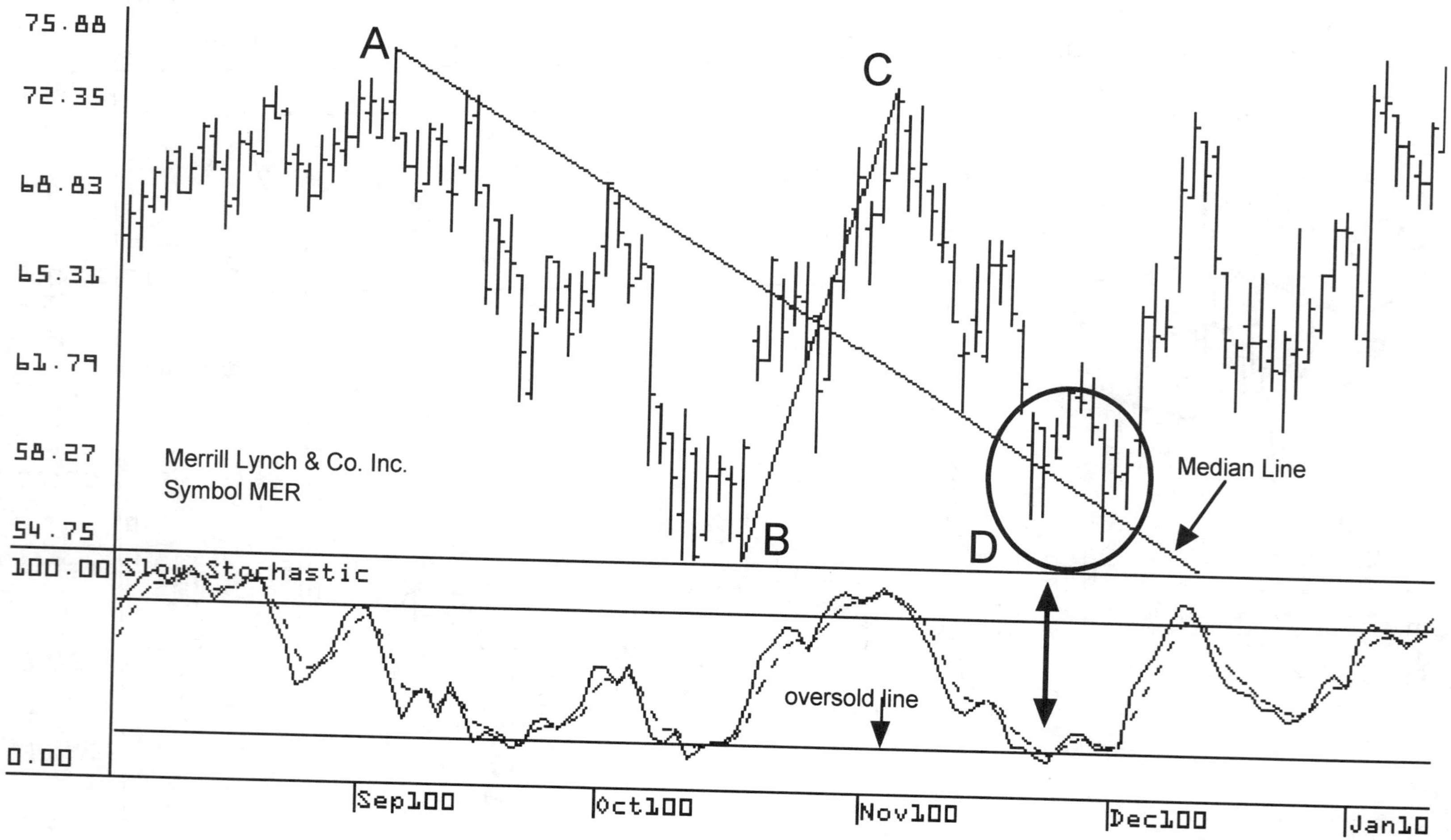

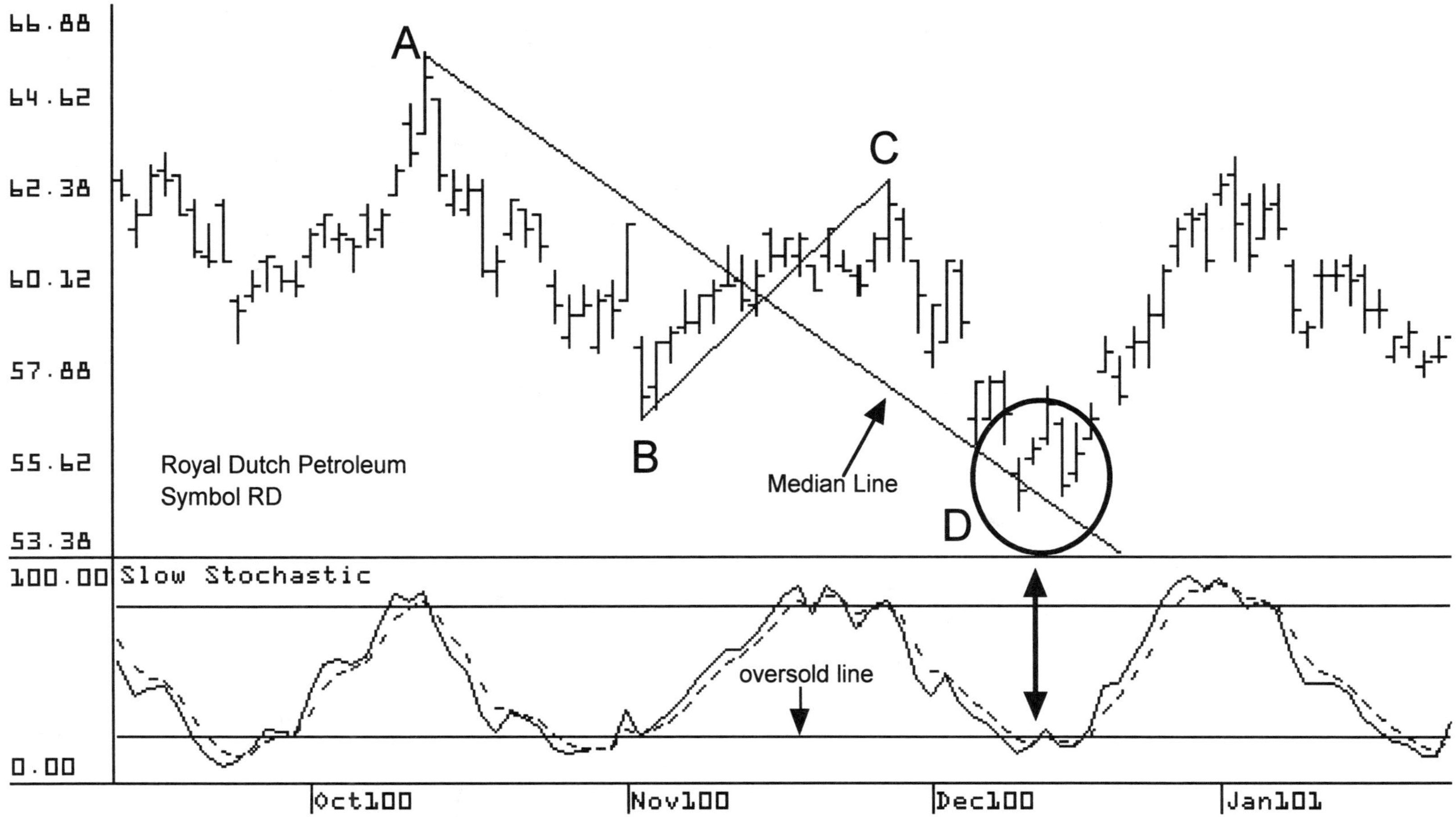

This page contains a chart for Royal Dutch Petroleum, symbol RD. A Median Line is drawn using pivots A, B, and C and a Slow Stochastic indicator is added to the chart. On this chart, the price falls to the Median Line at point D and the Slow Stochastic is also below the oversold line. This is a high probability swing trade setup at which a trader buys long the swing bottom at point D and holds for the next up swing.

Page 76

On this page is a chart for May 2002 Silver futures. A Median Line is drawn using pivots A, B, and C and a Slow Stochastic is added to the chart. On this chart the price falls to the Median Line at point D and the Slow Stochastic is also below the oversold line. This is a high probability swing trade setup point at which a trader buys long the swing bottom at point D and holds for the next up swing.

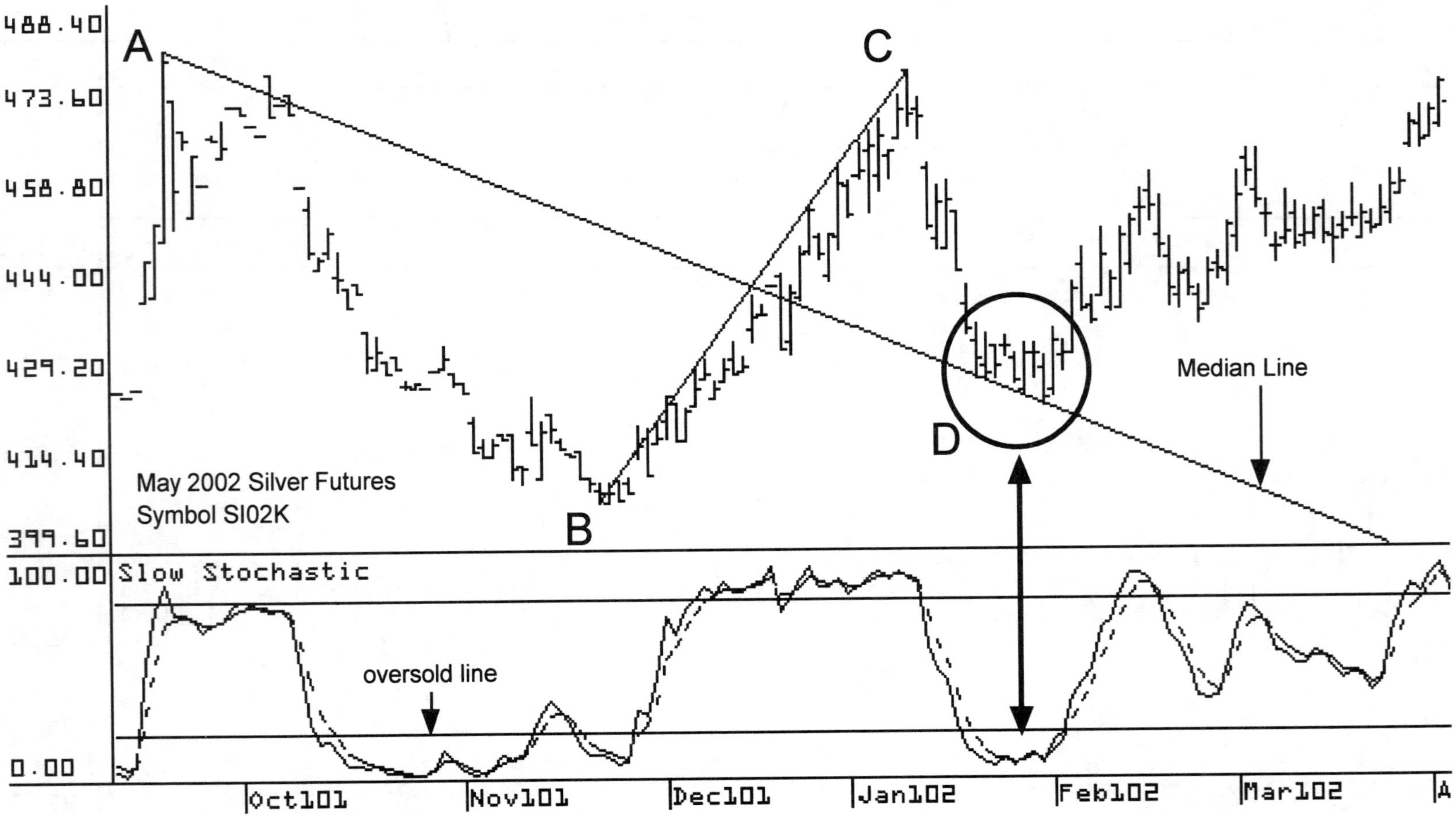

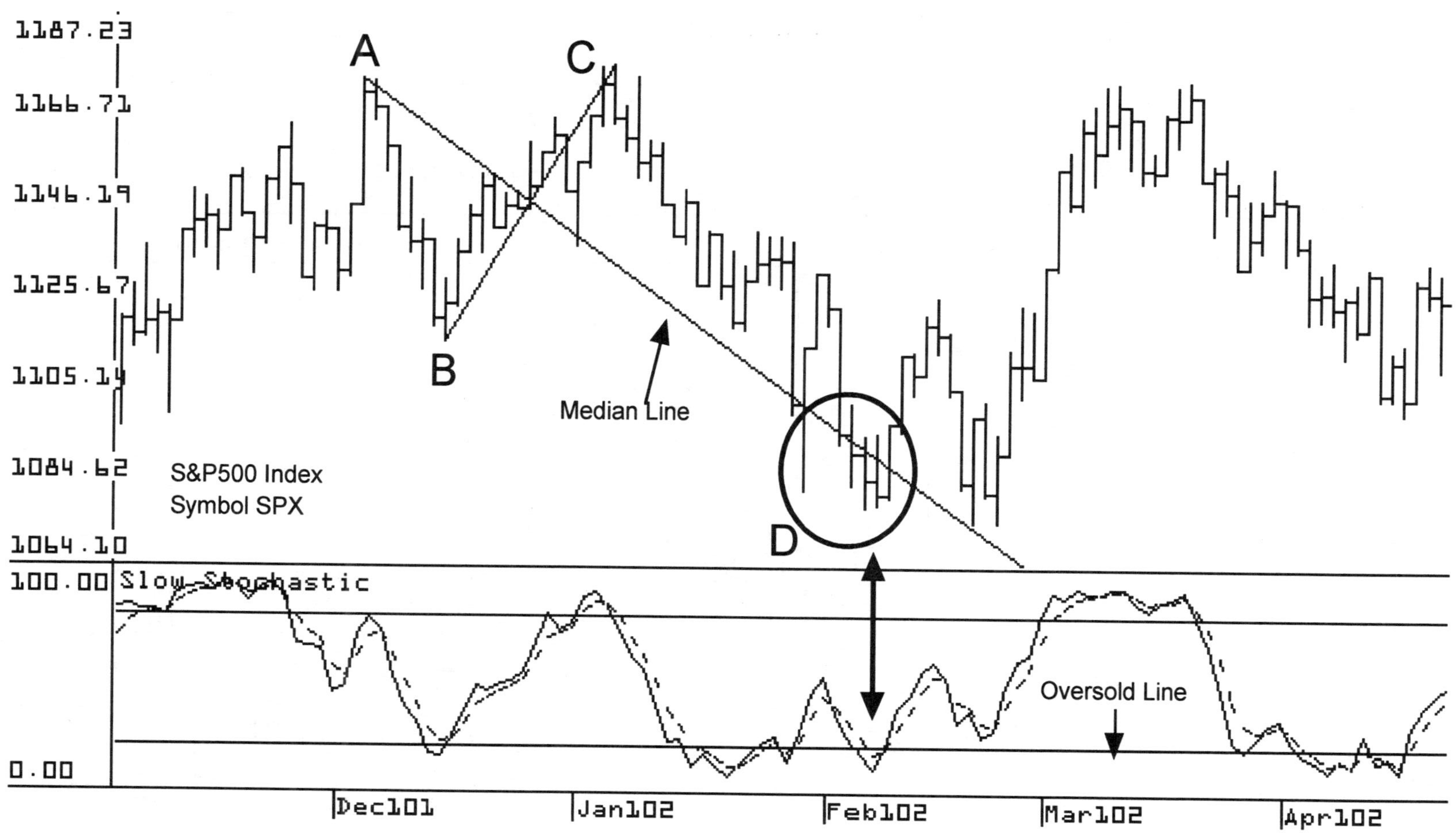

This page has a chart for S&P500 Index, symbol SPX. Pivots A, B, and C are used to draw a Median Line and a Slow Stochastic is also drawn on the chart. On this chart the price falls to the Median Line at point D and the Slow Stochastic is also below the oversold line. This is a high probability swing trade setup situation in which a trader buys long the swing bottom at point D and holds for the next up swing.

On this page is a chart for Tellabs, symbol TAB. A Median Line is drawn using pivots A, B, and C and a Slow Stochastic is positioned on the chart. The price increases from pivot C to the Median Line at point D and the Stochastic is also above the overbought line. This is a high probability swing trade setup. A trader sells short the swing top at point D and holds for the next down swing. Next, a second Median Line is drawn using pivots B, C and D. The price falls from pivot D to the second Median Line at point E and the Stochastic is also below the oversold line. This is another high probability swing trade setup. This time a trader buys long the swing bottom at point E and holds for the next up swing.

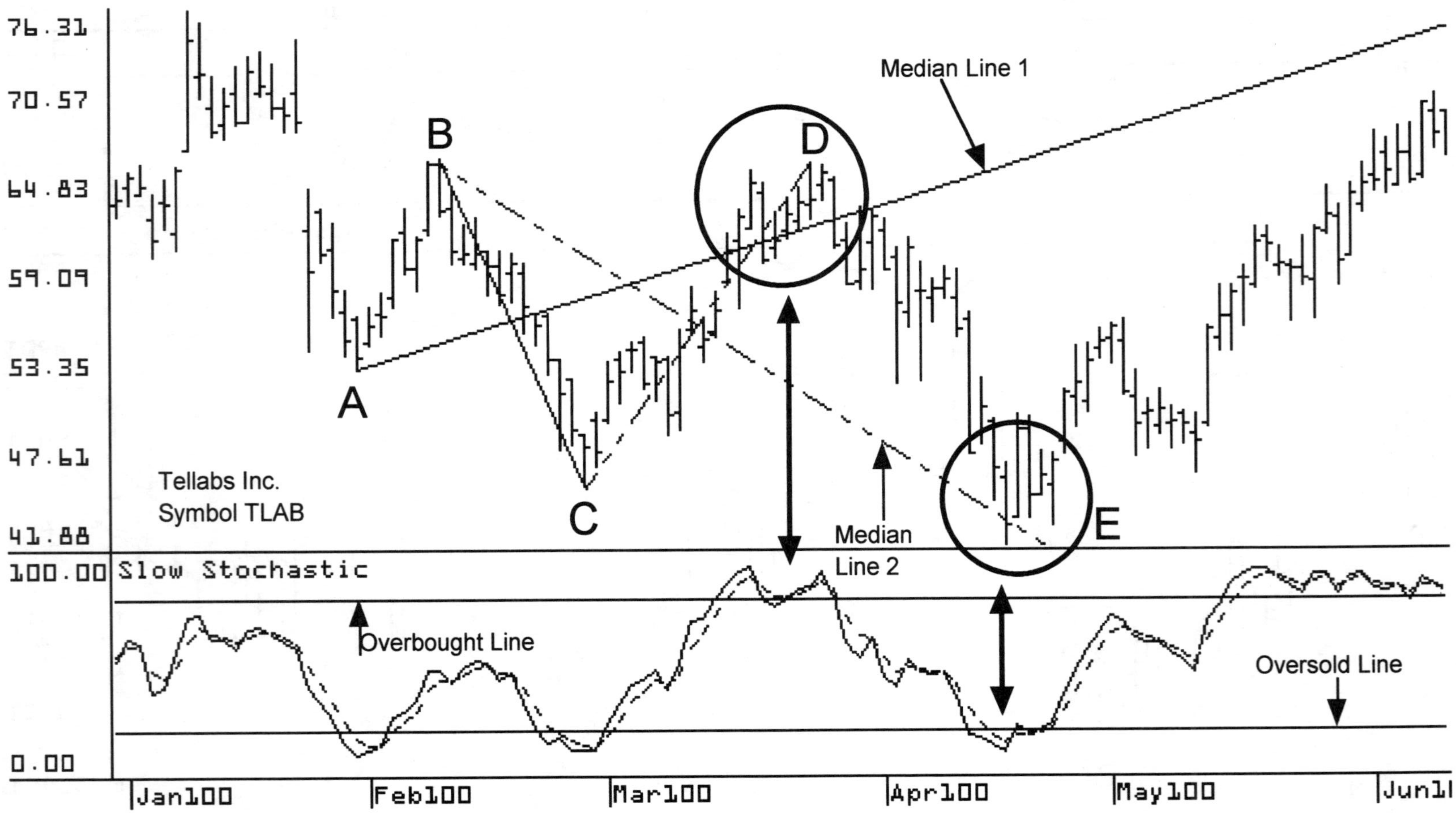

Page 78

The 50 Percent Pitchfork

Under some conditions, the Pitchfork is too steep to be of any trading value. This problem is addressed by the 50% Pitchfork developed at Austin Financial Group. This innovative Pitchfork is drawn using the same three starting pivots as the standard Pitchfork, but with a new set of drawing rules.

On the first diagram below, points A, B, and C represent three pivots used to draw a standard Pitchfork. The horizontal line, marked by the letter D, is the B-C midpoint. If pivot A is below D as seen on the diagram, the 50% Pitchfork is drawn with the 50% point between A and B instead of A. This 50% point between A and B is marked by the X.

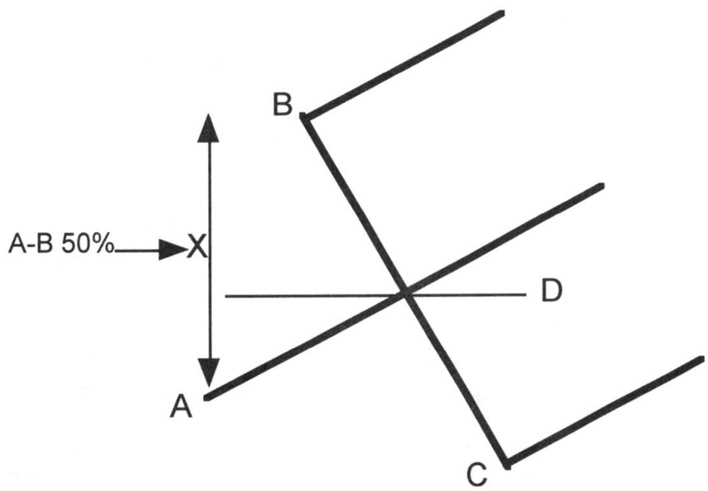

The diagram below shows the 50% Pitchfork calculated using points A, B, and C but it is drawn using points X, B and C. The Median Line which extends forward starts from X not A. If a comparison of the two diagrams on this page is made, it is evident that the 50% Pitchfork using the same three points A, B, and C can create a very different set of angles. In the top diagram, the Pitchfork slopes upward at a steep angle while the 50% Pitchfork in the bottom diagram declines downward at a gradual angle.

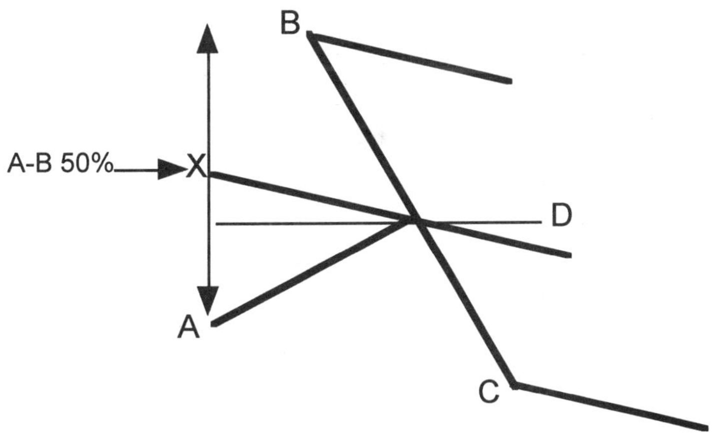

The first diagram below shows a normal Pitchfork drawn using points A, B, and C. When drawing a 50% Pitchfork, it is necessary to check if starting point A is above or below the B-C midpoint D. If A is above D, as seen on the diagram below, then the 50% Pitchfork is drawn with the 50% point between A and C instead of A. This 50% point between A and C is marked by the X.

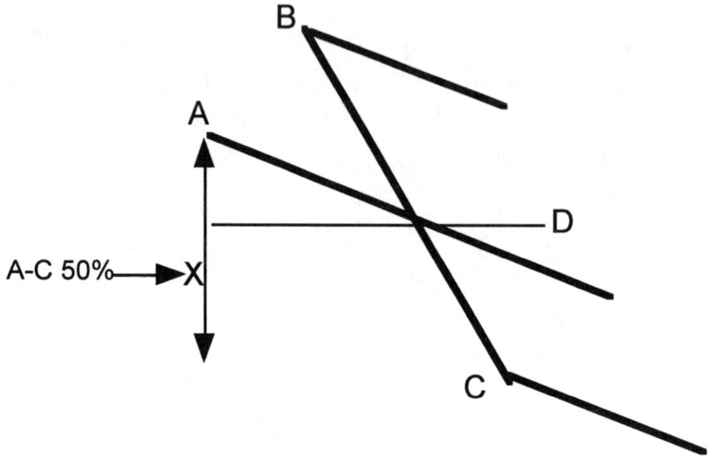

The diagram below shows that the 50% Pitchfork is calculated using points A, B, and C but is drawn using points X, B and C. It is important to notice that the Median Line which extends forwards starts from X not A. If the two diagrams on this page are compared, it is seen that the Pitchfork in the top diagram slopes downward and the 50% Pitchfork in the bottom diagram slopes upward. The Pitchfork in the top diagram also slopes at a steeper angle than the 50% Pitchfork in the bottom diagram. This shows that the 50% Pitchfork using the same three points A, B, and C creates a very different set of angles.

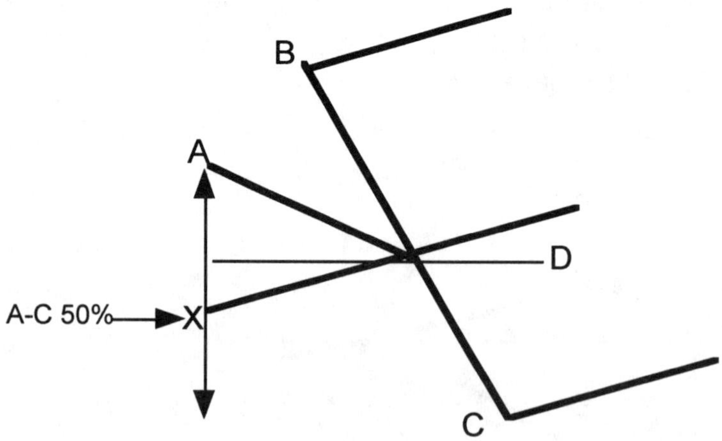

On this page there are two charts with the same price data. The top chart shows a normal Pitchfork and the bottom chart shows a 50% Pitchfork. The normal Pitchfork has a steep slope and covers only the swing immediately following pivot C. The 50% Pitchfork has a lower slope and correlates much better with the price swings beyond the first swing after pivot C. The 50% Pitchfork often works better than the normal Pitchfork when the market is moving sideways. Sideways markets often do not correlate well to the normal Pitchfork.

Normal Pitchfork

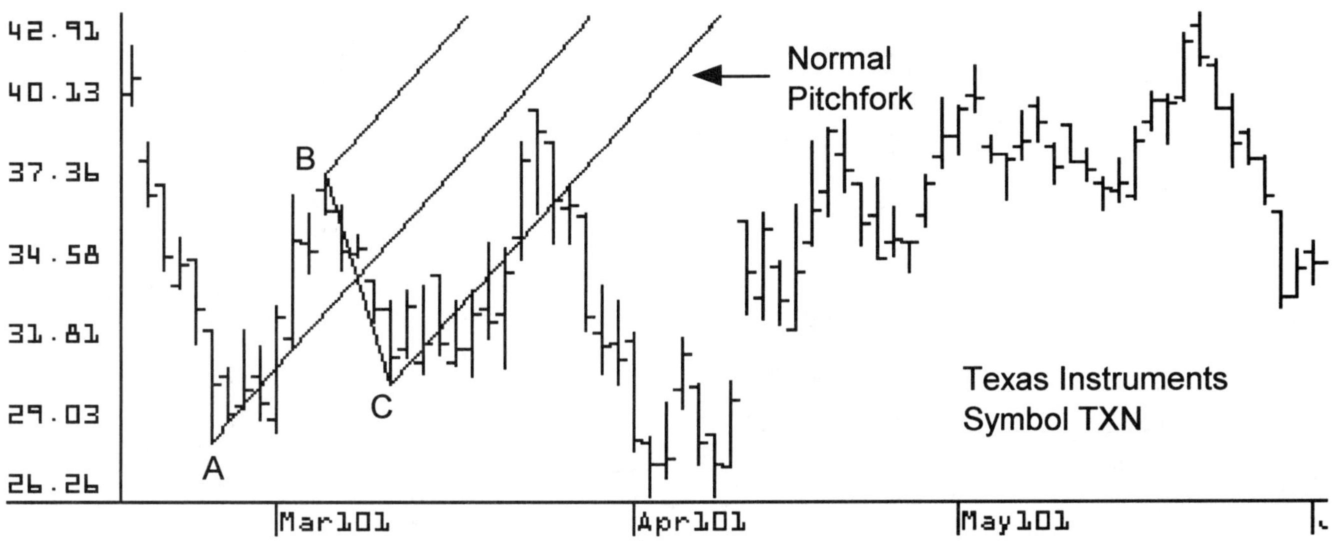

50% Pitchfork

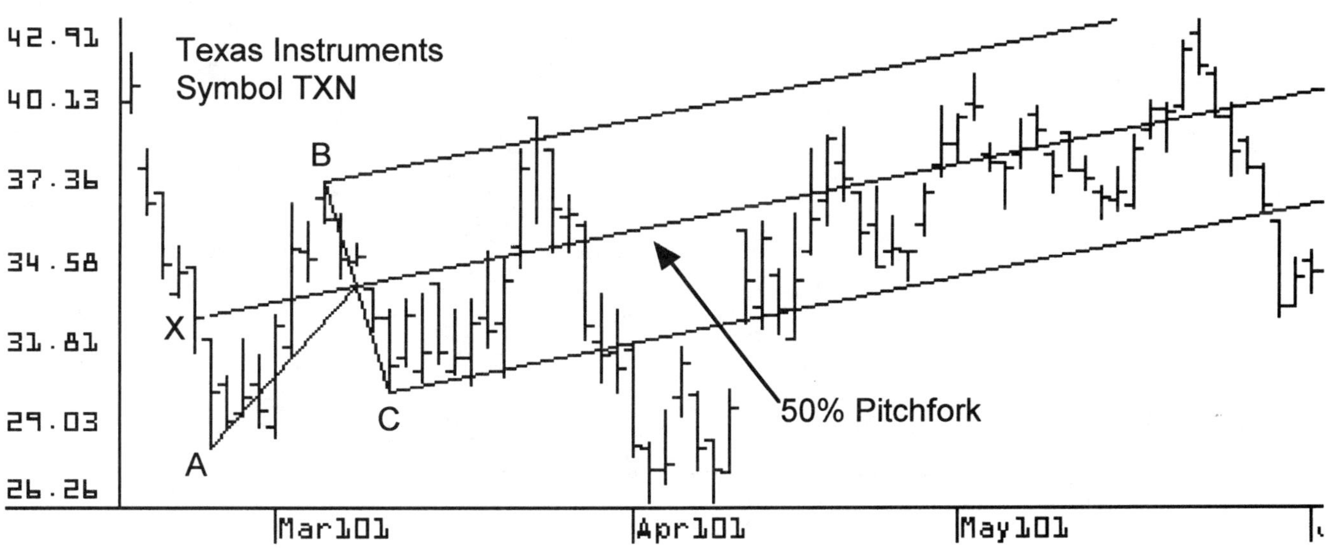

The chart on this page shows American Express, symbol AXP. The 50% Pitchfork is calculated with pivots A, B, and C but is drawn with point X, B, and C. After pivot C, the price swings stay between the 50% Pitchfork upper and lower parallel lines. This trendline channel created by the 50% Pitchfork correlates with the prices for almost five months.

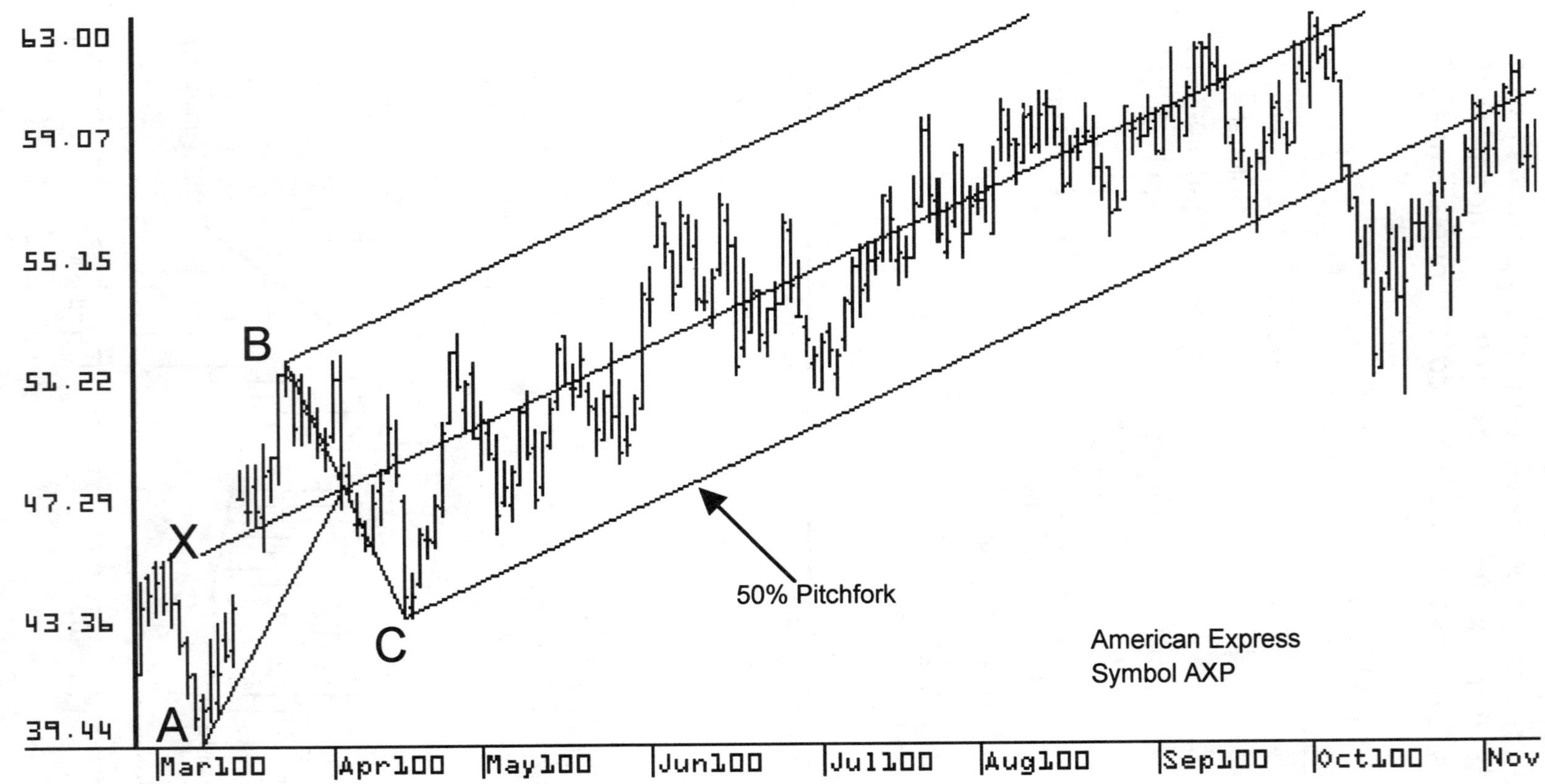

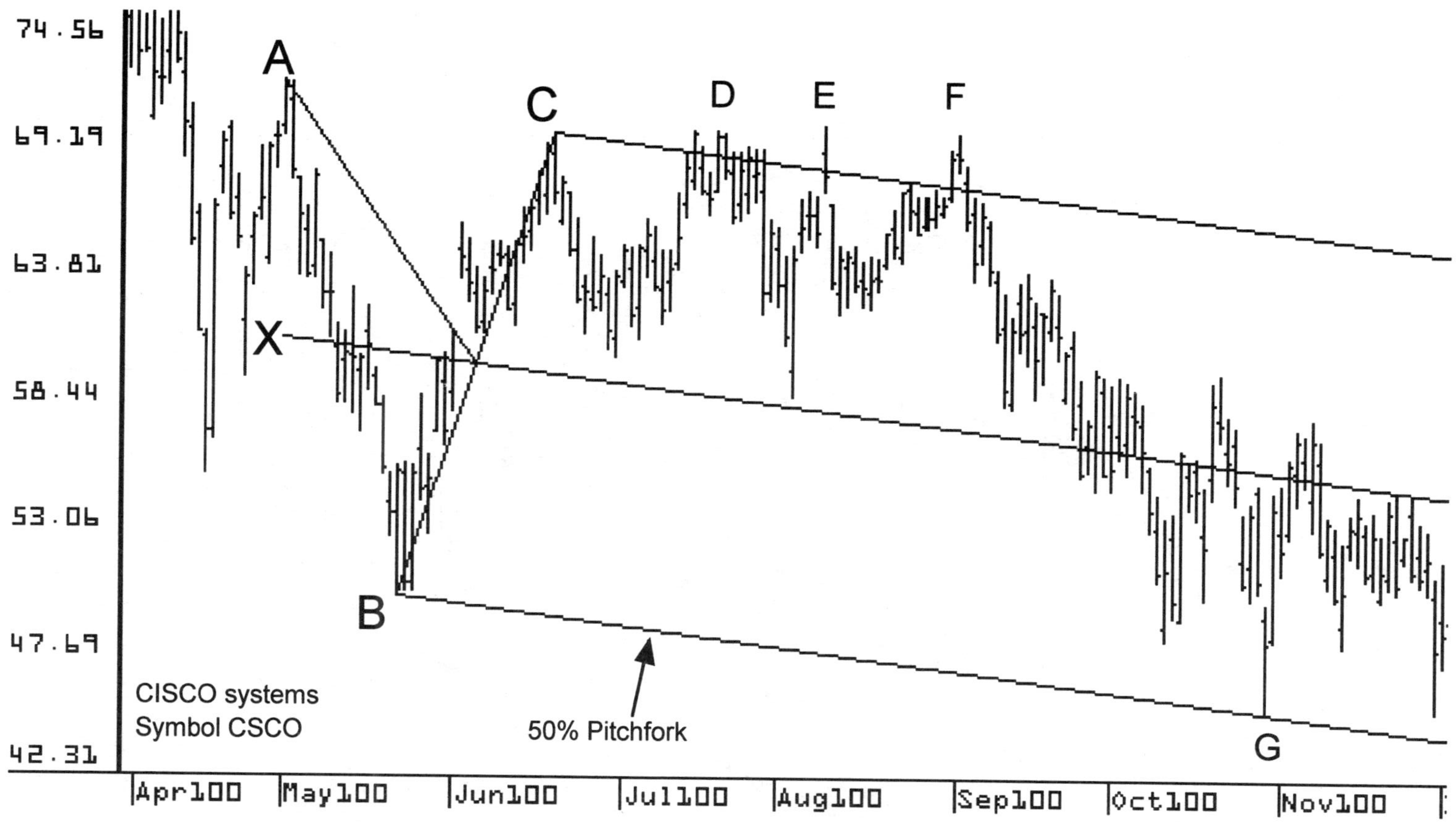

This page shows a chart for Cisco Systems, symbol CSCO. The chart shows a 50% Pitchfork which is calculated with pivots A, B, and, C but is drawn with points X, B, and C. After pivot C, the market swings move sideways and make tops against the upper parallel line at D, E, and F. Sideways markets often correlate very well with the 50% Pitchfork. After pivot F, the market falls and makes a bottom against the lower parallel line at G.

This page contains a chart for Motorola, symbol MOT. The chart calculates a 50% Pitchfork with pivots A, B, and, C but is drawn with point X, B, and C. After pivot C, the market makes a top against the upper parallel line at point D and a swing bottom against the lower parallel line at point E. The market makes another top against the Median Line at point F.

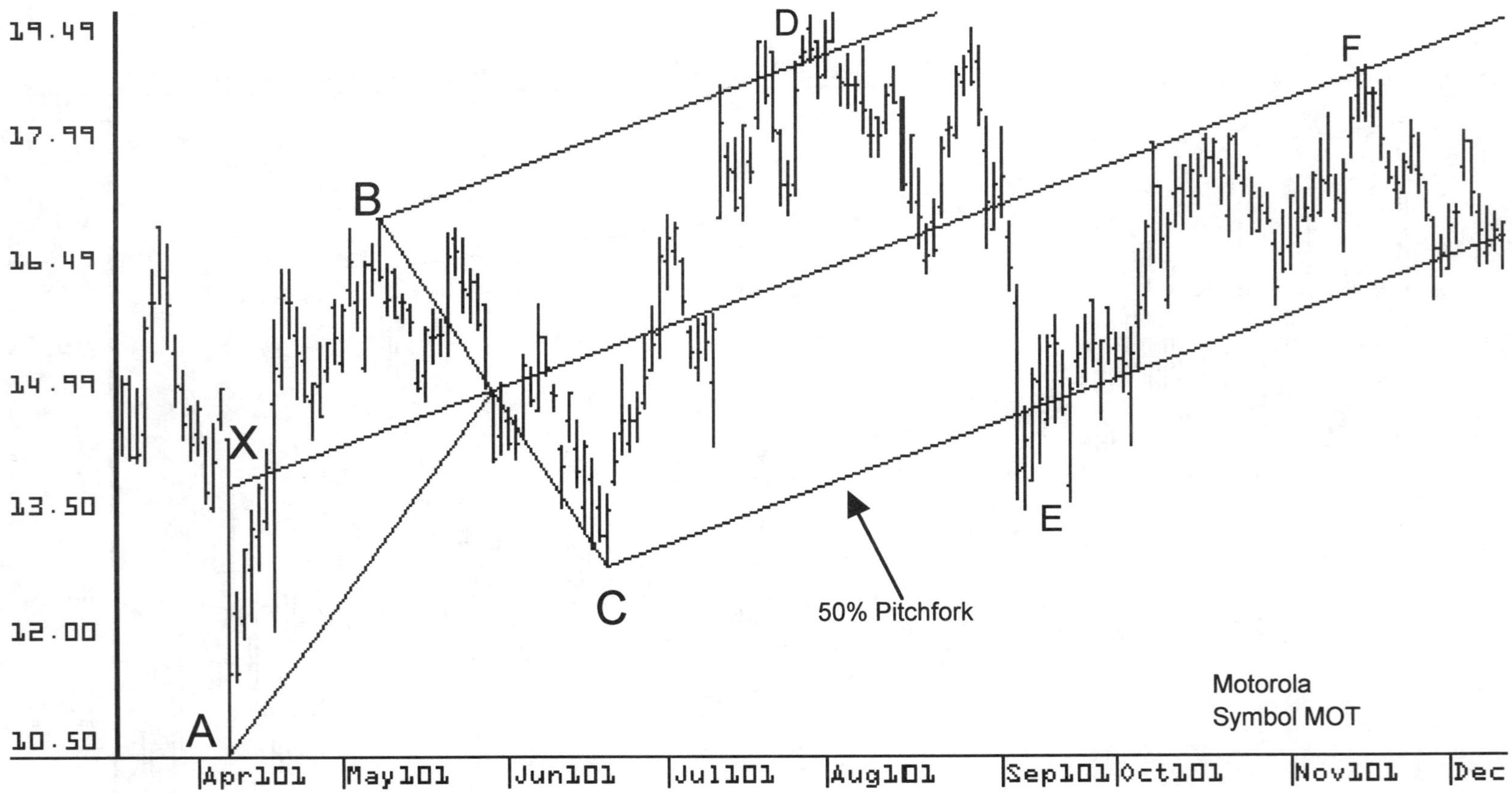

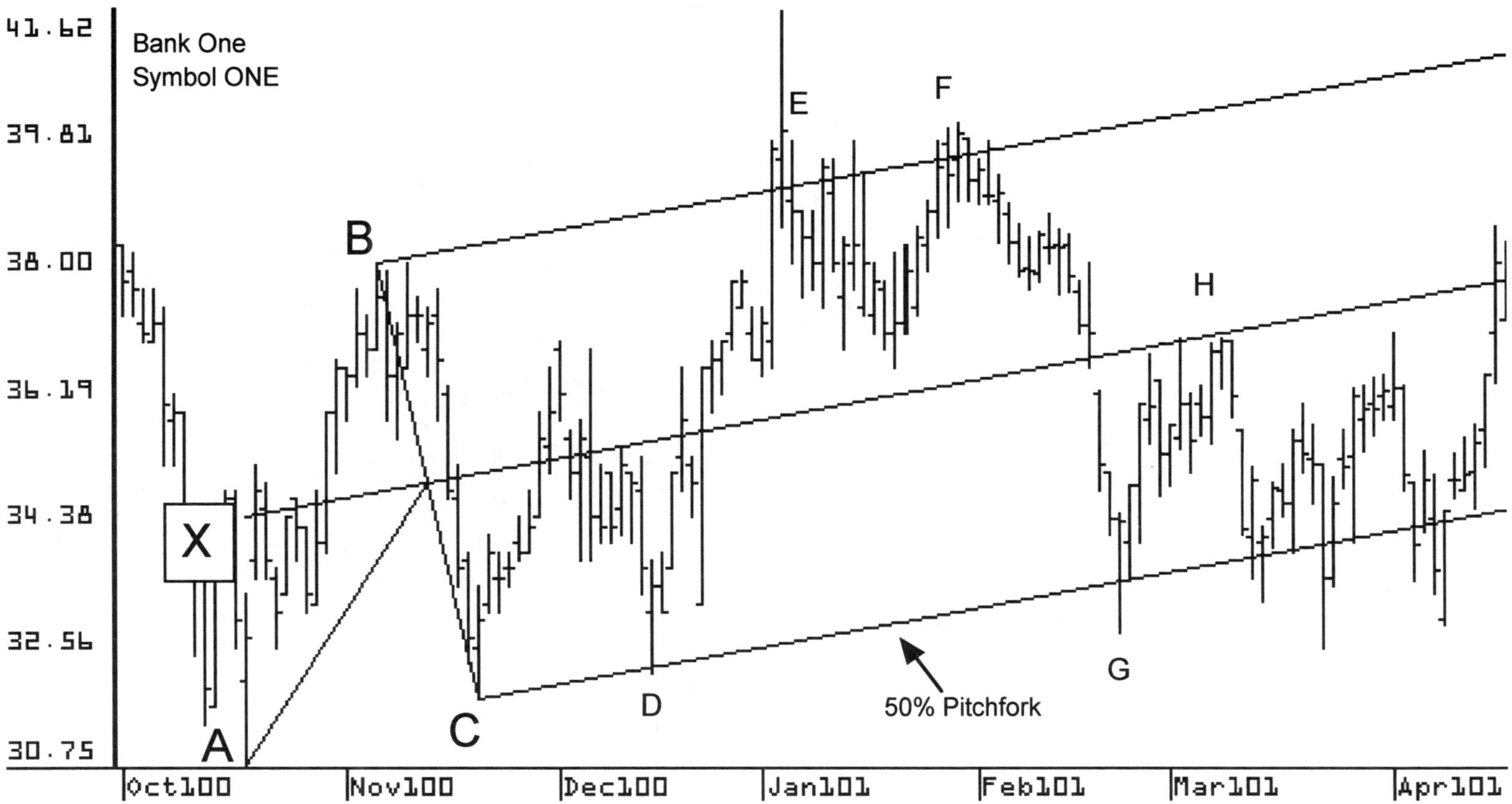

Data for Bank One, symbol ONE is used for this chart. The chart shows a 50% Pitchfork which is calculated with pivots A, B, and C but is drawn with point X, B, and C. After pivot C, the market makes bottoms against the lower parallel line at point D and G. The market makes swing tops against the upper parallel line at E and F. This market moves sideways with a mild upward slope after pivot C. This is an indication the market probably correlates better with the 50% Pitchfork than the normal Pitchfork.

Warning Lines work just as well with the 50% Pitchfork as with the normal Pitchfork. This page shows a chart for Novellus Systems, symbol NVLS. The chart calculates a 50% Pitchfork with pivots A, B, and C but is drawn with point X, B, and C. Also added to this chart are three Warning Lines below the lower parallel line. After pivot C, this 50% Pitchfork correlates very well with the swing tops and bottoms which form against the 50% Pitchfork Median Line, the upper parallel line and the lower parallel line. Some of these pivots occur at points E, F, G, H and I. There are also two pivots against Warning Line 1 at points D and J.

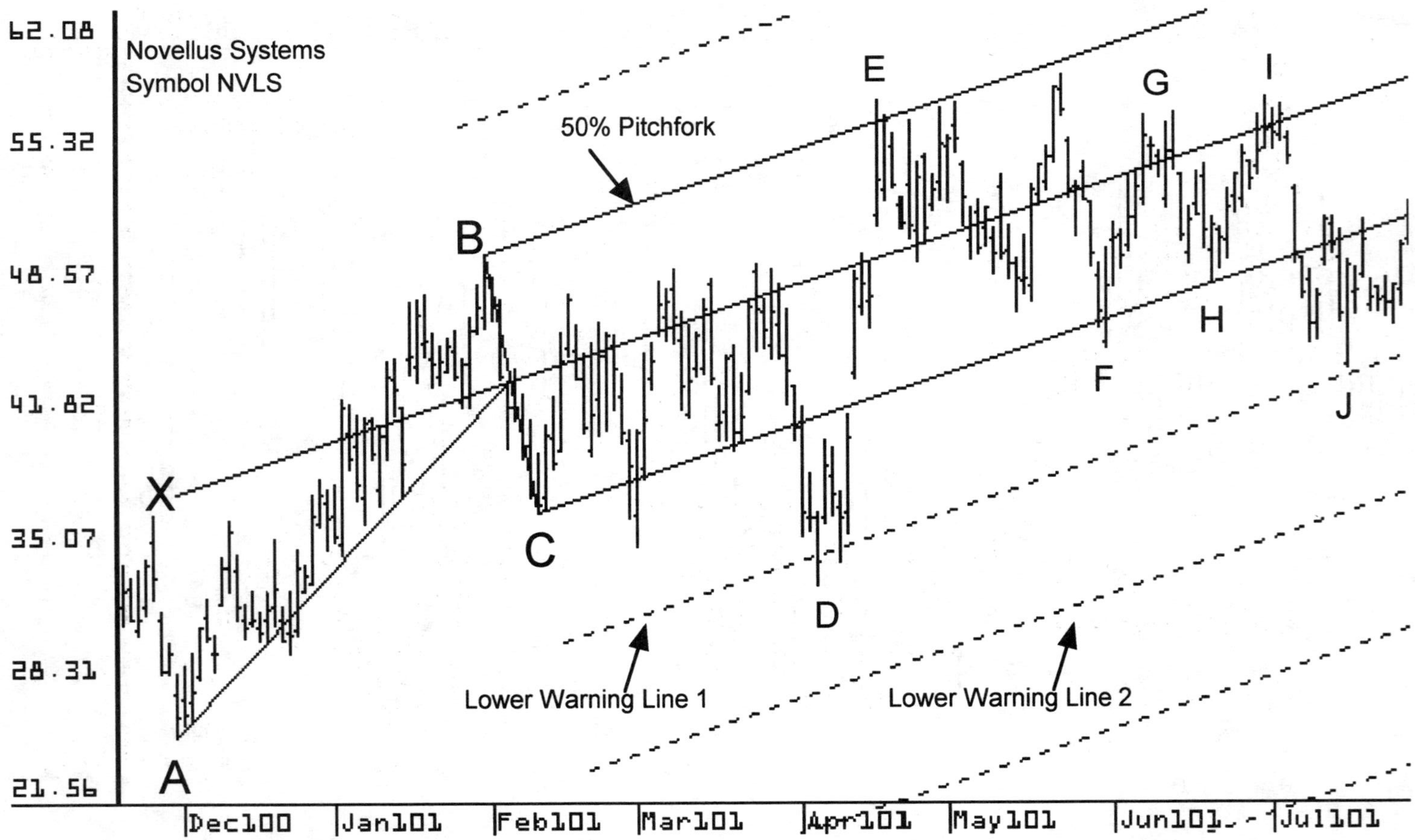

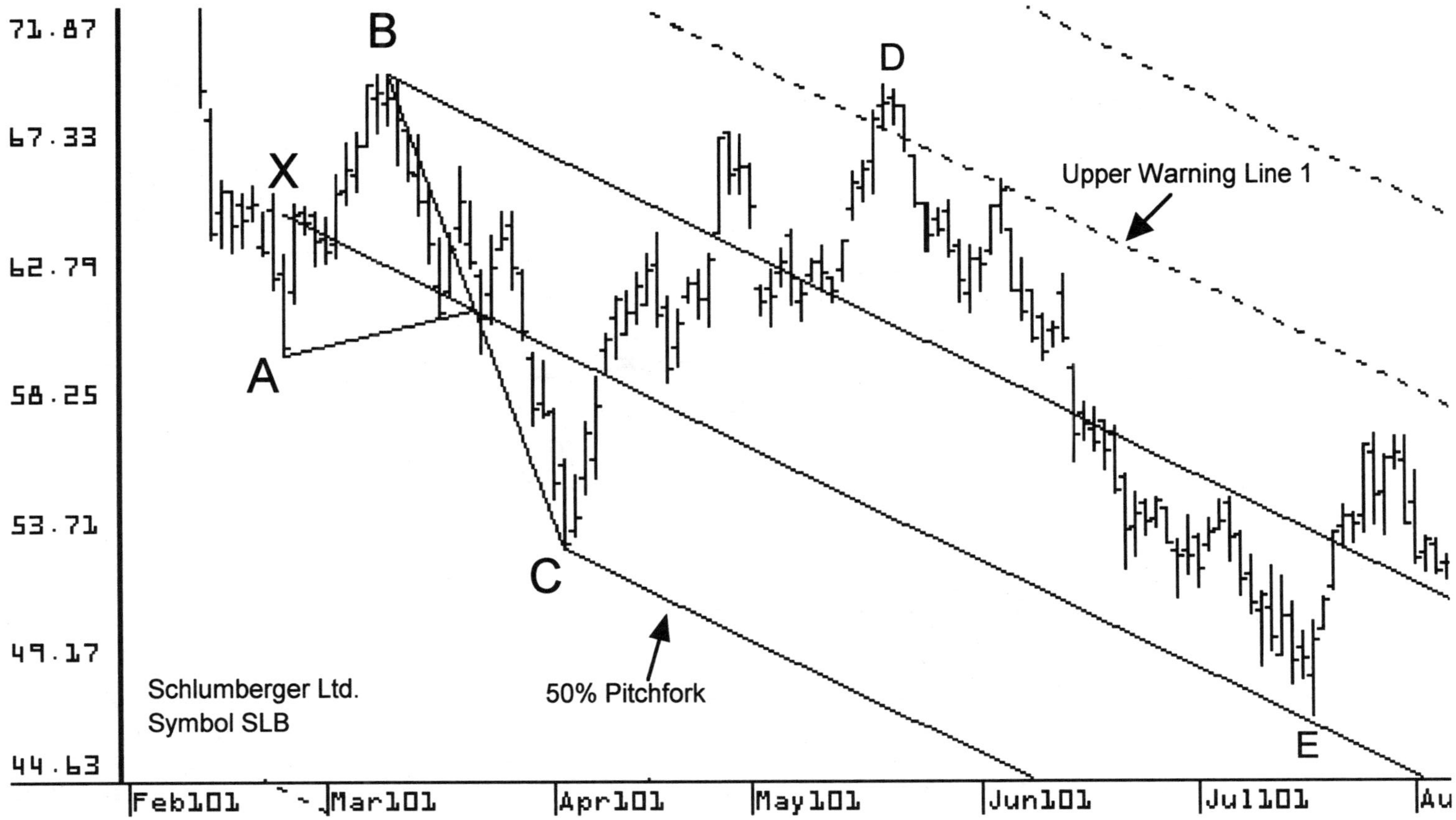

This page shows a chart for Schlumberger Ltd., symbol SLB. The chart shows a 50% Pitchfork calculated with pivots A, B, and C but is drawn with point X, B, and C. After pivot C, the market makes a significant swing top against the upper Warning Line 1 at point D. The market then falls very quickly coming to rest at the Median Line and makes a bottom at point E.

This page has a chart for Verisign, symbol VRSN. The chart shows a 50% Pitchfork which is based on pivots A, B, and C drawn with points X, B, and C. After pivot C, the market makes a significant swing top against the upper Warning Line 1 at point D. This is followed by a steep decline to the lower Warning Line 1 and a bottom at point E.

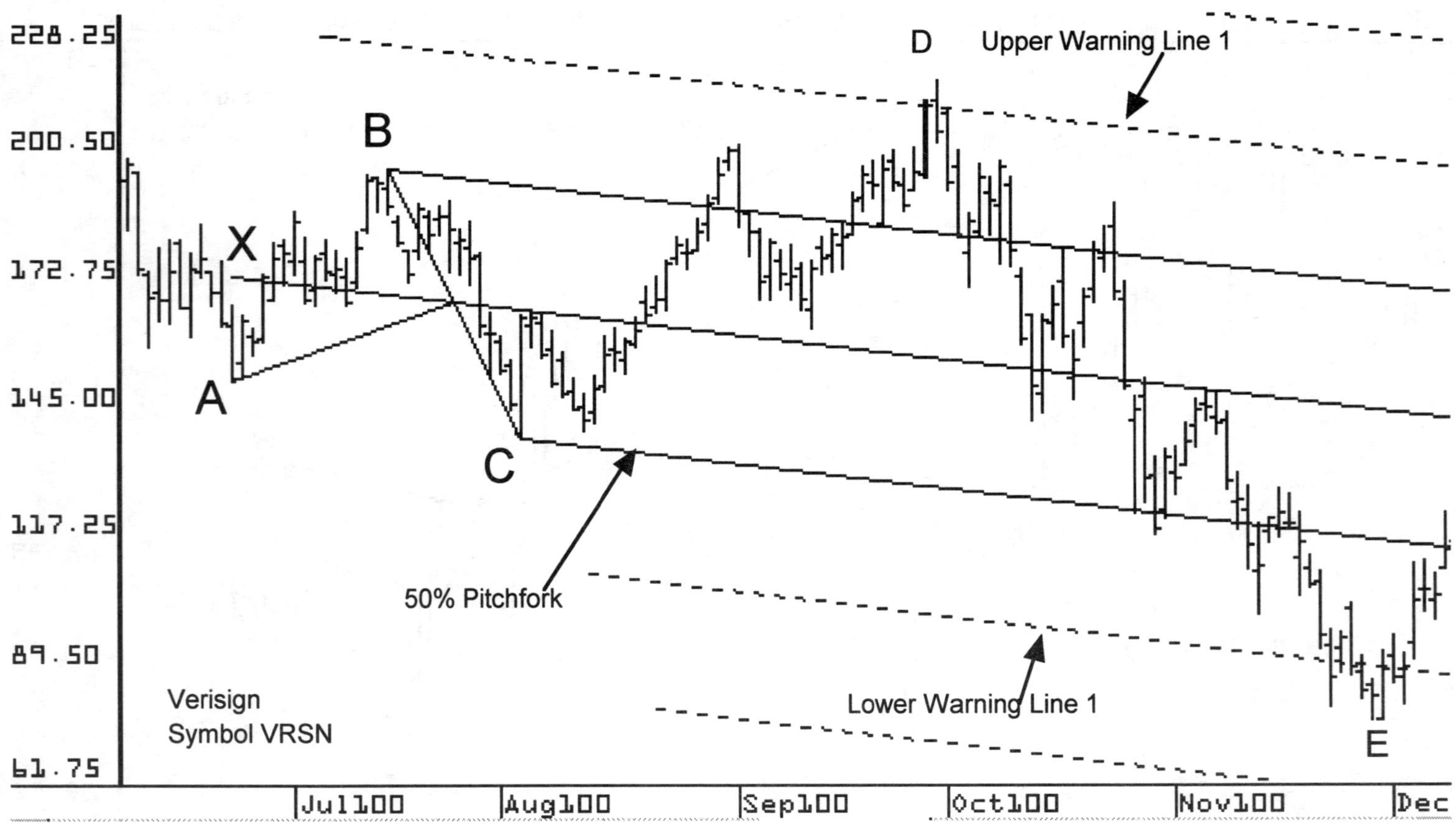

The Median Line Pivot Zone

When using the Median Line to swing trade pivots, it becomes very helpful to estimate when the price should reach the Median Line. Andrews stated that the price reaches a Median Line drawn from the most recent swings approximately 80% of the time. But how long should a trader wait for the price to reach the Median Line? Austin Financial Group developed a technique named the, "Median Line Pivot Zone," to estimate how long it should take for the price to reach the Median Line. The diagram below shows a Median Line drawn using pivots A, B, and C. The first step to calculate the Median Line Pivot Zone is to draw a Median Line and count the bar size of the two swings from A to B and B to C.

On the diagram below the size of swing A to B is shown as 10 bars and size of swing B to C is shown as 15 bars. Starting from the newest pivot used to draw the Median Line, in this case pivot C, count forward the number of bars in the larger of the two swing counts and mark this bar on the Median Line.

Finally, draw a rectangle from pivot C down to the mark on the Median Line. This rectangle is the Median Line Pivot Zone. Research at Austin Financial Group shows that the price usually reaches the Median Line before the end of the Median Line Pivot Zone. It is important to note that when the price touches the Median Line within the pivot zone, there is not a guarantee of a price reversal. What the Median Line Pivot Zone does is indicate that the market is moving in a cyclical fashion and can be used for swing trading. The next page has some rules for using the Median Line Pivot Zone.

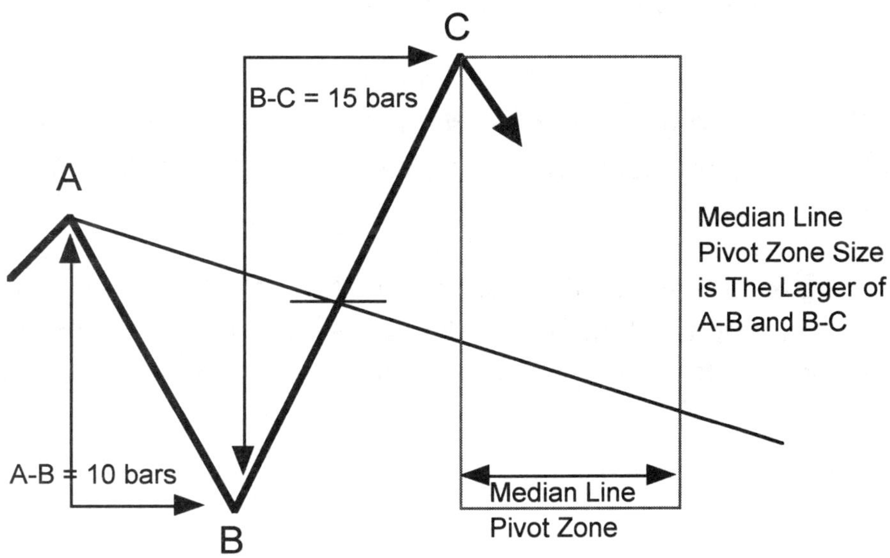

The diagram on this page shows the price ascending to the Median Line from a low at pivot C. This is simply the opposite of the diagram on the previous page.

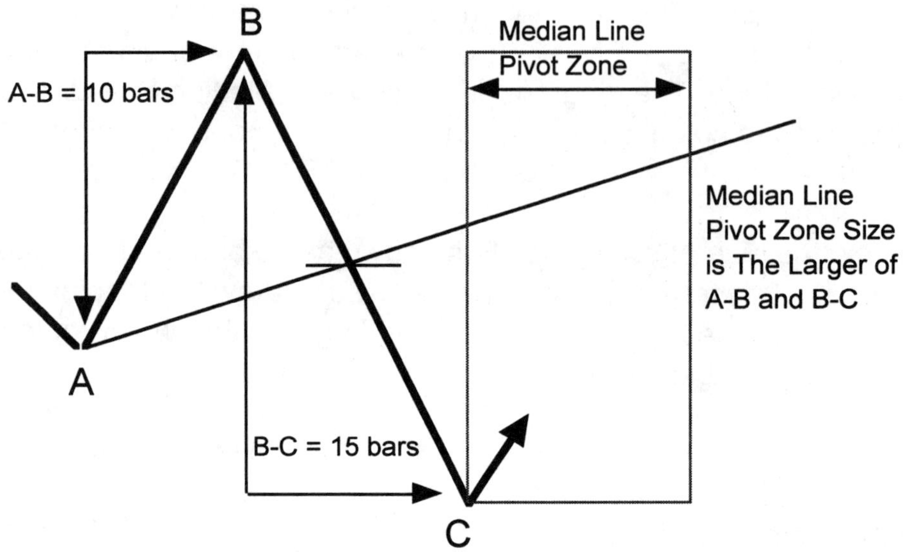

Median Line Pivot Zone Rule 1: If the price does not reach the Median Line inside the Median Line Pivot Zone, this indicates the market may not be in the appropriate position for swing trading at that time. In this situation, the swing trader takes extra caution or waits for the next swing.

Median Line Pivot Zone Rule 2: If the price does reach the Median Line in the Median Line Pivot Zone, this indicates the market is most likely suitable for swing trading. A trader starts watching for a pivot.

Median Line Pivot Zone Rule 3: When the price reaches the Median Line in the Median Line Pivot Zone, it will often end up touching the Median Line more than once before forming a pivot. This means a trader watches for a pivot but does not blindly enter the market expecting an immediate swing reversal.

Two charts for J.P. Morgan, symbol JPM are next. The first chart generates a Median Line using pivot A, B, and C. The swing from B to C is the largest with 29 bars. Starting from pivot C, a rectangle is drawn on this chart with the width of 29 bars. This rectangle is the Median Line Pivot Zone. Before trading the next swing, an investor watches to see the price decline to the Median Line inside the Median Line Pivot Zone.

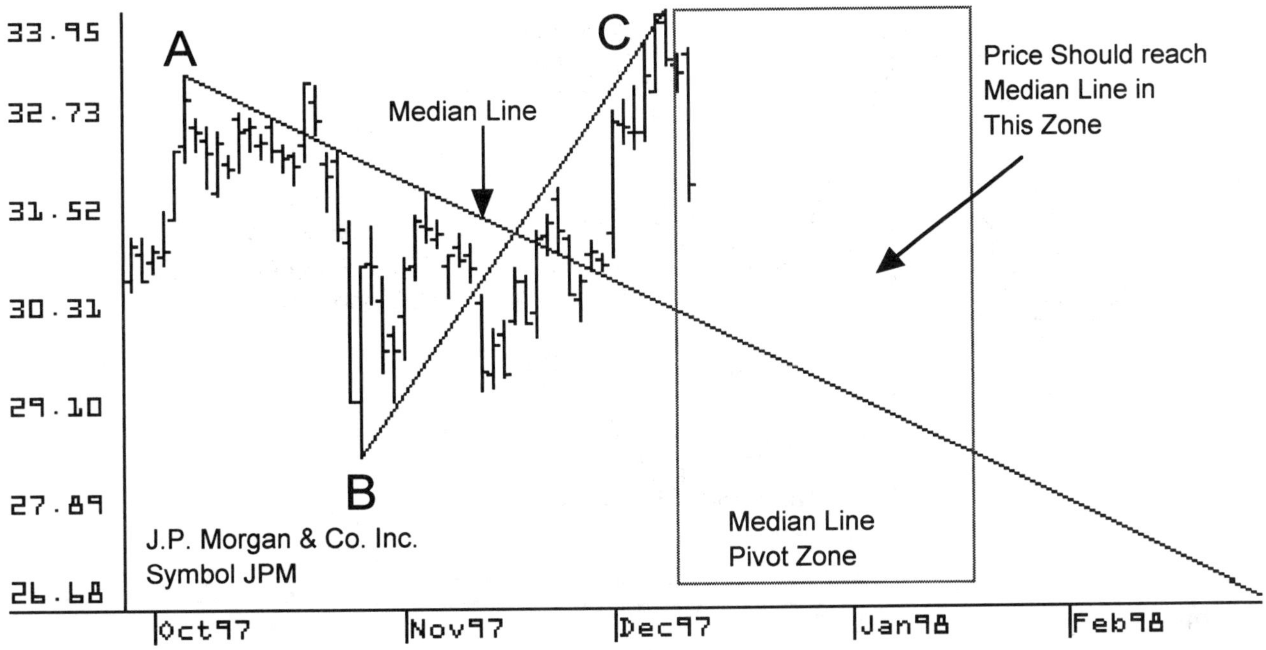

On the chart below, the price reaches the Median Line in the Median Line Pivot Zone. When this occurs a trader assumes the market is in a cyclical mode and starts watching for indications of a pivot bottom to trade.

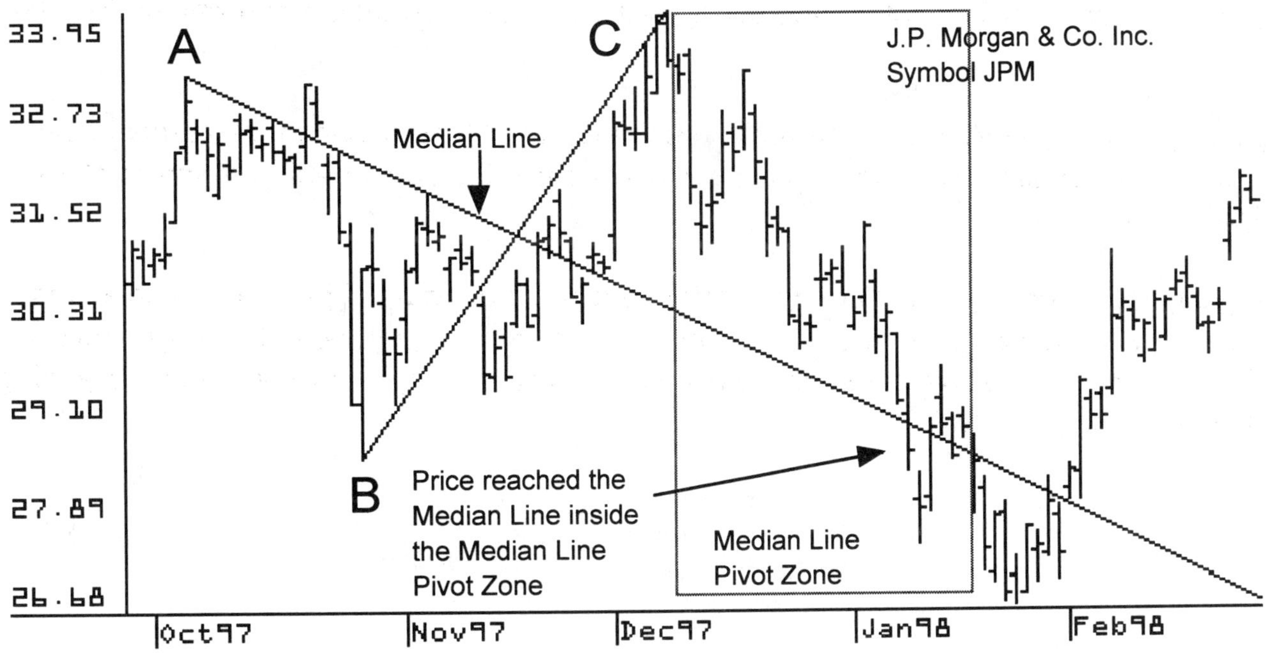

This page contains two more charts for J.P. Morgan, symbol JPM. The top chart shows a Median Line drawn using pivot A, B, and C. The swing from B to C is the largest with 25 bars. Starting from pivot C, a rectangle is drawn on this chart with the width of 25 bars. This rectangle is the Median Line Pivot Zone. A trader checks for the price to reach the Median Line inside the Median Line Pivot Zone before a trade on the next swing is considered.

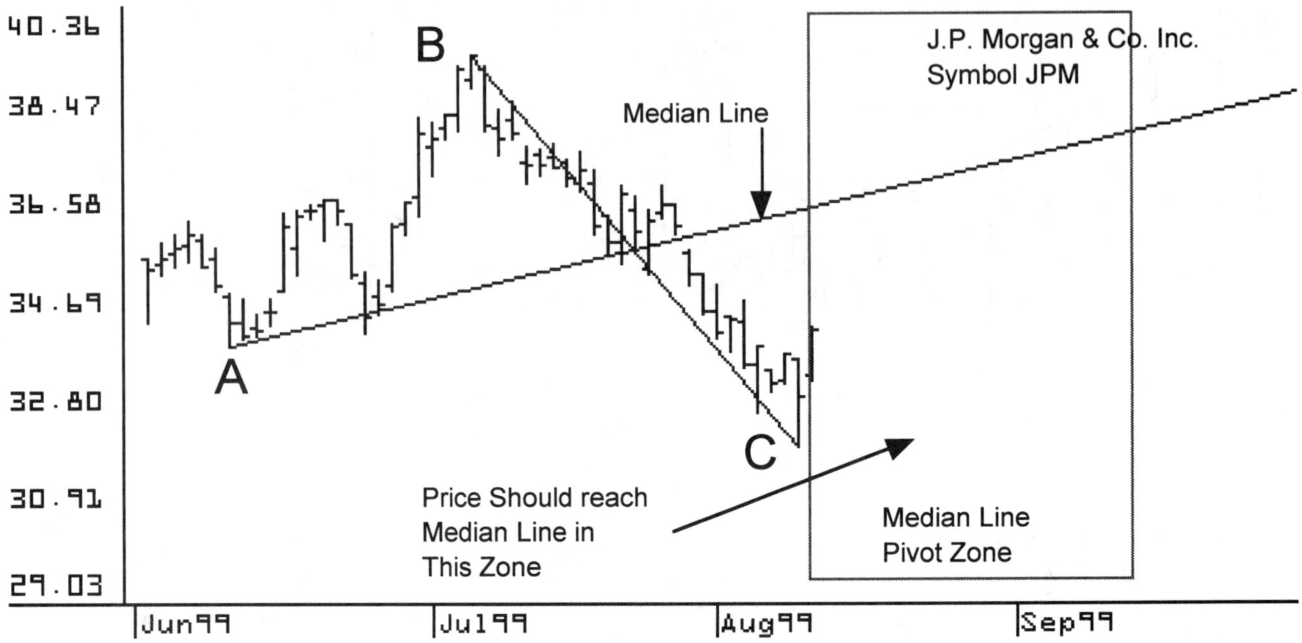

On the chart below, the price for J.P. Morgan reaches the Median Line in the Median Line Pivot Zone. When this occurs a trader assumes the market is in a cyclical mode and starts watching for indications of a pivot top to trade.

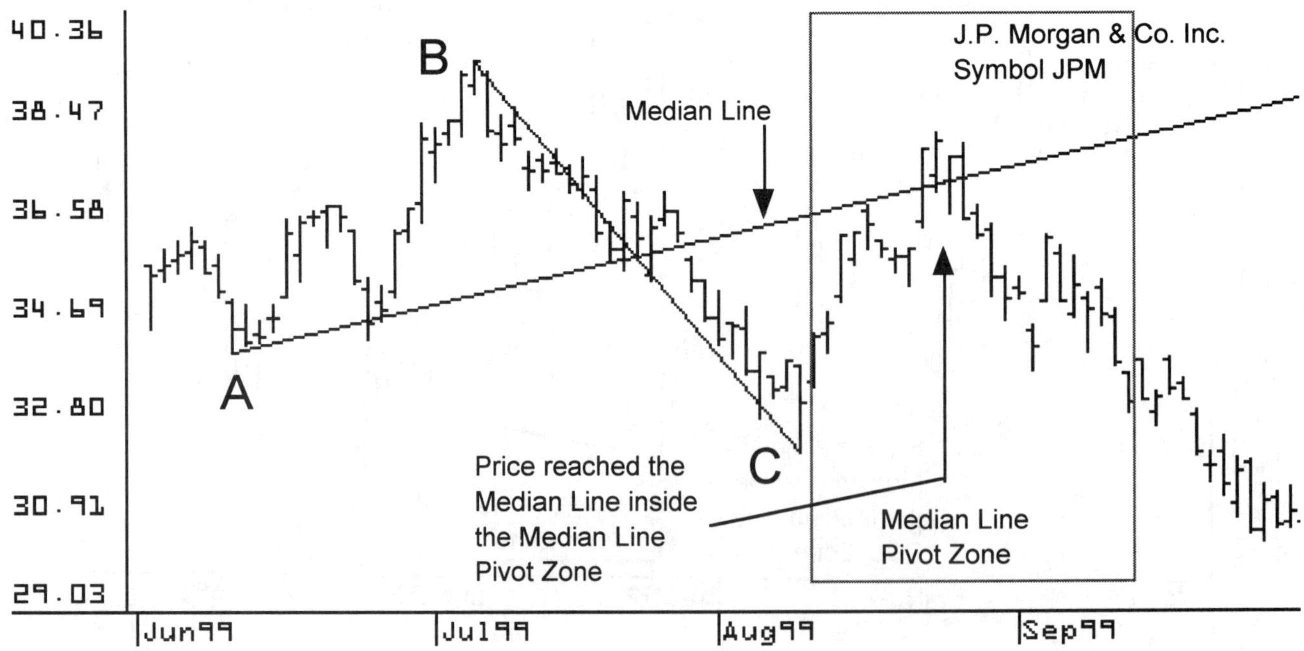

Here are two charts for Johnson & Johnson, symbol JNJ. The top chart shows a Median Line drawn using pivot A, B, and C. The swing from A to B is the largest with 11 bars. Starting from pivot C, a rectangle is drawn on this chart using the same width of 11 bars. This rectangle is the Median Line Pivot Zone. Preceding a trade on the next swing, a trader waits to see the price fall to the Median Line inside the Median Line Pivot Zone.

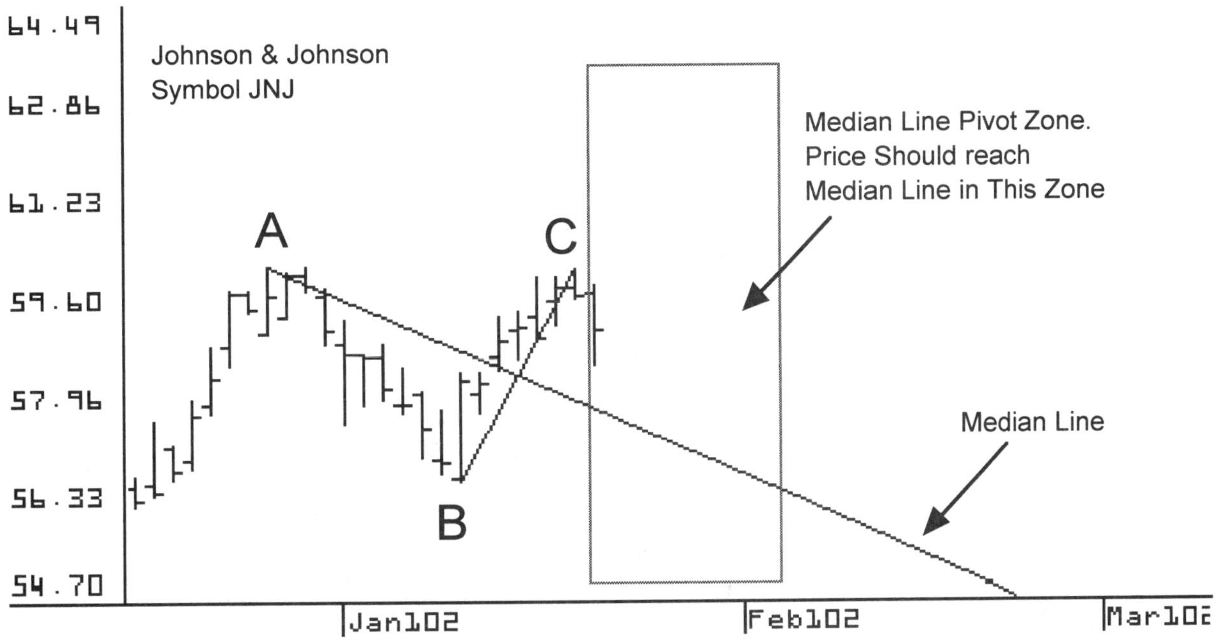

On the chart below you can see the price reaches the Median Line in the Median Line Pivot Zone. When this occurs a trader assumes the market is in a cyclical mode and starts watching for indications of a pivot bottom to trade.

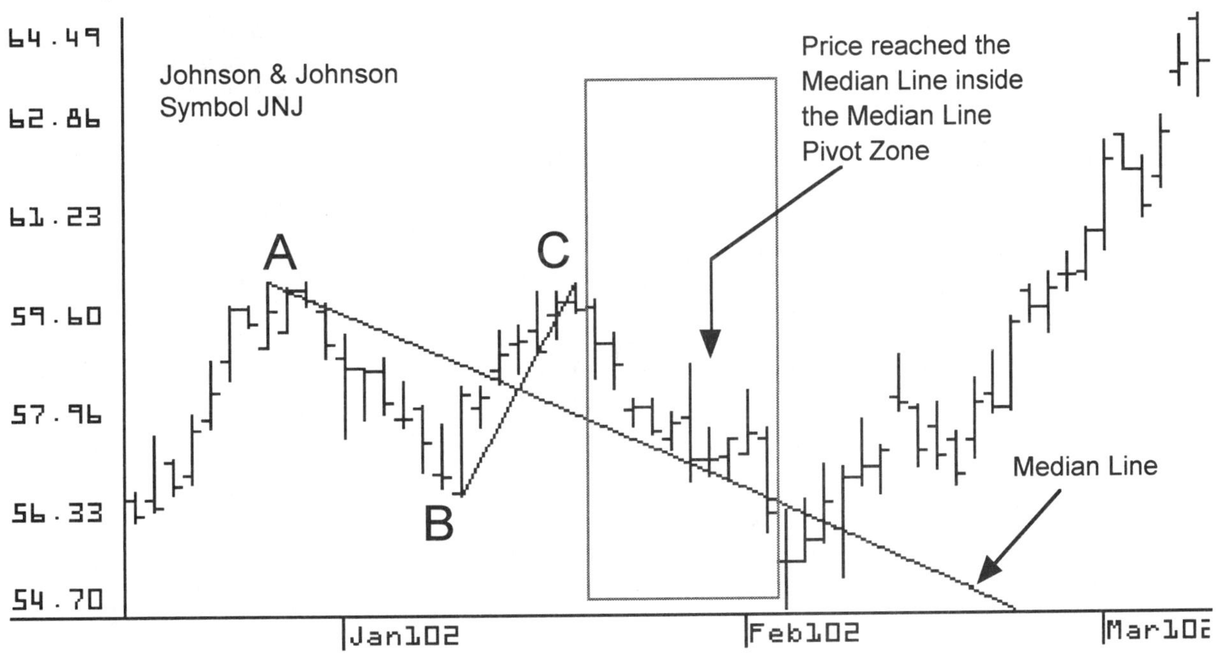

This page contains two charts for Merrill Lynch, symbol MER. The top chart shows a Median Line drawn using pivot A, B, and C. The swing from A to B is the largest with 31 bars. Starting from pivot C, a rectangular Median Line Pivot Zone with the width of 31 bars is drawn. The price needs to fall to the Median Line inside the Median Line Pivot Zone before an investor starts trading the next swing.

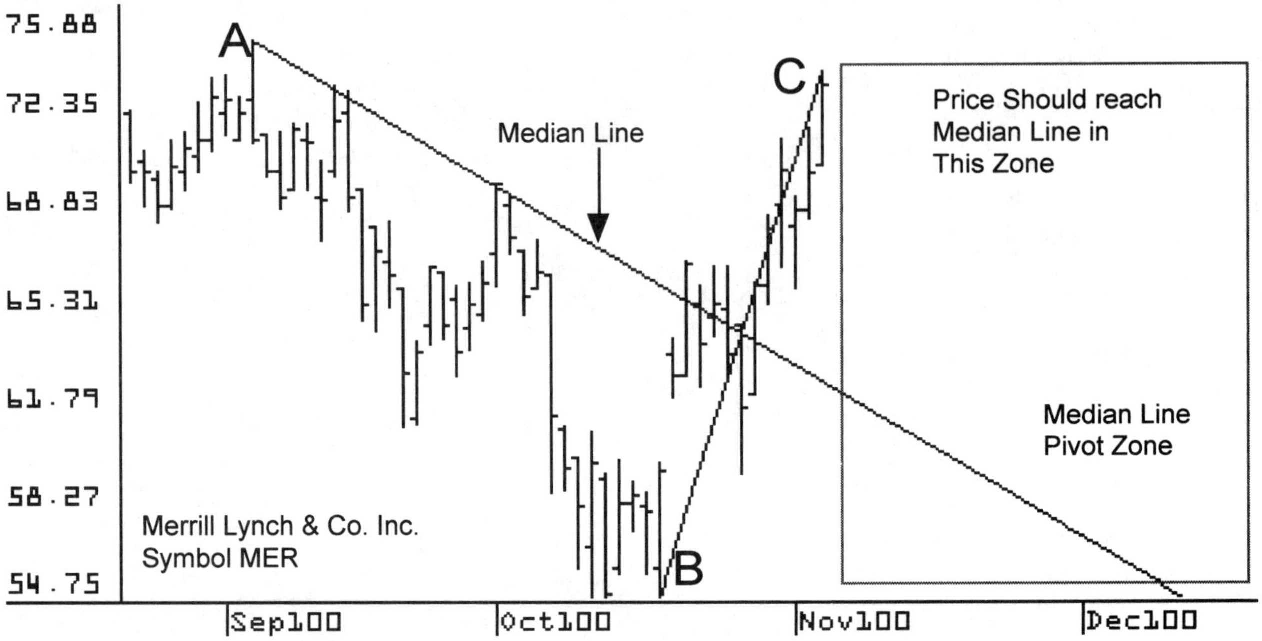

On the chart below the price reaches the Median Line in the Median Line Pivot Zone. A trader assumes the market is in a cyclical mode and starts watching for indications of a pivot bottom. When it occurs, a trade is considered.

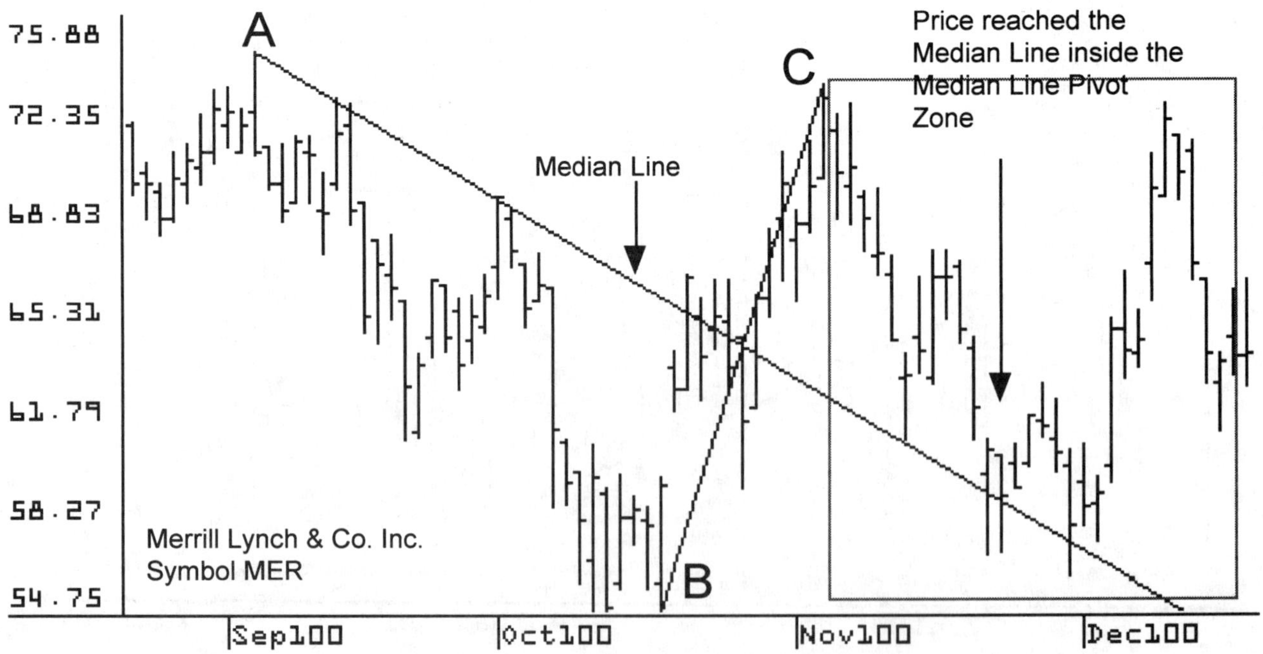

Royal Dutch Petroleum, symbol RD, is featured on the next two charts. The top chart shows a Median Line drawn using pivots A, B, and C. The swing from B to C was the largest with 18 bars. Starting from pivot C, a rectangle is drawn on this chart with the width of 18 bars. This rectangle is the Median Line Pivot Zone. Before considering a trade at the next swing, a trader wants to see the price fall to the Median Line inside the Median Line Pivot Zone.

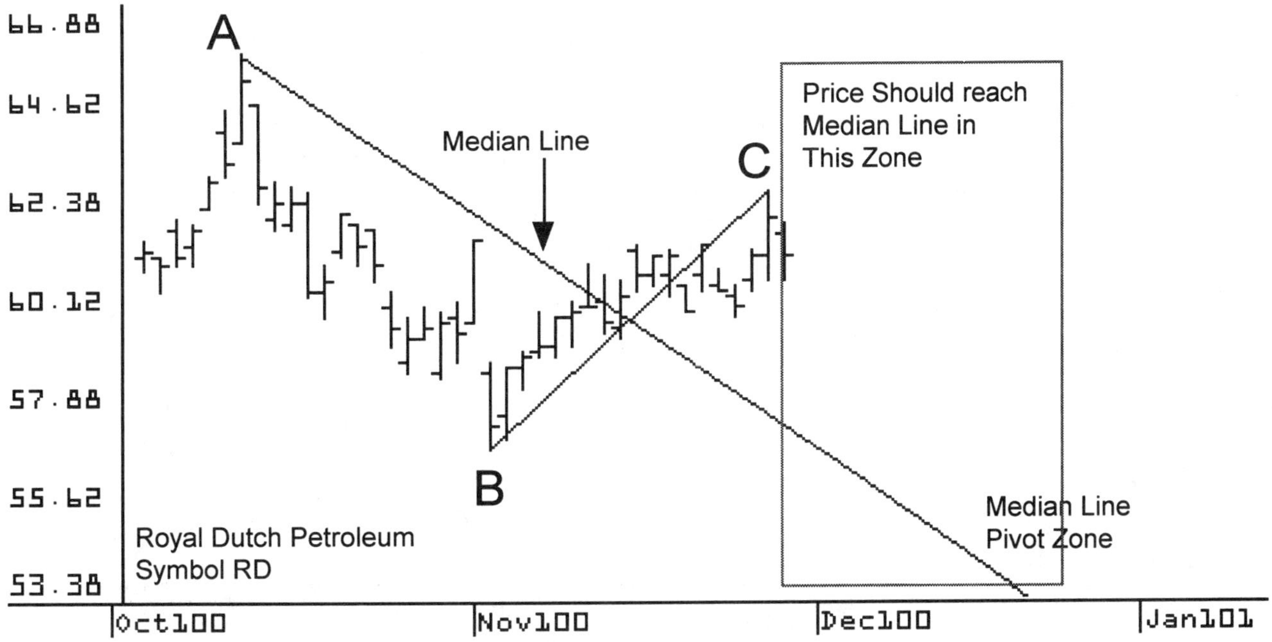

On the chart below you can see the price reaches the Median Line in the Median Line Pivot Zone. When this occurrs, a trader assumes the market is in a cyclical mode and starts watching for indications of a pivot bottom to trade.

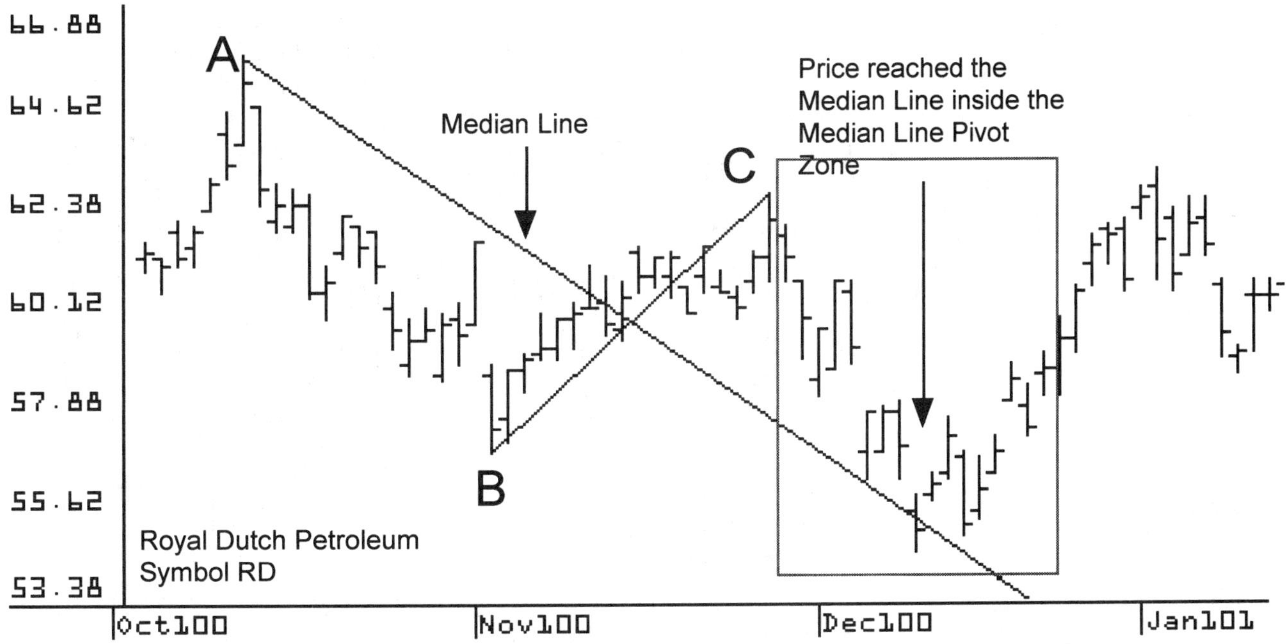

The next chart to study is the S&P500 Index, symbol SPX. The top chart shows a Median Line drawn using pivot A, B, and C. The swing from B to C is the largest with 15 bars. Starting from pivot C, a rectangular Median Line Pivot Zone is drawn with the width of 15 bars. Before a trader considers a transaction on the next swing, it is important for the price to fall to the Median Line inside the Median Line Pivot Zone.

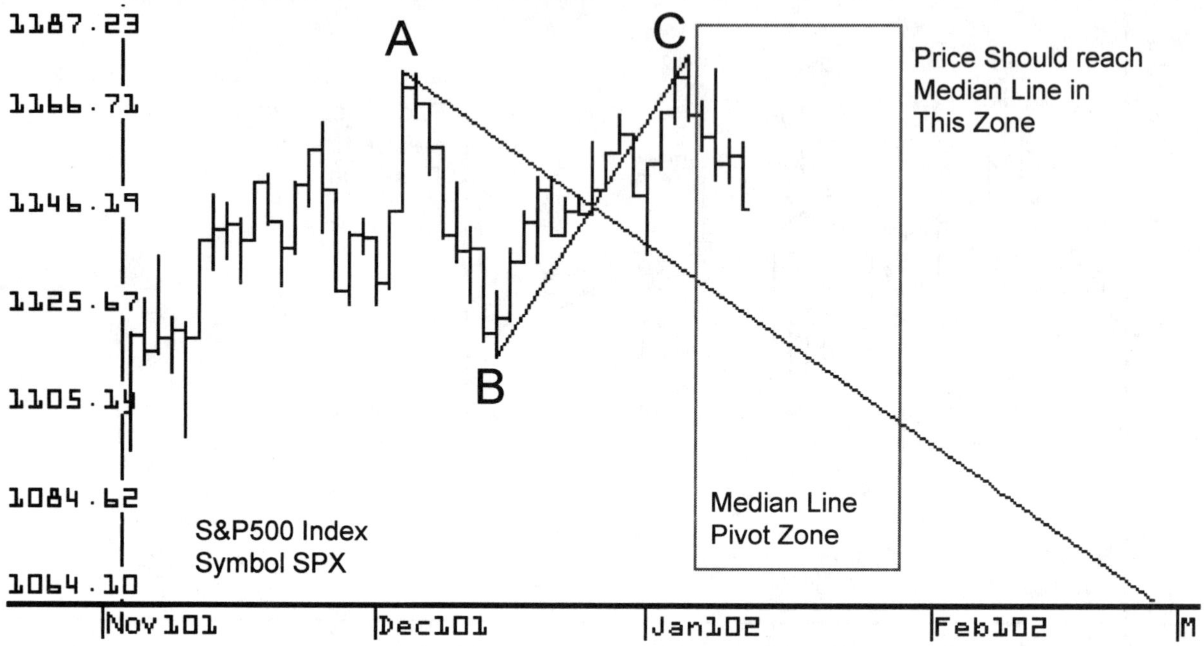

On the chart below, the price reaches the Median Line on the last bar of the Median Line Pivot Zone. When this occurs a trader infers that the market is in a cyclical mode and watches for indications of a pivot bottom to trade.

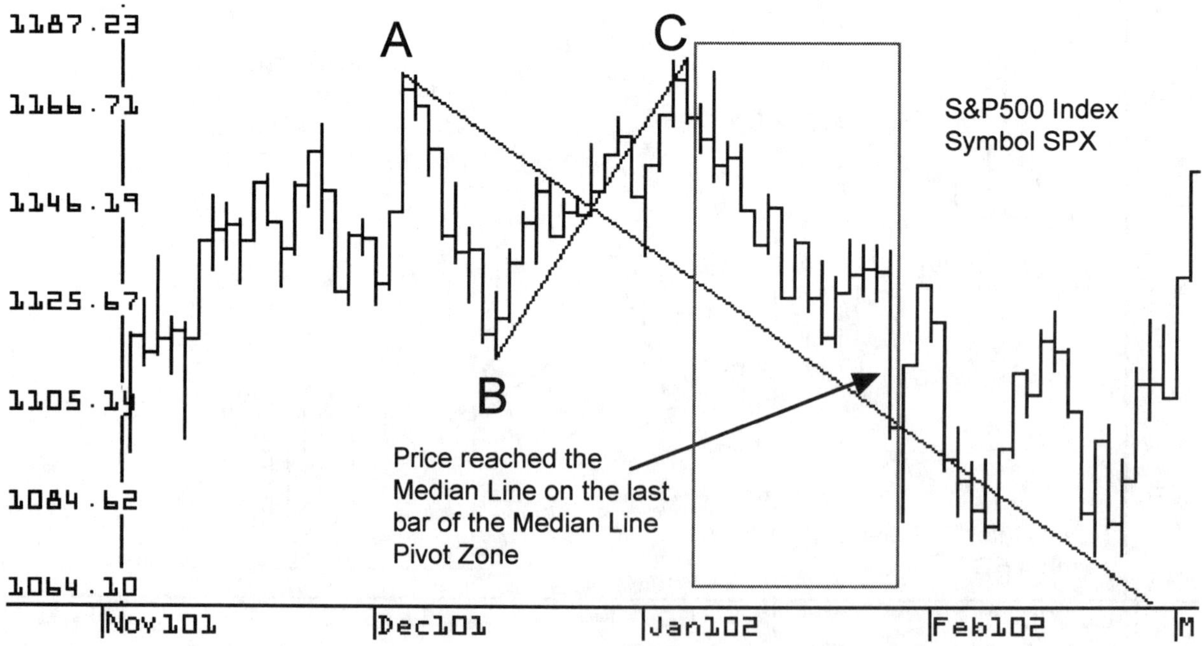

This page presents an example for Tellabs Inc., symbol TLAB. The top chart shows a Median Line drawn using pivot A, B, and C. The swing from B to C is the largest with 13 bars. Starting from pivot C, a rectangle is drawn on this chart with the width matching the largest swing of 13 bars. This rectangle is the Median Line Pivot Zone. In this example, the investor waits to see the price rise to the Median Line inside the Median Line Pivot Zone before considering trading the next swing.

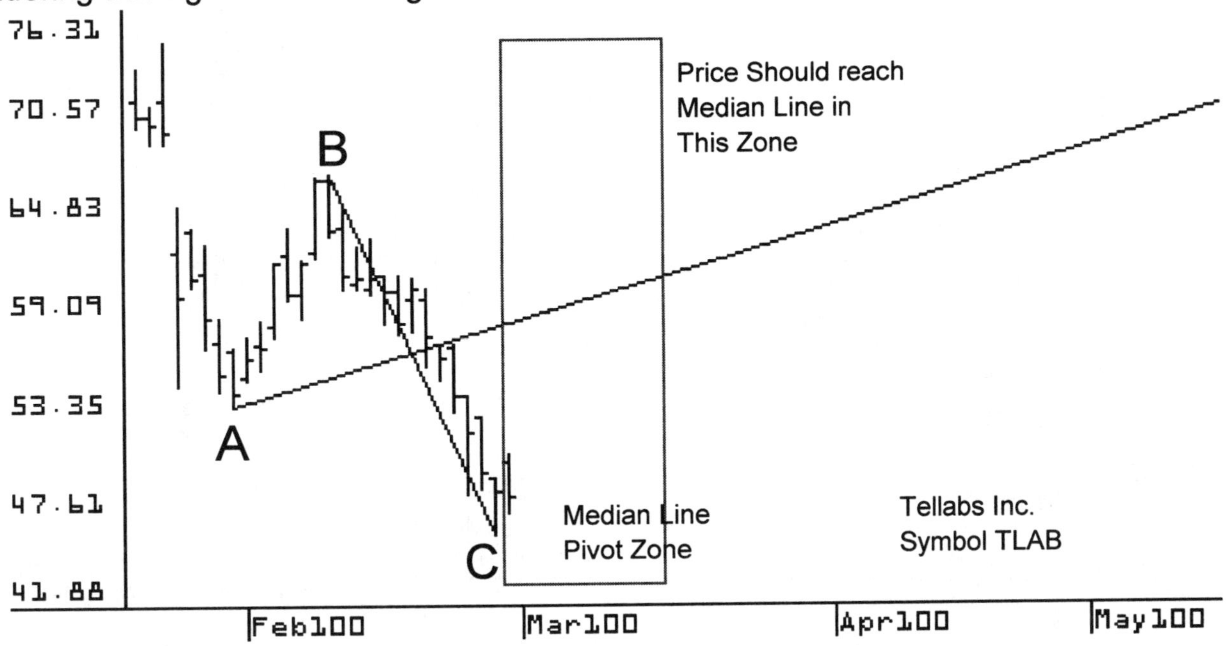

On the chart below, the price reaches the Median Line one bar before the end of the Median Line Pivot Zone. The chart on the next page is a continuation of this chart.

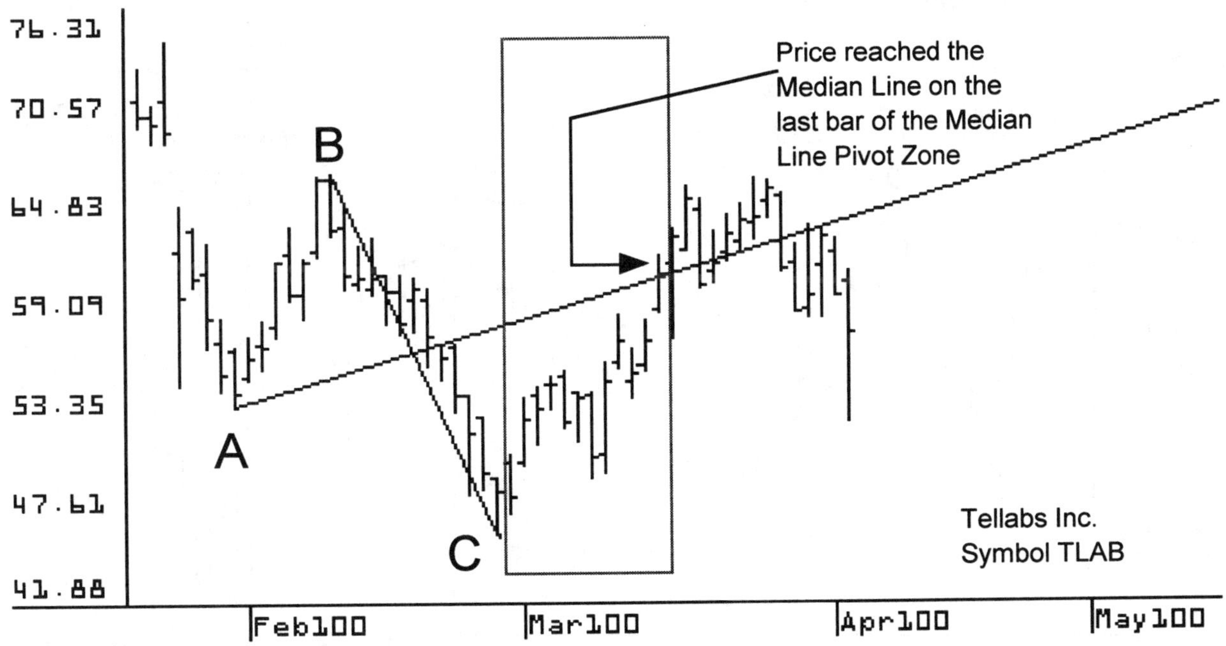

The two charts on this page for Tellabs Inc. are continued from the previous page. The top chart shows a Median Line drawn using pivots B, C, and D. The swing from C to D is the widest with 20 bars. Starting from pivot D, a rectangle is drawn on this chart with the width being 20 bars. Again, before an investor considers trading the next swing, the price needs to fall to the Median Line inside this zone.

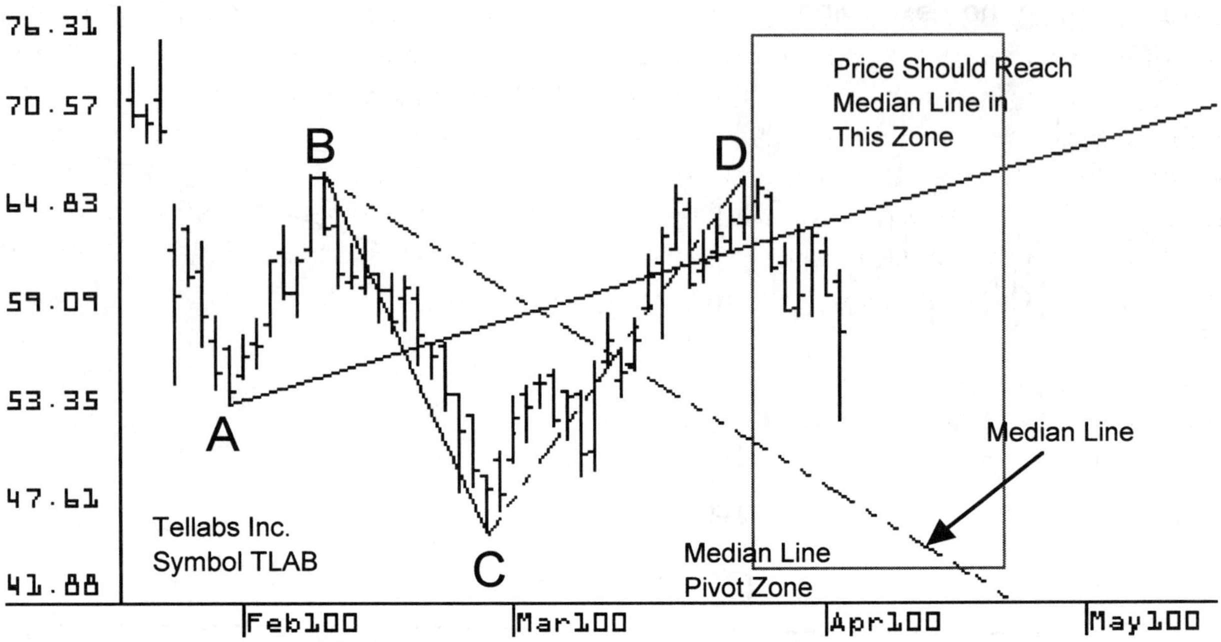

On the chart below, the price reaches the Median Line inside the Median Line Pivot Zone. When this occurs a trader assumes the market is in a cyclical mode and starts watching for indications of a pivot bottom to trade.

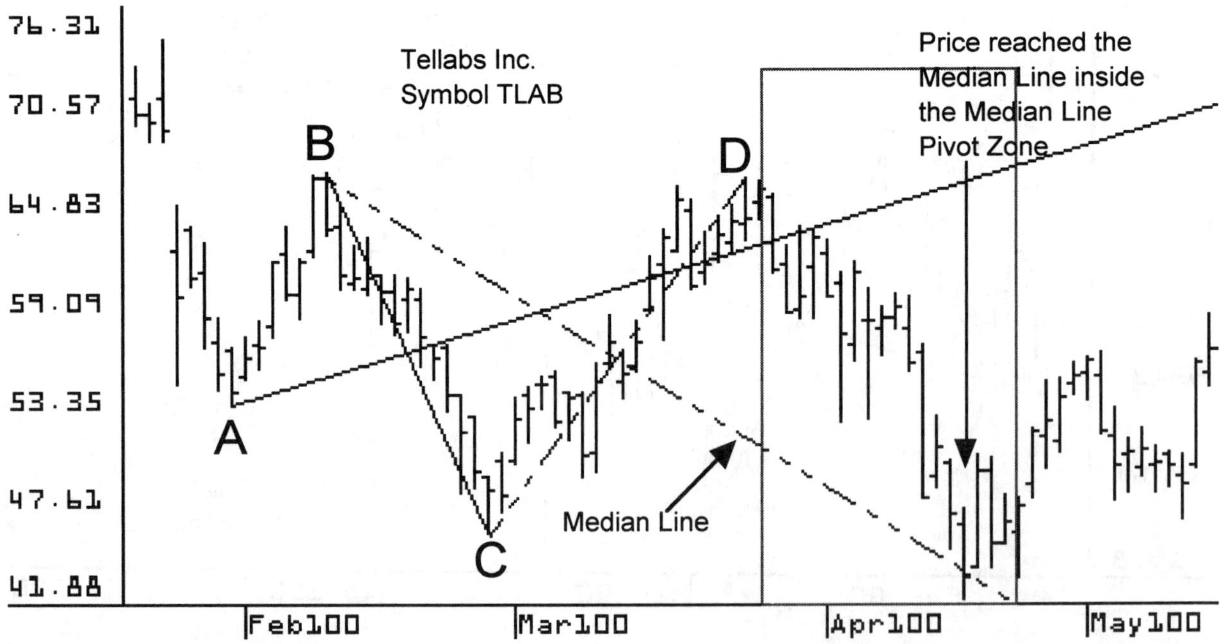

Action Reaction Method 3

Here is a variation of the Action Reaction Method which was developed at Austin Financial Group while research was conducted on support and resistance levels. This is a very specific application of horizontal action reaction lines. The diagram below shows a heavy black line which represents price swings. The price swings show a significant low at the bottom left of the diagram. After the price makes a significant low it often makes a small price swing upward before starting a new up trend. The top price of this first up swing after a major low is the location of the Center Line. The major low price is used for the location of the Action Line. The Reaction Line is then projected an equal distance above the Center Line as the Action Line is below the Center Line. On the diagram below, the location of the Center Line, Action Line and Reaction Line are displayed. The Reaction Line which is drawn using this method has a high probability of being a good resistance level.

The same setup is used with a major top. The Center Line is placed on the low price of the first down swing after a major top and the major top is the location of the Action Line. The resulting Reaction Line has an excellent chance of being a strong support level.

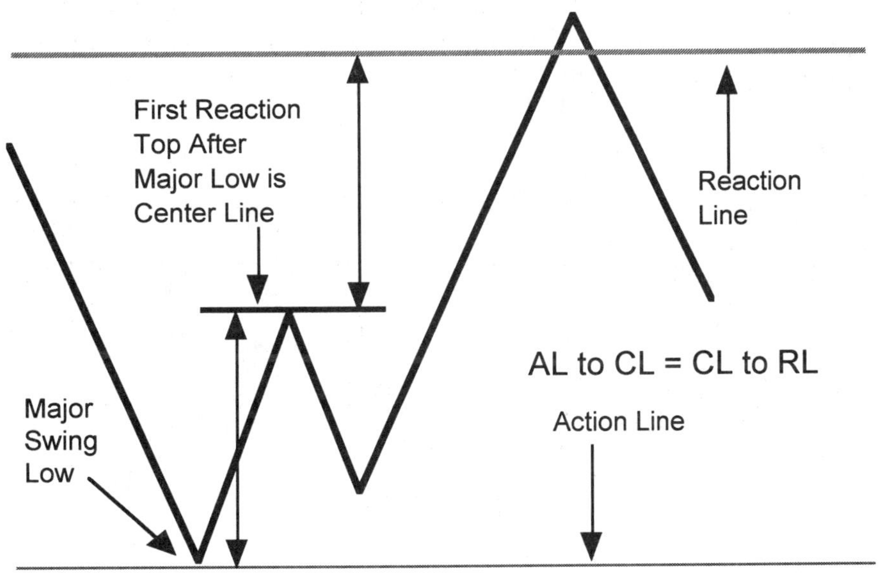

Below is an example of Action Reaction Method 3 using a chart for Teradyne, symbol TER. A major low is identified on the bottom left of the chart. The Center Line is drawn as a horizontal line across the top of the first swing upward after the major low. The Action Line is drawn as a horizontal line aligned with the major low. The distance between the Center Line and the Action Line is projected upward from the Center Line and the Reaction Line is drawn at that price. It is seen on the chart below, that the price moves upward until it reaches the Reaction Line and makes a top at point A on the Reaction Line.

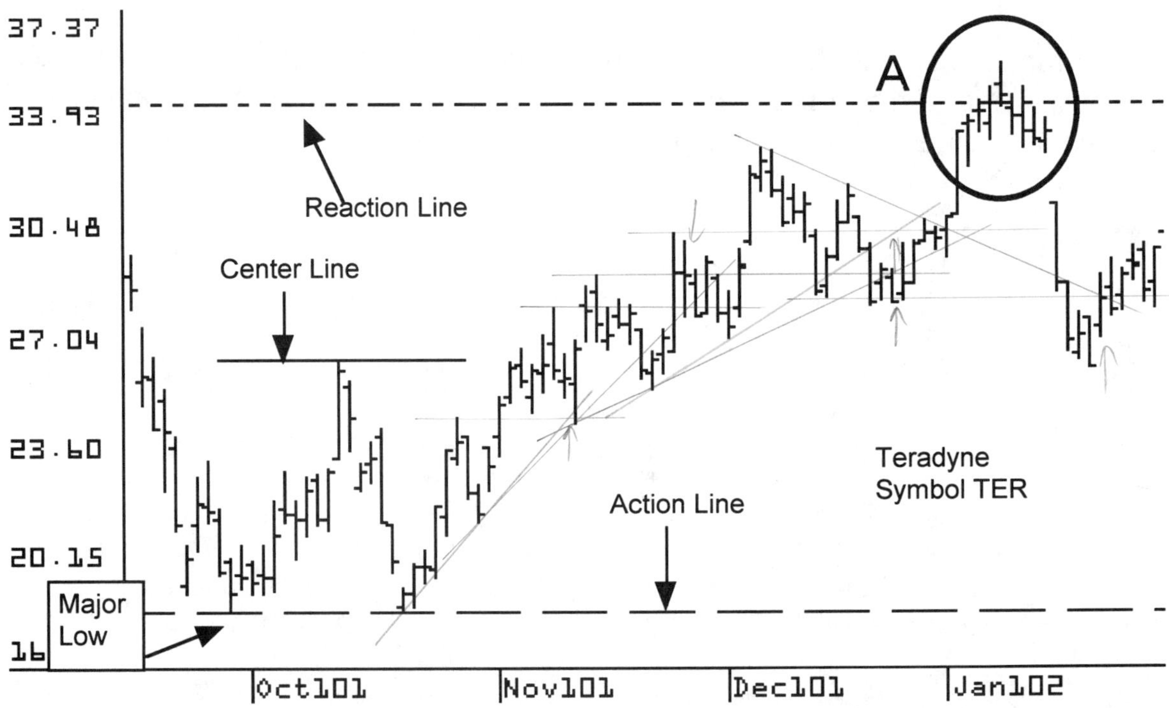

This page's chart is for EMC Inc., symbol EMC. On the chart below, the horizontal Center Line is placed against the top of the first small up swing after a major low is made. The Action Line is drawn as a horizontal line aligned with the major low. The Reaction Line is drawn above the Center Line, an equal distance between the Center Line and Action Line. The price moves up and makes two important swing tops against the Reaction Line at points A and B.

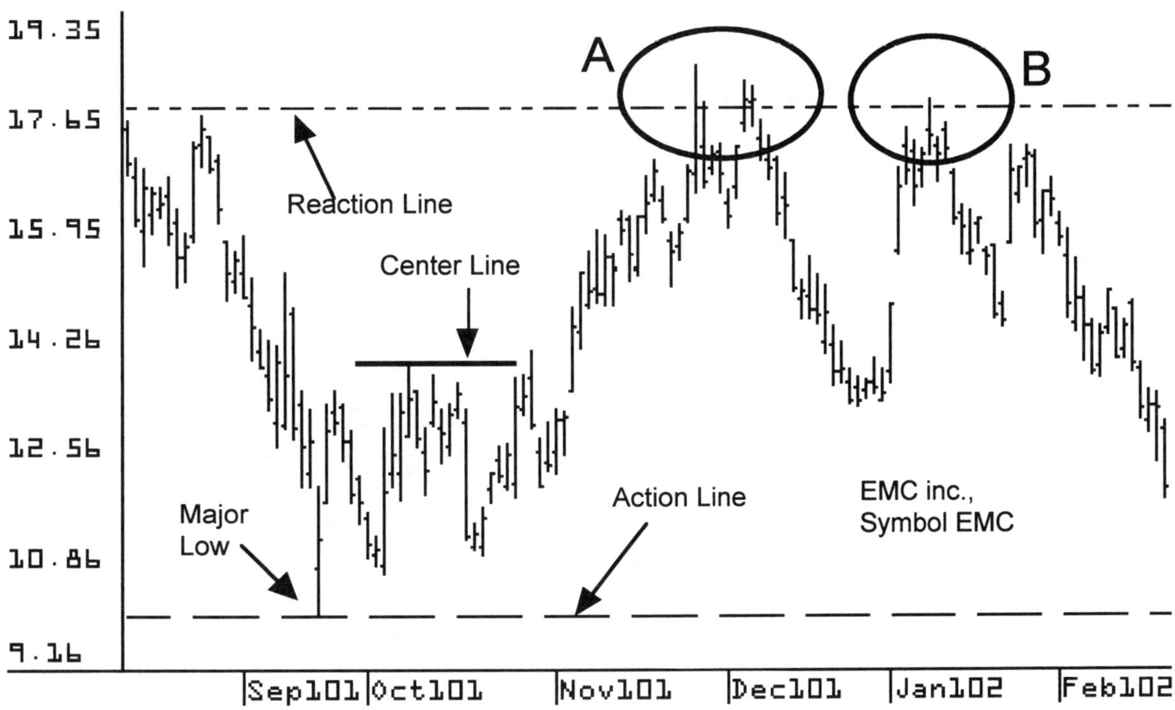

Here is a chart example for NASDAQ 100 shares, symbol QQQ. The Center Line is drawn as a horizontal line against the low price of the first down swing after a major top. The Action Line is drawn as a horizontal line against the major top. The Reaction Line is drawn below the Center Line the same distance as between the Center Line and the Action Line. In this case, the price falls to the Reaction Line and makes a swing bottom at point A.

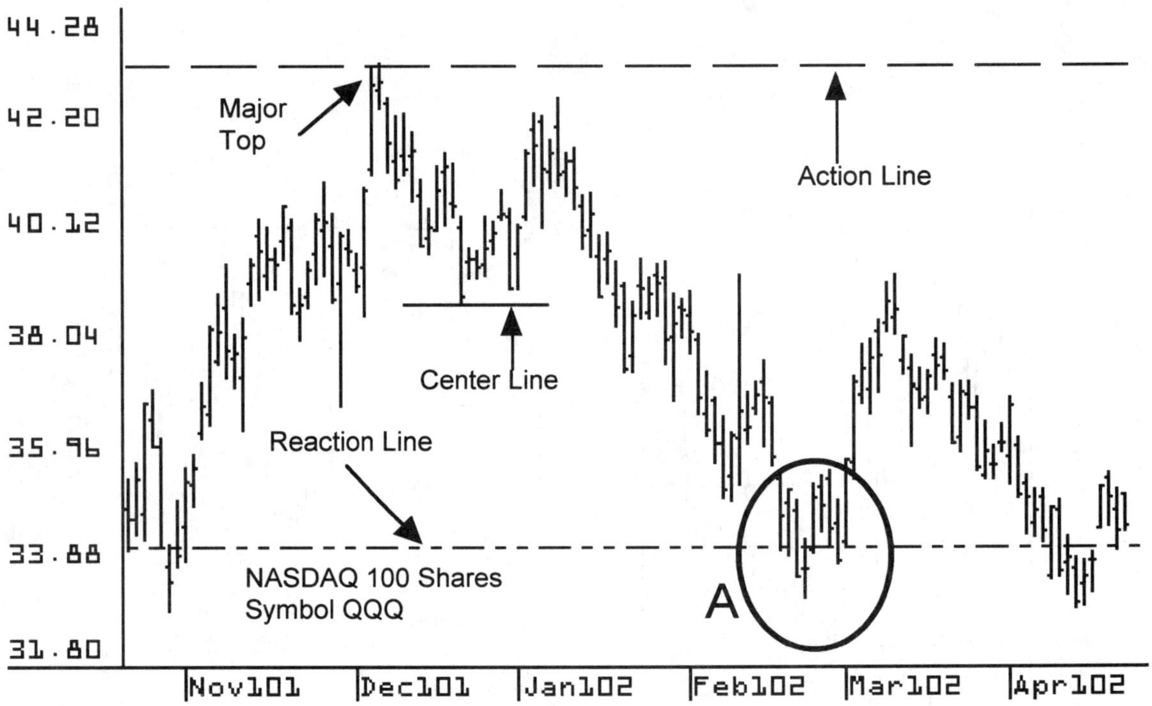

Marriott, symbol MAR is used for the next chart. On this chart, the horizontal Center Line is placed against the top of the first small upward swing after a major low is made. The Action Line is drawn horizontally, and aligned with the major low. The distance between these two lines is calculated. The Reaction Line is drawn above the Center Line the same distance as between the first two lines that are drawn. The price moves up and makes a swing top against the Reaction Line at point A.

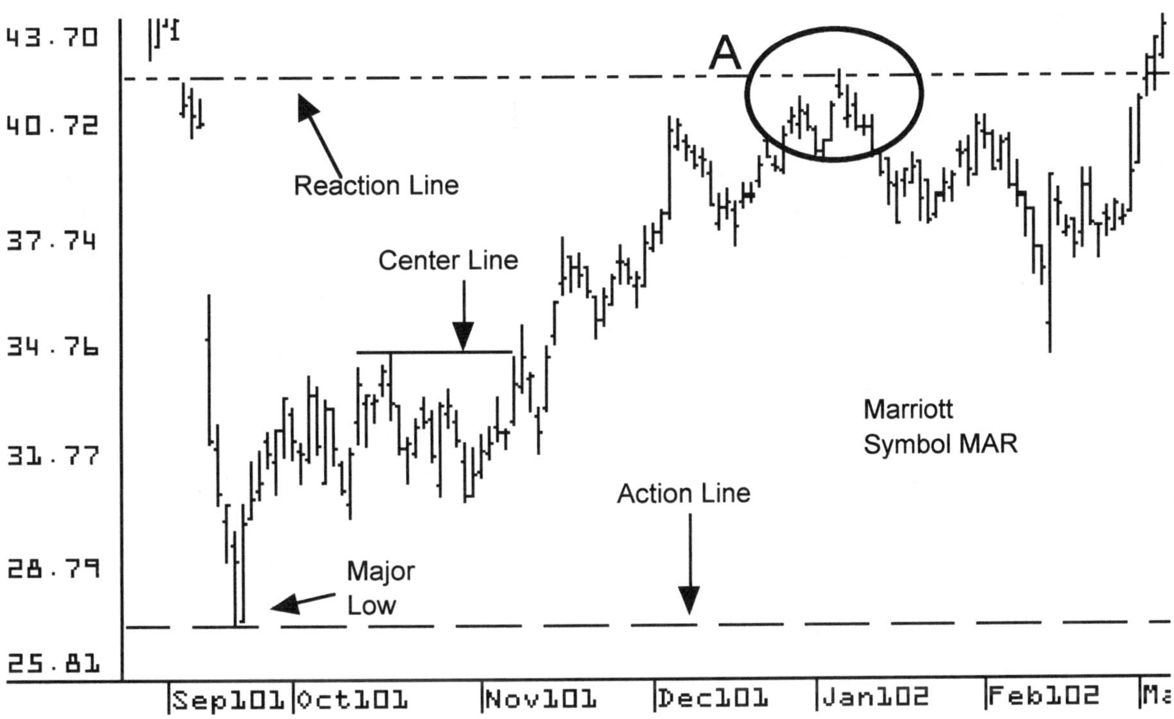

The Super-Pitchfork

While using the Action Reaction Methods at Austin Financial Group, it was noticed that some historical pivots used to align the Action Lines worked better than others. Reaction Lines from the recent past, worked best. To say this another way, the greatest correlation with the near future is the recent past. Based on this observation the Pitchfork and the Action Reaction Methods were combined to created the Super-Pitchfork.

The chart on this page shows the details of the Super-Pitchfork. Utilization of this technique begins with drawing a Pitchfork involving pivots A, B, and C. Next, the line from pivots B to C is used as the Action Reaction Method Center Line. Pivot A is then used as the alignment point for the Action Line.

The next step applies the distance from pivot A to the Center Line as a measurement for drawing Reaction Lines at equal increments into the future. The chart below exhibits three Reaction Lines which are equal distances apart. This integrates the Pitchfork and the Action Reaction Method by using the same three pivots A, B, and C for both methods. This is the Super-Pitchfork.

Point D on the chart below is important. At this point, the price reaches the Super-Pitchfork Median Line and Reaction Line 1 at the same time. A trader wants to see the market make a pivot where two lines intersect. It is very common to see pivots form just before or just after two lines intersect on the Super-Pitchfork.

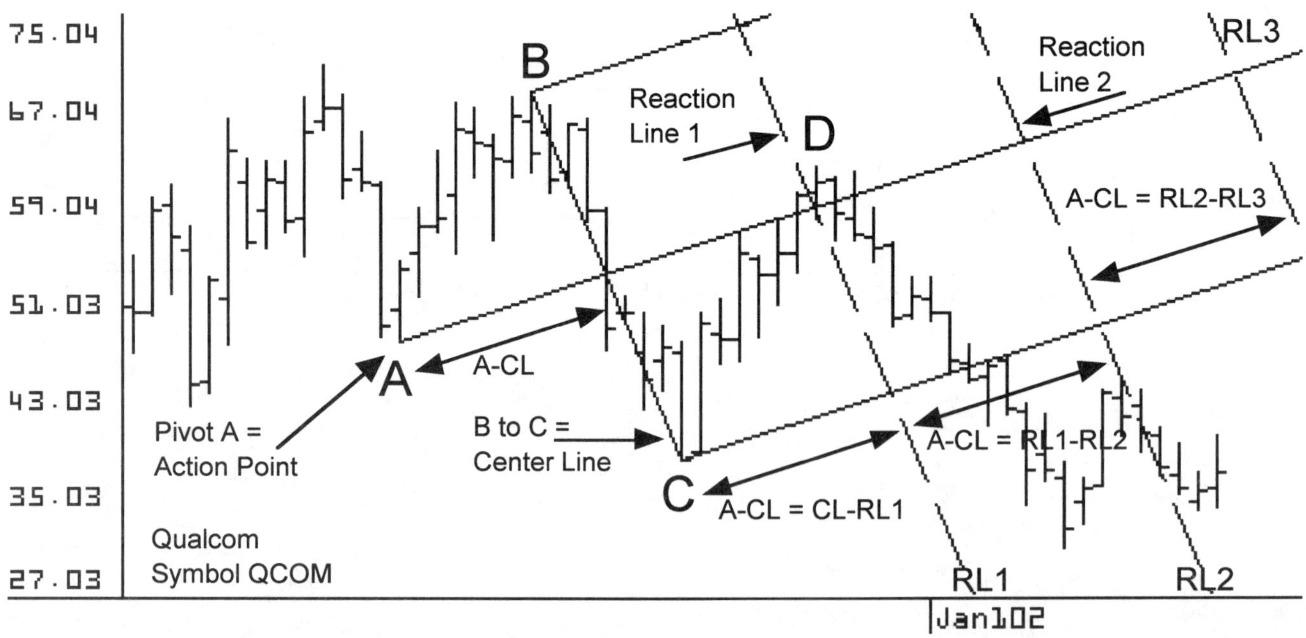

The top chart on this page is for Network Associates, symbol NET. A Super-Pitchfork is applied to this chart using pivots A, B, and C. The price makes a pivot at point D where the Median Line crosses Reaction Line 1.

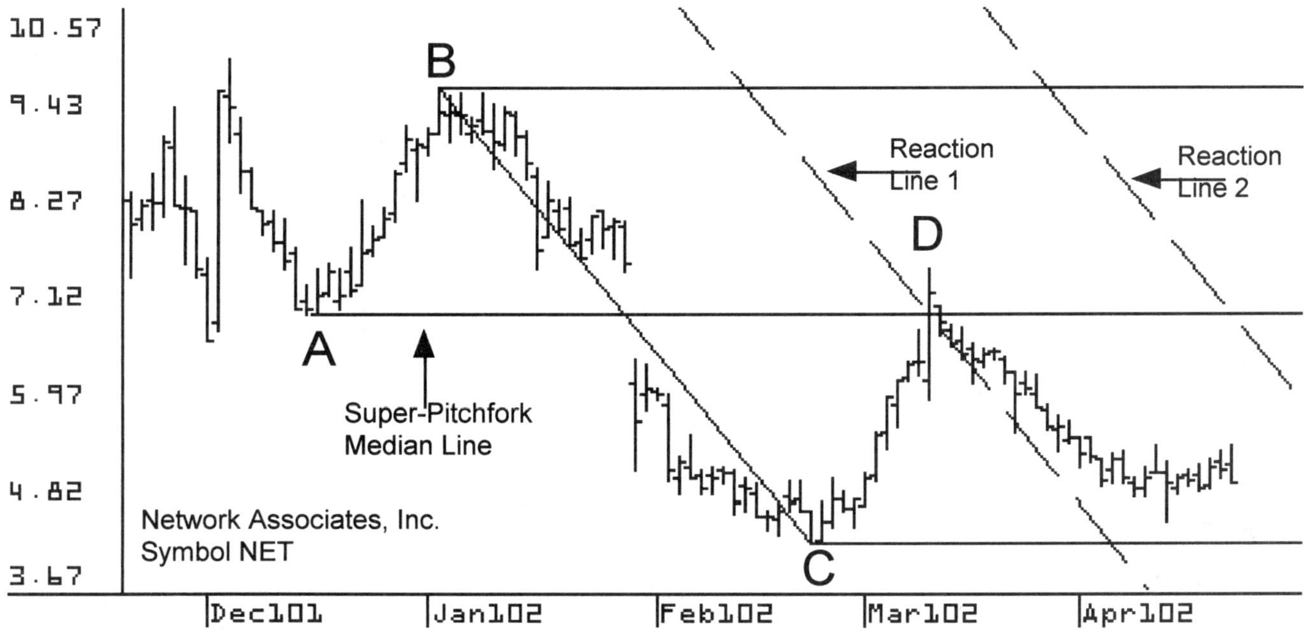

The chart below shows Knight Trading Group, symbol NITE. Pivots A, B, and C are used to draw a Super-Pitchfork. The price makes a pivot at point D where the Median Line crosses Reaction Line 1.

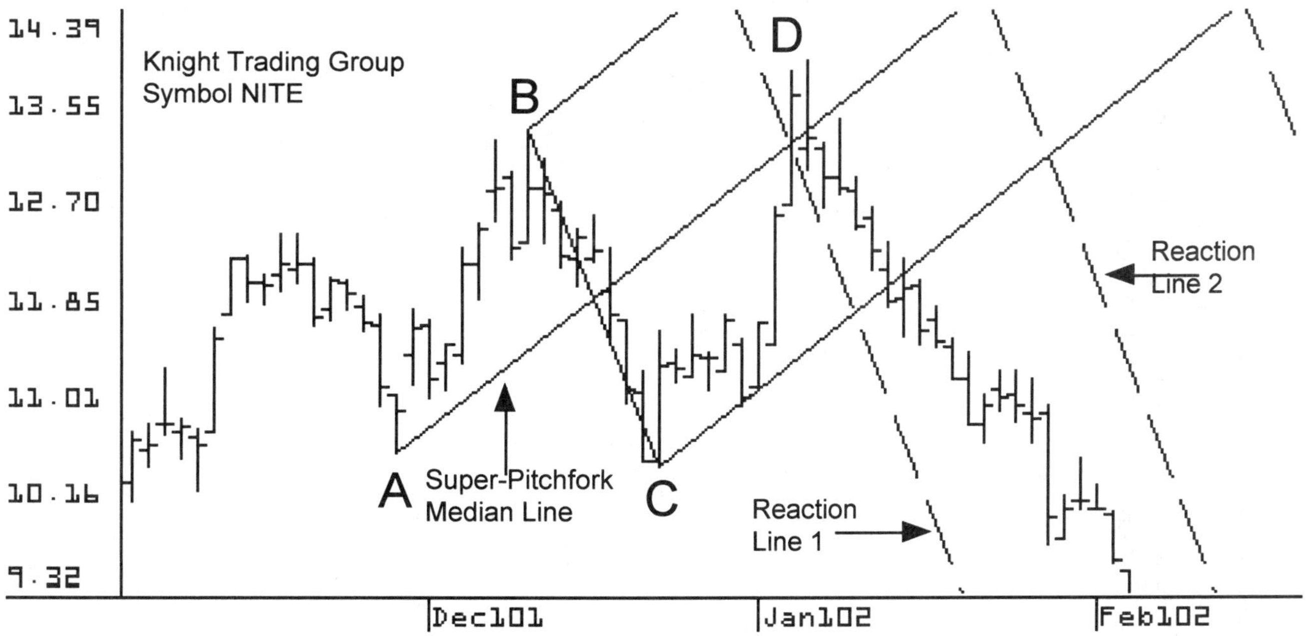

Verisign, symbol VRSN, data is used on the next chart. The Super-Pitchfork is drawn using pivots A, B, and C. The price makes a pivot on the Median Line at point D just before Reaction Line 1. The price also makes a pivot just after Reaction Line 2 at point E. It is very common to see market pivots form immediately preceding or immediately following the Super-Pitchfork Reaction Lines.

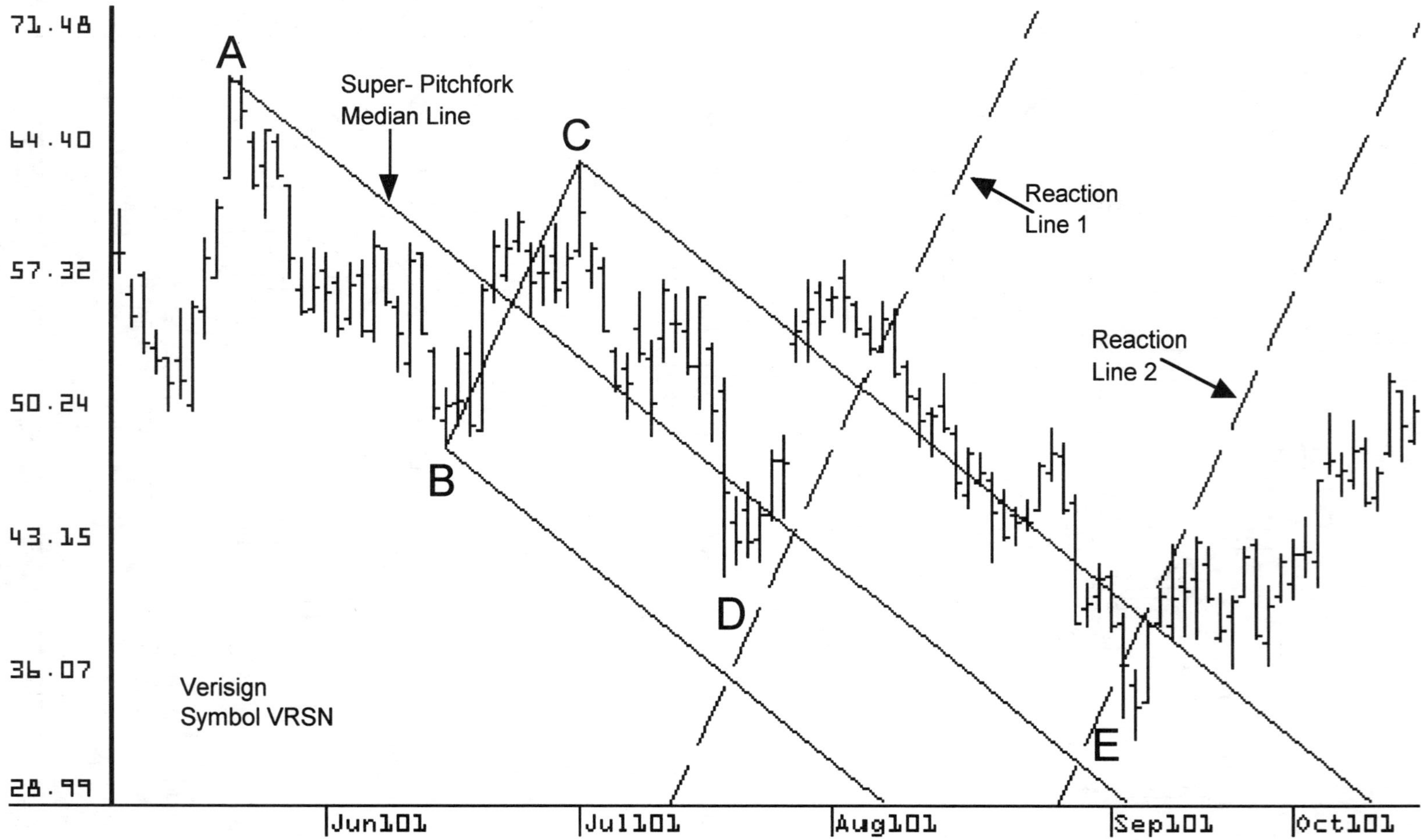

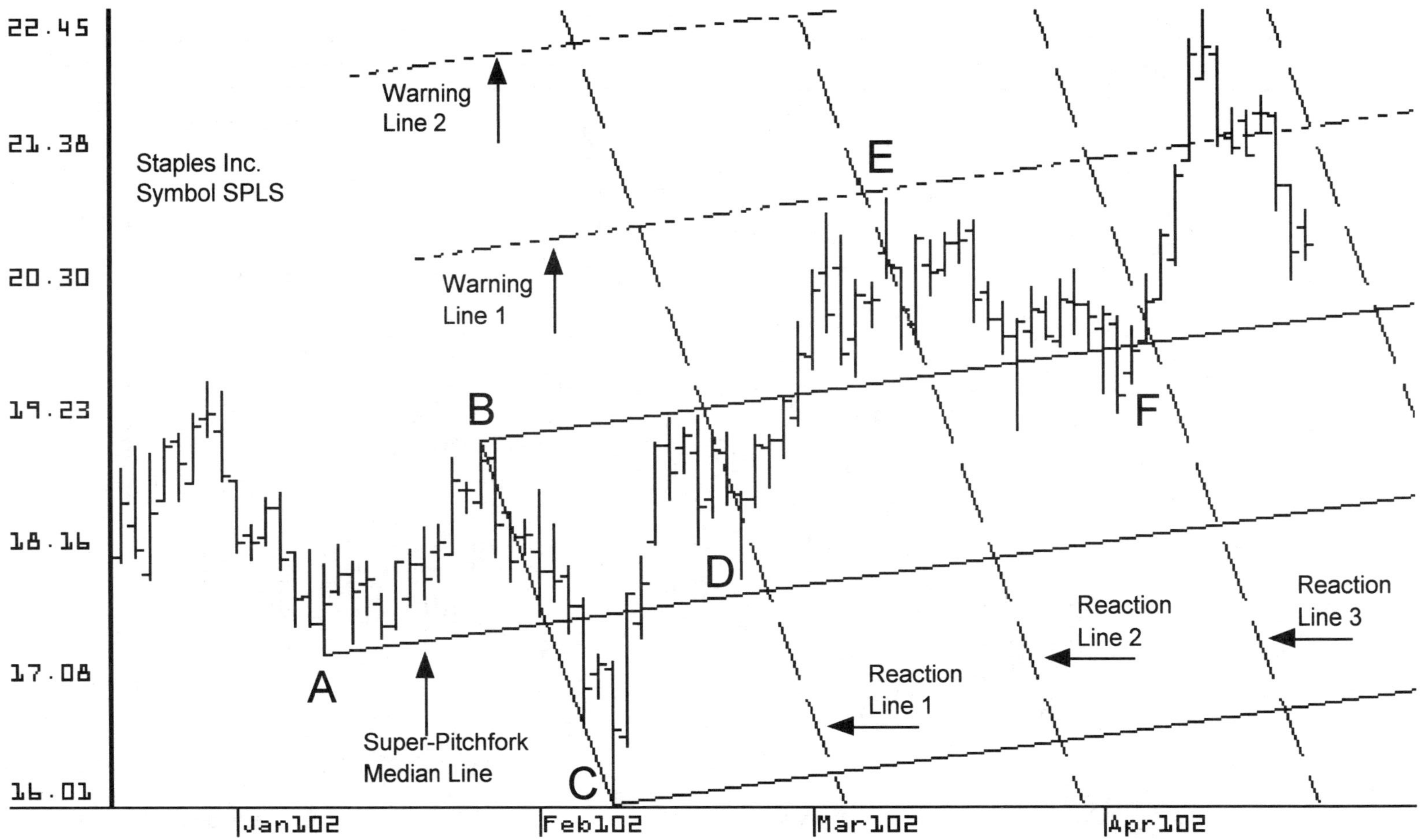

The chart on this page shows Staples Inc., symbol SPLS. Pivots A, B, and C are used to draw a Super-Pitchfork. After pivot C, the market moves up to the Super-Pitchfork upper parallel line. The market moves sideways for a few bars until the price reaches Reaction Line 1 at point D. After point D the market moves up to point E where Reaction Line 2 crosses Warning Line 1. After point E the price falls to point F where Reaction Line 3 crosses the Super-Pitchfork upper parallel line.

Comcast Inc., symbol CMCSK is used in the next example. The Super-Pitchfork is drawn using pivots A, B, and C. After point C the price moves up to point D where Reaction Line 1 crosses the Median Line. The price also makes a top at point E where Reaction Line 3 crosses the Median Line.

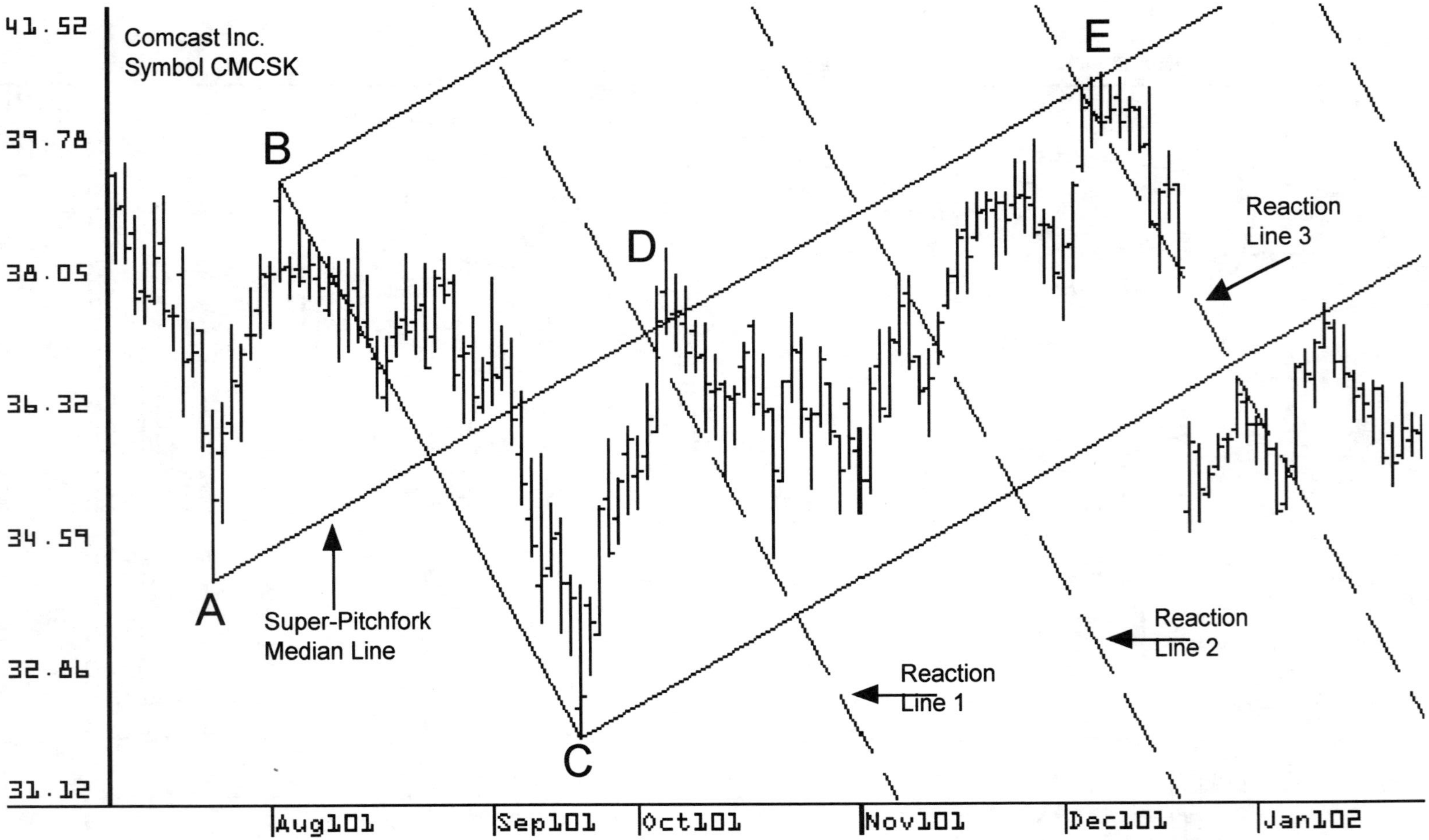

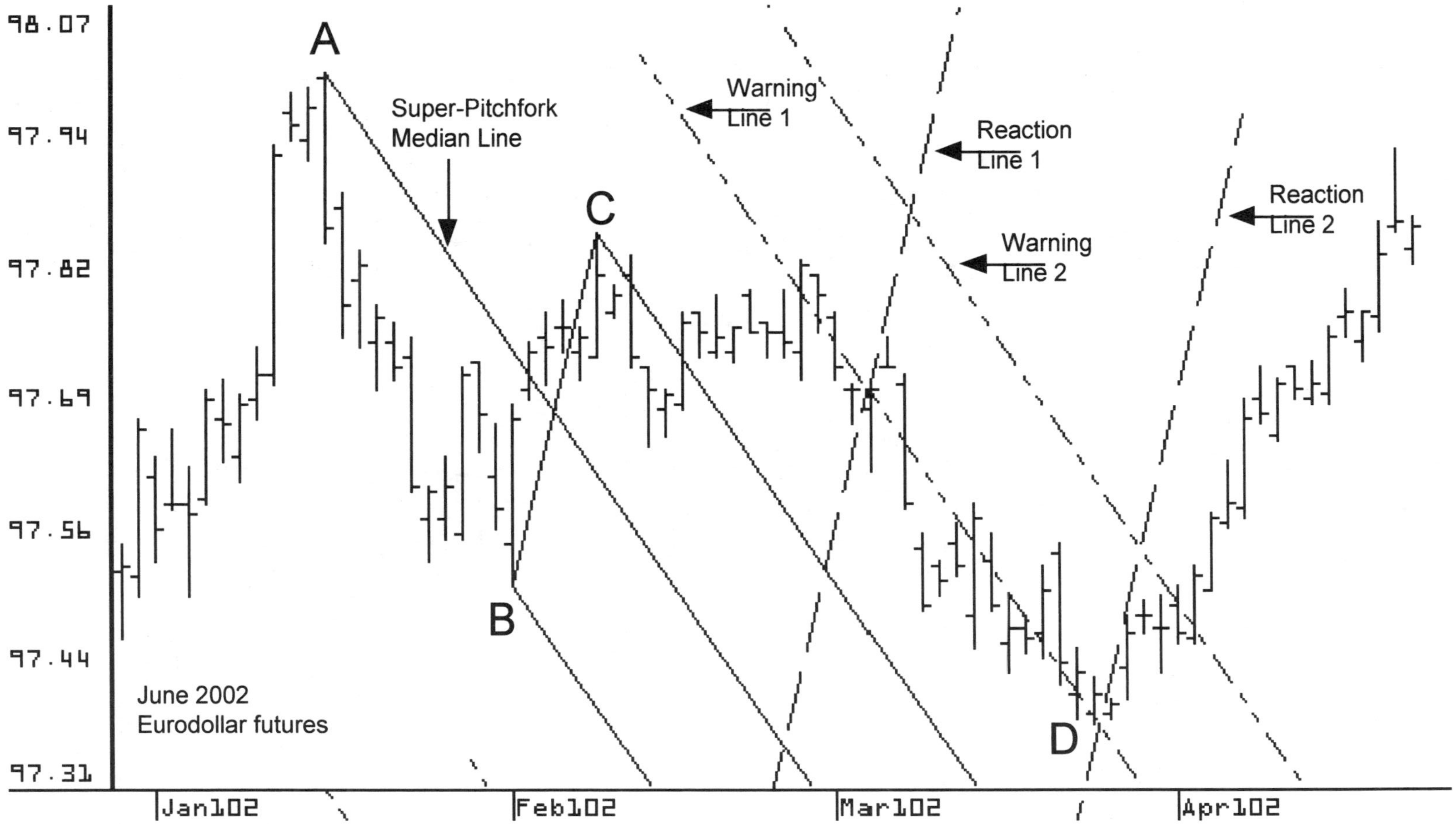

The data for June 2002 Eurodollars futures is used in the chart on this page. Pivots A, B, and C are used to draw the Super-Pitchfork. After pivot C, the price falls and makes a bottom at point D where Reaction Line 2 crosses Warning Line 1.

The chart on this page shows Eli Lilly, symbol LLY. The Super-Pitchfork is drawn as usual, using pivots A, B, and C. This market makes swing tops at points D, E, F and G against Reaction Lines 1, 2, 3 and 4 respectively.

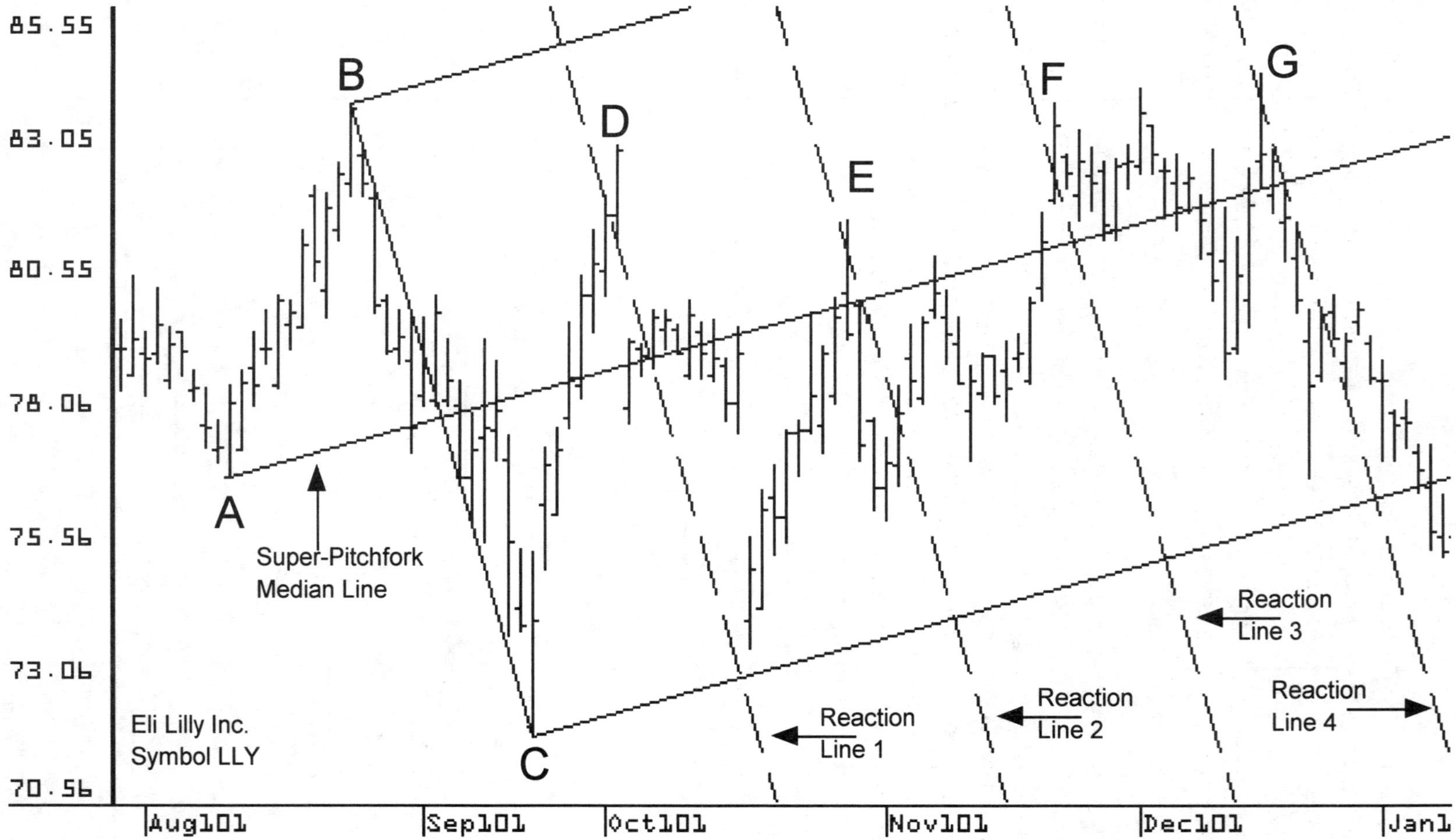

Conclusion

This book was designed to have unique content which would not be found in any other book on a trader's book shelf. I believe this book has succeeded well in doing just that. Over the past ten yeas there have been almost no books published which are devoted exclusively to trendline methods and I have never seen a book devoted exclusively to exploring Alan Andrews' trendline methods. For this reason there is no bibliography at the end of this book listing other sources for learning about Andrews work. As far as I know, there are none available to the general public.

If you have been a trader for a few years, I am sure you have been exposed to different types of trendlines. For example most traders have heard of W.D. Gann's price and time angles or regression trendlines. After researching trendline methods for over a decade, I am convinced Andrews' trendline methods are the best you will ever see. The correlations to the markets which can be found using other trendline methods are only intermittent. Other trendline methods will correlate to the markets enough to catch your eye but not enough to make profits trading. In my opinion, the Andrews trendline methods have the highest correlation to market movements of any trendline methods and can be used as the foundation of a profitable trading method.

The charts in this book were made using the MarketWarrior software. Information about this program can be found at http://www.marketwarrior.com.

End.